AMERICAN HEGEMONY AND THE TRILATERAL COMMISSION

Cambridge Studies in International Relations is a joint initiative of Cambridge University Press and the British International Studies Association (BISA). The series will include a wide range of material, from undergraduate textbooks and surveys to research-based monographs and collaborative volumes. The aim of the series is to publish the best new scholarship in International Studies from Europe, North America and the rest of the world.

D1351231

CAMBRIDGE STUDIES IN INTERNATIONAL RELATIONS

AMERICAN HEGEMONY AND THE TRILATERAL COMMISSION

STEPHEN GILL

*Associate Professor of Political Science,
York University, Toronto*

CAMBRIDGE UNIVERSITY PRESS
Cambridge, New York, Melbourne, Madrid, Cape Town, Singapore,
São Paulo, Delhi, Dubai, Tokyo

Cambridge University Press
The Edinburgh Building, Cambridge CB2 8RU, UK

Published in the United States of America by Cambridge University Press, New York

www.cambridge.org
Information on this title: www.cambridge.org/9780521424332

First published 1990
First paperback edition 1991
Reprinted 1995
Re-issued in this digitally printed version 2009

A catalogue record for this publication is available from the British Library

ISBN 978-0-521-36286-3 Hardback
ISBN 978-0-521-42433-2 Paperback

For my father, Rowland Gill

CONTENTS

FIGURES

x

TABLES

ACKNOWLEDGEMENTS

This book was made possible because of the generosity of a large number of people. First and above all, I would like to thank Dr Stephen Burman, of Sussex University, for several years of encouragement and critical but always thoughtful and constructive help, as both a thesis supervisor and as a friend. To him, I am greatly indebted. At one point he may have believed the project was unfinishable, but his doubts were never revealed:

> He had been eight years upon a project for extracting sunbeams out of cucumbers, which were put into phials hermetically sealed, and let out to warm the air in raw inclement summers. (Jonathan Swift, *Voyage to Laputa*)

This study of the Trilateral Commission would not have been possible without the kind co-operation of its members and staff, large numbers of whom gave freely of their time for interviews and consultations. In particular I am most grateful to Mr Charles Heck, the North American Director of the Commission, for all his assistance while the research was being carried out. It is a tribute to his open-mindedness that the thesis and this book were ever produced.

In addition, I am obliged for support, friendship and encouragement to Dr Martin Durham and Dr Neil Malcolm. I would also like to thank Dr Steve Smith, the general editor of this series, for always being willing to give encouragement and advice when it was needed. The venture to publish this book was supported by Professor David Lane and Professor Susan Strange and I am appreciative of this. Although not personally involved at any point in the project, the writings of Professor Robert Cox have been an important inspiration in the conceptualisation of this book. I also owe a considerable intellectual and personal debt to David Law, who has been both my most ruthless and most generous academic critic. It goes without saying that my association with such a good and stimulating friend has meant a great deal to me over the years.

Beyond these academic and professional acknowledgements, many people were helpful to me on my travels in Europe and North America whilst I was gathering information. They are not mentioned here by name, however, this does not mean that their kindness is forgotten. In particular, I would like to thank my friends Scott Kenworthy and George Kohn for always showing me the best American hospitality. I am also deeply grateful to my wife and best friend, Jill Kirby, for her support during the task of writing this book. Finally, I would like to thank my mother, Millicent Gill, for her love and her devotion to my father as his life spirit was taken from him. I hope this book is worthy of his memory.

1 INTRODUCTION

This study seeks to contribute to the development of a historical materialist theory of international relations. It does this, first, by offering an interpretation of changes in the international power and hegemony of the United States during the 1970s and 1980s, in the context of change in the world political economy. Such change involves, amongst other issues, the question of co-operation and conflict in the relations between the major capitalist states, notably those of North America, Western Europe and Japan. Second, it analyses the importance of the Trilateral Commission and similar American-sponsored private international relations councils.[1] The latter are seen as indicative of the internationalisation of civil society and what I call the 'transnationalisation of the state'. These questions are considered in the context of a changing 'global political economy' which consists of a set of interacting and dynamic social forces operating at *both* domestic and international 'levels'. The concept of the global political economy, one which includes the social force of competing theorisations, perspectives and ideologies concerning the 'politico-economic world' held by different sets of interests, serves as the basic ontology for the study.[2]

For the purposes of this book 'Trilateralism' can be defined as the project of developing an organic (or relatively permanent) alliance between the major capitalist states, with the aim of promoting (or sustaining) a stable form of world order which is congenial to their dominant interests. More specifically, this involves a commitment to a more-or-less liberal international economic order.

FOCUS OF THE STUDY

In this study the central problem of analysing Trilateralism is seen as inseparable from ongoing theoretical and practical debates about the changing nature of American hegemony. This is because the

1

Trilateral Commission can be conceived of as an expression of shifts in dominant ideas and possibly practices in the American foreign policy establishment and, to a certain extent, its counterparts elsewhere.[3]

Our study addresses what, in the conventional terminology of Anglo-Saxon international relations, would be called three 'levels of analysis' (global, international and domestic) and one basic methodological issue. These involve:

(i) Changes in the global political economy and their implications for order, conflict and co-operation amongst the 'Trilateral' countries (Canada, the United States, Japan, and the members of the European Community, except Greece).

(ii) The role of the United States in these changes.

(iii) The role of private international relations councils. Their significance, it will be argued, lies partly in the fact that they help us to understand connections between the 'domestic' and 'international' levels in the political economy.

The methodological point concerns the role of ideology and consciousness in the study of political economy. The Gramscian approach which I adopt gives weight to 'ideological apparatuses' in explaining the nature of global hegemony, order, conflict and co-operation. This point is specifically elaborated through analysis of the case of the Trilateral Commission, where attention is paid to the construction of international networks of identity, interest and ideas, and their representation through institutional linkages.

Let us now outline the substance of the study. Chapter 1 elaborates our main concerns and aims. Chapters 2 and 3 introduce and apply different theoretical perspectives which help to constitute the political economy, as well as seek to explain its basic dynamics. Chapter 2 focuses on the realist, neorealist and liberal theories which together serve to constitute the hegemonic perspective of the American foreign policy establishment (and the bulk of the United States' membership of the Trilateral Commission). These approaches are contrasted, in Chapter 3, with Marxist perspectives. A case is made in favour of historical materialist theory for explaining the questions at issue. In this context the chapter extends, at the international level, the Gramscian concepts of the state, civil society, hegemony, historic bloc, and organic intellectual.[4] In this chapter ideological and political forces are related to material forces, notably those promoting the tendency towards a deep-seated integration of the world political economy, and those which may constrain these tendencies, such as those represented by national security structures.

Chapter 4 criticises the widely-accepted argument that American

2

international power and hegemony declined substantially during the 1970s and 1980s, opening up the possibility of a disintegration of the postwar international economic order into economic spheres-of-influence and protected regional blocs, akin to the situation in the 1930s. Rather, American centrality in the global political economy has changed and in some respects has been re-emphasised. Thus arguments concerning 'hegemonic decline' are misplaced. Chapter 5 offers an alternative, historical materialist interpretation, and advances the argument that the changes of the 1970s and 1980s are best seen as a 'crisis of hegemony', a crisis which involves a structural transformation in the nature of the postwar politico-economic order, and the political consensus between the states and civil societies of the major capitalist nations. This is not a crisis in American power *per se*, rather it is a change in the relationship between key social forces within the constitution of the global capitalist order. It is argued that this change cannot be adequately understood using a concept of the state as a domestically autonomous rational actor, unproblematically aggregating national interests.[5] In particular, my analysis emphasises the complex interrelationship between state and civil society in the metropolitan capitalist countries, links which connect state and civil society at both 'domestic' and 'international' levels, and the way these links can be understood. In order to do this I introduce an analysis of the cumulative power of internationally mobile capital within the global system, and develop a novel, synthetic concept of the 'power of capital'.

Chapters 6 to 8 focus on the Trilateral Commission and associated institutions. Chapter 6 examines the origins and formation of the Commission, and Chapter 7 examines its organisational form and networks of interest. Chapter 8 assesses its evolution and development in terms of debates about changes in Trilateral and global relations. Special attention is given to the construction and maintenance of networks which link together the internationalist elements of the civil society of each of the Trilateral countries, helping to cement their military, political and economic linkages. In particular I consider to what extent the Trilateral Commission is dominated by American material interests and frameworks of thought. It is argued that the political influence of the Trilateral Commission on United States administrations has been most pronounced on economic rather than military questions.

Chapter 9 reconsiders the main arguments and evidence, and recapitulates the theme of a crisis of hegemony. It also applies the criteria for evaluation of different theoretical approaches noted below.

ANALYSING THE TRILATERAL COMMISSION

Despite the existence of private international forums like the Trilateral Commission since the turn of the century, very little systematic attention has been paid to them in the major accounts of international relations in the twentieth century.[6]

This might be seen as ironic given that the United States, where both the Commission and a large number of other such councils originated, is generally considered to be the birthplace of the modern study of international relations, as well as having the largest and best-resourced research community in this field.[7] Moreover, many commentators have noted the high degree of interchange between private individuals, academics and policy makers in the sphere of United States foreign policy.[8] Many such individuals are, or have been, members of the private councils under discussion. Despite such a silence in the literature, this book argues that a careful study of the Commission helps to shed light on important ideological and social processes in the global political economy. The membership and networks associated with the Commission stretch to the other Trilateral countries and beyond.

In this study, our exposition and analysis of the Commission is based on a categorisation developed from the three types of (transnational) social forces, identified by Robert Cox. These are: material capabilities, institutions and ideas.[9] These generally originate in the economic structure but interact in a dynamic and dialectical way at three levels: production relations (broadly defined), state-civil society complexes and in historically specific 'world orders'.

With reference to the first of Cox's categories, *material capabilities*, many members have, or have had, substantial links with many of the largest and most resourceful transnational corporations, the activity of which is part of the process of the internationalisation of capital. The cumulative effects of the internationalisation process might be said to constitute a major structural change in the global political economy since the 1930s. Other members have been leaders of state institutions which carry considerable military as well as economic power. Our second category, *institutions*, relates to the substantive argument concerning the 'transnationalisation' of a state, a phenomenon which partly involves a range of political and institutional responses to the internationalisation of economic activity. Many Commission members have held high government office, notably in the fields of finance and economics, foreign affairs and national security, as well as in international organisations. The Commission is also

4

viewed as one type of institutional response to the structural changes noted above.

The third category of *ideas* can be related to the concept of ideological apparatuses, and their relationship with the first two of our categories. The Trilateral Commission's *Triangle Papers*, co-authored by North Americans, West Europeans and Japanese, embody a range of dominant perspectives in the study of international relations, political economy and sociology. These are drawn from commensurable academic traditions. They are written from positions compatible with the material interests of dynamic elements of transnational capital, as well as the outlook of many centrist and some right-wing politicians and officials in the Trilateral countries.[10] These ideas can be viewed as of practical significance, in so far as they not only reflect but also possibly serve to develop the consciousness of Trilateral elites, and the agenda for their discussions of global questions. The Commission aims to foster 'trialogue' and co-operation between the three 'regions' and is concerned with the conditions for, and possibility of, the construction of a more congruent set of relationships between the 'Trilateral' nations.

It is hoped, therefore, that this book will help to unravel what one writer has called the 'enigma' of the Trilateral Commission.[11] That it is an enigma can be explained by the fact that first, nearly all of the literature on the Commission has been polemical and journalistic, and, perhaps because of this, no previous study has analysed the Commission in terms of a theoretical debate using appropriate criteria to evaluate the evidence. Second, all studies published to date have lacked primary sources. This book, in contrast, is based on a wide range of primary sources, including over 100 extensive interviews with members. Third, the bulk of what has been written focused on the early years of the Commission's existence, when it had achieved a certain notoriety after ex-member President Jimmy Carter chose more than twenty of its members to fill senior positions in his administration.[12] For example, the only book-length study to date was based on research completed in 1979, which allowed for the first six years of the Commission's existence.[13] This study, based on research mainly completed in 1986, is thus able to analyse the Commission's development over a timespan which is the minimum necessary to give an adequate interpretation of its development.

IDEOLOGY, IDENTITY, INTERESTS AND POLITICAL CULTURE

Let us now return to the methodological issue posed earlier: the role of ideas in the study of international relations, and the particular question of order. Ideology, ideas and institutions are, of course, only one aspect of the constitution of order, since an historical order will involve a combination of coercive and consensual aspects of power. This combination helps to structure the relationships between states, class and group forces and social movements. Moreover, any given order may benefit some more than others. A particular order may be defined by some groups and political leaders as being in the 'national interest', or in terms of 'class' or group interests.

Our methodological question can, of course, be approached in different ways. One is by using a psychological-anthropological concept of belief systems.[14] I prefer, however, to use a Marxist concept of ideology. The term 'belief system' suggests something more cognitive than what I have in mind. Ideology, in my view, though analytically distinct, is not independent of other social forces, but interacts with them in a dialectical way. A concept of ideology can only make sense, therefore, if it is placed in a social theory.

As Jorge Larrain has argued, ideology has both a positive and a negative meaning.[15] The negative usage corresponds to the Marxist idea of false consciousness, an idea which rests upon a separation and opposition between science and ideology, truth and illusion, and the false and real interests of social classes. Whether a distinction between real and false interests exists in practical terms is often doubtful, since it presupposes the capacity to distinguish clearly between the two. Nonetheless, there are accepted criteria to allow judgements on this issue, such as levels of affluence, material rewards allocated to different groups and classes, their respective life-chances and life-expectancy, and the degrees of freedom, broadly defined, that each enjoys. If a given order systematically promotes particular, rather than general interests (however defined), then the questions, 'in whose interests, why and how?' are significant ones which social scientists need to address.

The positive strand refers to ideology as the expression of the world view of a class, or fraction of a class, which may be expressed, for example, in ideologies of nationalism. Ideologies struggle to define and sustain a concept of 'real interests' for different classes and nations, relative to other concepts. This often entails the negative aspect of reproducing attitudes and values in other classes and nations which serve to undermine their respective interests. Thus the concepts of interests and order, like power and freedom, are essentially contestable.[16]

Seen from this perspective the development of ideology is an ongoing social and political process which can take place at a number of levels: the level of groups, classes, nations and world orders. Different ideologies, 'not only coexist, compete, and clash, but also overlap, affect, and contaminate one another'.[17] Thus the ideological war between the Soviet Union and the United States operates in parallel with a struggle between classes and group interests within and across different states. As Goran Therborn argues, in the context of such battles two things can be said to occur. First, an actor needs to secure the 'right to speak', to be heard and respected. Second:

> he or she must assert the overriding relevance of a particular kind of identity, say that of 'workers' as opposed to 'Christians', 'Englishmen', or 'football fans'. This mode of interpellation therefore implies the assertion that certain features of the world are more important than others – for example, exploitation rather than interdependence . . .[18]

A relevant example, which we will consider in this book, is the conflict between, on the one hand, mercantilist perspectives, which lay stress on rival national interests (and which can be associated with 'national capital' and some elements of organised labour, as well as the security complex), and economic liberal perspectives stressing an interdependent world, with a high degree of mutuality of interest among nations (which can be associated with transnational capital). These perspectives were engaged in a struggle over the definition of 'national interests' and the conduct of American foreign policy in the 1970s and 1980s. In Gramscian terms, each of these ideologies was associated with rival historic blocs of political forces. These blocs transcended social classes, with elements of capital and labour involved in each constellation.

In this context, it is also crucial to pay attention to the relationship between ideology and political culture. For example, scientific and policy-making communities and networks develop their own subcultures, and ways of seeing and interpreting the world which may or may not be congruent with the popular political culture. However a congruence between foreign-policy elites and the mass of the population, at least at a minimum, may be vital for political mobilisation. To be effective, the subculture must be not only cohesive, but able to incorporate new ideas and social forces. The danger is that the elite may become separated from important forces in the civil society. This is germane to both 'domestic' and 'international' levels of analysis.

At the global level, an emphasis on culture is important for a study of Trilateralism, both in terms of the analysis of the international fraternity of elites the Trilateral Commission has sought to develop (very few women have been involved) and, more generally, in terms of cultural limits to a convergence between the Enlightenment traditions of the West, and the Confucian traditions of Japan. Trilateralists are concerned to foster changes in identification across nations. As such, cultural contrasts may be a great obstacle, especially given Japanese xenophobia and nationalism and the widespread, often racist, resentment at Japanese economic success in the West. Similar, though less dramatic, cultural contrasts also apply to American perceptions of the identifications with Western Europe.[19] One way of transcending such limits may be through a global spread of the liberal concepts of the market, possessive individualism, consumerism, interdependence, efficiency and welfare. These concepts are central to the arguments made in many of the Commission's *Triangle Papers*.

ON PERSPECTIVES

Let us now define the term perspective and show how this concept is applied in this book. Perspectives encompass the theoretical and practical outlook, world view and identity of different constellations and coalitions of political and social movements and institutions. A perspective involves not only an ideology but also a theory which is adopted by, or related to, certain interests. As Robert Cox notes:

> Theory is always *for* someone and *for* some purpose. All theories have a perspective. Perspectives derive from a position in time and space, specifically social and political time and space. The world is seen from a standpoint definable in terms of nation or social class, of dominance or subordination, or rising of declining power, of a sense of immobility or of present crisis, of past experience, and of hopes and expectations of the future. Of course, sophisticated theory is never just the expression of a perspective. The more sophisticated a theory is, the more it reflects upon and transcends its own perspective; but the initial perspective is always contained within a theory and is relevant to its explication. There is, accordingly, no such thing as theory in itself, divorced from a standpoint in time and space. When any theory so represents itself, it is the more important to examine it as ideology, and to lay bare its concealed perspective.[20]

8

Elsewhere, Cox has linked various perspectives in the debate over Third World attempts to promote a New International Economic Order during the 1970s to networks and patterns of interest.[21] One of these, the 'establishment' perspective, is attributed to a set of intellectuals and institutions centred in the United States. This included the Trilateral Commission, the New York Council on Foreign Relations, the Ford Foundation, the Brookings Institution and certain parts of the directorates of the International Monetary Fund, the World Bank, and the Organisation for Economic Co-operation and Development. Here prevails the 'world view' of the most dynamic elements of transnational capital and certain sections of the governments of the largest capitalist countries. This is 'the view from the top'. These institutions have interlocking memberships, similar aims and congruent sets of ideas, the latter of which Cox characterised as 'monopolistic' liberalism. This doctrine (in my view better named 'oligopolistic liberalism') stresses market efficiency (entailing international capital mobility) over the goals of equity and redistribution.

Likewise, the dependency theorists of Latin America are linked to what Cox called the 'Third World Forum', although the range of theoretical positions within this constellation of forces is much broader than in the 'establishment' view. This reflects the diversity and divisions between and within Third World countries, as well as varying degrees of national power. This perspective also includes some economic liberals, some social democrats and international Keynesians of the Brandt/Palme type, but also many who advocate quasi-autarkic strategies of intellectual as well as economic self-reliance for the Third World, often involving strategies of 'delinking' from the capitalist world economy. I would also point out that many of the Third World leaders in this forum are in fact 'catch up mercantilists' who merely borrow some of their rhetoric from theories of imperialism and dependency. These views are generally made from the 'bottom' of the inter-state hierarchy.

To apply this argument further, postwar American liberal internationalism, with its appeal to universality, can be seen in an analogous way to Friedrich List's view of nineteenth-century ideologies of free trade as a means of justifying British imperialism and mercantilism.[22] The concern with declining hegemony and with the prospect of a disorderly world economy was, and still is, central for the 'establishment' perspective. Many Third World theorists continue to prioritise the questions of international inequality and injustice, whereas for establishment liberals the key issues are political order and economic efficiency. The latter perspective is the globally hegemonic one, although its hegemony is contested. As such, it serves to configure the definition of problems and the formal agenda in the major international economic organisations.

As is noted above, little empirical work has been done on the ways in which transnational groups come to constitute their common interests and shared identity, enabling them to co-operate fruitfully. Despite the apparently long-standing nature of this phenomenon, the study of such formations at the world level is still in its infancy. However, much work is needed to make sense of such social forces, and to explain the salience and resilience of different perspectives in contemporary international relations. Thus the perspectives discussed here should be viewed as *part of* the global political economy. They are bound up with the construction of interests and identity for individuals, groups, classes and nations. They are at least indirectly important for the political mobilisation of constellations of social forces. This argument holds irrespective of what might be termed the 'scientific' status of each perspective.

CRITERIA FOR EVALUATION

My comments on culture and ideology, and on perspectives should not be taken to imply that I am advocating a relativist approach to social scientific explanation. On the contrary, despite the fact that all social scientific explanation is theory based and cannot be wholly value-free, there are methodological criteria which theories must meet in order to advance their claim to be relevant. These criteria include *scope, consistency,* and *reflexivity.*

With respect to reflexivity, I mean the ability to explain the emergence and predominance of certain types of explanation. Since the historical materialism I adopt incorporates the existence and place of other theories in its explanation of social forces and social change in the global political economy, that is *as part of* the object of analysis, it is both reflexive and broad in scope. Also, because of its attention to the problematic role of ideas and institutions it extends the usually rather narrow functionalist attribution of interests and ideas to class or group position in most of the Marxist literature, as well as giving a more comprehensive explanation of global order and change. Through its stress on the importance of ideas, identities and institutions, it is perhaps able to overcome some of the economism found in cruder variants of Marxism and in determinist realist and world systems accounts of the rise and fall of hegemonies. In this sense, a key aim of this book is to show the greater comprehensiveness and consistency of the Gramscian perspective, with respect to the issues under consideration.

2 REALIST AND LIBERAL PERSPECTIVES

The purpose of chapters 2 and 3 is to sketch the contours of the theoretical debate concerning world order and conflict and co-operation between the major capitalist states. It is argued that realism characterises the mainstream outlook of the American security complex, whereas the liberal and neorealist views are more associated with American international business, and the liberal flank of the foreign policy establishment. A synthesis of the liberal and realist positions is represented in the mainstream outlook of the Trilateral Commission.

REALISM AND MERCANTILISM

Realism is the oldest approach to the study of international relations, and can be traced back as far as Machiavelli and Thucydides.[1] Recent exponents of realism include E. H. Carr, Hans Morgenthau, and the latter's self-proclaimed disciple, Robert Gilpin.[2] Mercantilism can, for the purposes of this study, be seen as an economic policy variant of realism. Robert Keohane notes that the recent critique of this perspective 'seems only to reconfirm the centrality of Realist thinking in the international political thought of the West'.[3]

Let us now sketch the nature of realism. According to Gilpin, realism is underpinned by three basic assumptions. These are, first, that international (that is inter-state) relations are inherently conflictual, with anarchy the rule, order, justice and morality the exceptions. Power is the ultimate arbiter of politics. Second, realism reflects a pessimistic view of human nature in which the primary motivations are the quest for power and security, as well as greed and fear. Third, the 'essence of social reality is the group', since *homo sapiens* is a tribal species: loyalty is given first to the family, then the tribe and ultimately the nation. The realist approach combines aspects of essentialism (in

11

so far as it may be grounded in the Augustinian concept of original sin and in the assumption that there is a basic continuity in the nature of international relations) with an existentialist concept of international action. That is, realists assume that international life is akin to a Hobbesian state of nature, in the form of struggle between the conflicting wills of different states. This struggle takes place under conditions of international anarchy, that is, the absence of an order-producing force, such as a world government.

For realists then, the basic unit of analysis in the study of international relations is the state. The nature of states is held to be similar, in so far as each is a territorial entity which has a concept of its national interest which guides policy. The nature of the anarchic inter-state system places rational constraints on the unrestrained pursuit of such interests, for example, through the mechanism of the balance of power. In its neo-realist (as opposed to historical) variant, this theorisation is based upon an individualist concept of structure, in that the international system is, in essence, seen to consist of discrete states interacting under a condition of anarchy which each must take as given. In this structural context, realists take the common view that security is a zero-sum game, and thus more security for one state must mean less security for another (although many modern realists are quick to acknowledge that nuclear weapons may mean less security for all).

Given the emphasis on security and the survival of the state, it is not surprising that realists stress the primacy of politics in their concept of political economy, with the state as the primary actor. The identity and definition of the state rests on the existence of other states, as does the question of the state's external autonomy. More powerful states are less externally constrained than others, provided that they have sufficient internal autonomy rationally to conduct foreign policy, notably in the sphere of national security. As such, the 'domestic' and 'international' levels are only analytically separate, since it is acknowledged that domestic interests motivate and shape state policy. Even in a powerful state, domestic autonomy may be constrained by strong coalitions of forces (such as a military–industrial complex), thus preventing aggregation or rational pursuit of 'national interests'. For example, the complex nature of American civil society, the atomisation of its political institutions, and the phenomenon of 'interest group liberalism' often prevent the formation of a coherent concept of the national interest.[4] This undermines any interpretation of the American state as a rational actor.

Nonetheless, domestic and international aspects of the political economy are linked since 'national capital' may operate internationally. Since the state's central concerns are security and survival, foreign economic policy, as well as military policy, is assessed in terms of the degree to which it reduces vulnerability, maximises security, and increases the relative wealth of the nation. This viewpoint also informs the view of co-operation with other states: this is most likely to be judged worthwhile if it maximises *relative* as opposed to *absolute* gains for one's own nation. By contrast, the gist of the liberal view, as exemplified in the Ricardian theory of comparative advantage, lies in its stress on the absolute welfare gains from international co-operation.

In this light, a typical realist policy prescription would be to call for a strategy of national self-sufficiency, at least for 'strategic industries'. Failing this, it should endeavour to obtain guaranteed access to crucial technologies and commodities for domestic industry. In this context regulation of trade and capital flows is essential; strategic commodities should be stockpiled (the Pentagon and the United States Department of Energy built up huge stockpiles of oil and minerals in the 1980s); and foreign firms in strategic sectors should be either excluded from the domestic economy (as in post-1945 Japan) or carefully controlled by the state. Therefore, national (public or private) control over technology and productive knowledge is at the heart of realist policy prescriptions, since advanced technology underpins modern military and industrial power. Realists generally argue that technology and some capital imports should be encouraged, provided that they do not create a situation of dependency or vulnerability. For example, from an American viewpoint, an important objective would be to suck in West European and Japanese technology whilst attaching tight national security controls as to its use by foreign powers, as has been the case in negotiations concerning participation in the Strategic Defense Initiative. By contrast, technology exports, at least for arms-related industries, are seen as dangerous unless very strict controls can be applied (such as in the Pentagon's traditional policy of a high technology embargo towards the Soviet bloc).

For realists, an interventionist role for the state in the economy is crucial. This is especially the case for developing strategic industries, notably those using high technology. In the American case such interventionism often is carried out under the banner of national security, by the Pentagon and other security agencies. In the 1980s, the Pentagon returned to its immediate postwar role of catalysing the regeneration of America's scientific and technological base, attempting to increase the rate of productivity growth. In an era where

13

knowledge and production are ever more closely interrelated, American realists have argued for careful policies to encourage skilled immigration (for example by lowering American income tax rates relative to those overseas, as in the 1986 Tax Act). Skilled emigration, however, is seen as undesirable. Such interventionism contrasts starkly with liberal perspectives which stress economic openness and the need for international mobility of factors of production in order to maximise economic efficiency, and, therefore, the absolute gains to global welfare.

Realist policies also have a historico-cultural dimension, with political mobilisation seen as achieved primarily through patriotism and nationalism. Influenced by the German nationalist ideas of Hegel and Fichte, Friedrich List made the quintessential realist argument concerning the developmental and mobilisational qualities of cultural nationalism. Writing in 1841, he argued:

> Between each individual and entire humanity . . . stands *the nation*, with its special language and literature, with its peculiar origin and history, with its special manners and customs, laws and institutions, with the claims of all these for existence, independence, perfection and continuance for the future and with its separate territory; a society which, united by a thousand ties of mind and of interest, combines itself into one independent whole . . . and . . . is still opposed to other societies of a similar kind in their national liberty, and consequently can only under the existing conditions of the world maintain self-existence and independence by its own power and resources. As the individual chiefly obtains by means of the nation and in the nation, mental culture, power of production, security and prosperity, so is the civilisation of the human race only conceivable and possible by means of the civilisation and development of the individual nations.[5]

What can we make of these arguments when they are applied to the United States, with its history of immigration and ethnic hetero-geneity? Clearly, American nationalism has never been based upon common descent, ancestry, religion or, to a lesser extent, tradition. Rather, as Kohn has observed, it is rooted in the universal *idea* of liberty, understood as a 'natural' human right, valid ultimately for all human beings. American civilisation has, therefore, an 'assimilative power' which 'transformed many millions of the most diverse immigrants into a "new race of men"'. This was 'made possible by this "universality" of American nationalism'.[6]

Such a universal appeal is clearly a strength of American nationalism (or 'Americanism'). This contrasts with the cultural xenophobia of, for example, Japan and the Soviet Union. However, 'Americanism' has contradictions from a realist point of view, since the American idea of liberty is both possessively individualist and negative in nature. It stresses individual liberty, the right to acquire property, and minimal interference from government. American political culture is strongly anti-statist, with widespread fear of 'big government' and a traditional opposition to the existence of a permanent military establishment.

American realists, therefore, are drawn to stress selected aspects of Americanism. Since realists advocate the idea of a strong, relatively autonomous state, and *raison d'état*, justifications of the state's international policies are usually couched in terms of defending and extending American values on a world-wide basis (for example in the doctrine of Manifest Destiny). In the post-1945 context, with the growth of a massive military establishment, such legitimation has taken the form of Cold War concepts in a climate of permanent insecurity and preparedness for war. As President Eisenhower suggested in his farewell address, the growth of the military-industrial complex (of which he was a key architect after World War II) may substantially undermine key aspects of the American liberal-democratic and constitutional tradition.

From a realist viewpoint, too strident an anti-communism might be foolhardy, since it could lead to the United States squandering its power and resources to contain communist forces in regions of only secondary importance: the war in Vietnam is the classic example. Moreover, Vietnam brought with it the breakdown of the national consensus (or 'workable dissensus', to use the phrase of Thomas L. Hughes) on what Robert Tucker called 'the purposes of American power', as well as the domestic politicisation of foreign and military policy.[7] The defeat in Vietnam led to an agonising reappraisal of the American place in the world, and, for a time, the security complex was placed on the defensive. Its resources were reduced, its legitimacy was at an all-time low.

Nonetheless, what Richard Falk has termed a 'hyper-consensus' arose within the establishment in the mid-1970s on the need to reverse a perceived decline in American military power.[8] This was expressed in the return of containment as the centrepiece of American strategy. There were different versions of this, ranging from Robert Tucker's concept of 'realist containment' (premised on military primacy but applied to the 'vital interests' of the United States), to an 'unlimited ideological containment', advocated by neo-conservatives such as Irving Kristol and Norman Podhoretz. The latter not only entailed military supremacy but also a world-wide anti-communist ideological, political and economic offensive. The most restrained of the new concepts was 'containment without confrontation' which synthesised the concept of detente with approval of a steady increase in American military power.[9] The latter concept was closest to the mainstream view expressed in the Trilateral Commission in the late 1970s and 1980s, especially by its European members.

Tucker's argument suggested that, rather than all-out containment of communism, anti-Sovietism was a more sensible method for gaining support for stronger military forces. Neo-containment was still able to draw support from the currents of Manicheanism in the political culture: the United States would continue to deliver the world from evil, atheistic Soviet communism. From this vantage point, the neo-conservatives' proposals were undesirable since they were beyond simply sustaining the security of the United States and its key allies (as well as politically undermining the *rapprochement* with China). An all-out quest for military supremacy over the Soviet Union would threaten future American economic performance. This would, in the long term, undercut the basis of the military strength of the United States.

In conclusion, co-operation is difficult to achieve in a realist world: realists see inter-state conflict as either inevitable or an ever-present possibility, almost irrespective of the ideological predispositions of states. The anarchic structure of the inter-state system makes the pursuit of national security part of a zero-sum game, where one state's gain is relative and represents, therefore, another's loss. This anarchic environment may even be negative-sum, if technological developments in weapons systems cause states to feel even less secure.

REALISM AND THE INTERNATIONAL ECONOMIC ORDER

Let us now turn to the problem of international economic order. For realists, the balance of power between states is crucial and, if the balance changes, the level of conflict in the 'inter-state system' may rise, after a period of relative equilibrium. In contrast to Marxism, historical change and levels of conflict are often seen as underpinned by a basic structural continuity, despite cycles where power balances shift, and empires or hegemonies rise and decline. As Gilpin acknowledges, the central assumption of *War and Change in World Politics* is that 'the nature of international relations has not changed fundamentally over the millennia'.[10]

This assumption enables realists either to suggest probable scenarios, or else to make predictions concerning international order.

Stable, co-operative and relatively peaceful international systems are frequently associated, notably by American realists, with periods of hegemonic domination. Kenneth Waltz, for example, suggests that although the bipolar postwar system dominated by the superpowers is somewhat unstable, it is nonetheless much more stable than a balance of power system involving a larger number of states.[11] Thus the issue is not ideology or political philosophy, but the distribution of power.

Consistently present in the American literature is the view that high levels of conflict (economic as well as military) are more likely in periods of prolonged hegemonic decline (and implicitly if the hegemon seeks to reverse its decline by military means). Part of the reason for this is that when the capacities of the hegemon decline, this encourages a 'Gaullist' response on the part of other states, since they will be encouraged to break the international rules set by the hegemon and more forcibly assert their national interests.

What this means is that, for realists, strong political and military foundations are conditions of existence of a liberal international economic order. As Gilpin argues, discussing the 1970s and early 1980s:

> the crisis of the world economy . . . was at least in part a consequence of the erosion of . . . political foundations: the relative decline of American hegemony, the increasing strains within the anti-Soviet alliance, and the waning of the commitment to liberal ideology . . . The political cement of the economic system is dissolving with the eclipse of American hegemony and related political changes.[12]

In addition, one aspect of a realist analysis of such changes is that, under conditions of declining hegemony, the political commitment of the United States to the maintenance of the international economic order has been weakened. This is because of the greater weight in policy-making of what can be termed a nationalist bloc of forces in the domestic political economy. The weight of these forces was reflected in a shift in American policies in a 'domesticist' (i.e., nationalist) and more unilateral direction, particularly during the Nixon years, and in the first Reagan administration. Domesticist forces were countervailed by internationalists, who argued for a more co-operative and globally-oriented American economic policy.

In the United States during the 1970s and 1980s the 'domesticist' outlook was to be found across the conventional left–right political spectrum. In a more extreme, ideological form, it was linked to generally conservative and right-wing organisations such as the Committee on the Present Danger, the Coalition for Peace through

17

Strength, the Lehrman Institute, and to a lesser extent, the Hoover Institution and the Heritage Foundation. It was also to be found, however, in the mainstream views of organised labour (in the AFL-CIO) and amongst some liberals in the Congress, such as Richard Gephardt, the Democratic contender for president in the 1988 campaign. More fundamentally, such a realist view lay at the heart of the geopolitical outlook of America's military-industrial complex, as well as the politico-economic vantage point of those domestic producers (capital and labour) threatened by increased foreign competition and/or the internationalisation of production.

Crucial for our discussion then, is the orientation to economic policy imparted by a realist view of the world. Such policy is seen as an instrument of political objectives. To be effective, such policy requires the assertion of national economic sovereignty. A Trilateral Commission report, premised on the internationalists' central concept of interdependence, criticised this notion (seen as underpinning the 'domesticism' and unilateralism of the first Reagan administration's economic policies) as being fundamentally misguided: 'In essence, real economic sovereignty now falls far short of nominal economic sovereignty even for the United States – though 'autonomy illusion' (to use a phrase coined by Robert Keohane) remains prevalent even in informed American circles.'[13]

In addition, realists who share Gilpin's assumption of an essential continuity in international relations do not accept the liberal argument that the growth of postwar 'interdependence' has brought with it any change in the nature of inter-state rivalry. Rather, they maintain that it has intensified some of its (economic) manifestations, and complicated the task of defining and 'defending' the 'national interest'. Since realists lay considerable emphasis on the state shaping national responses to international forces, it is not surprising that their view of interdependence is that it derives from state policies, and that international 'regimes' are seen at best, as epiphenomenal configurations of inter-state power. Moreover, inverting Marx's base-superstructure metaphor, realists criticise the extreme exponents of the interdependence school for assuming the primacy of economic and technological forces, neglecting the more fundamental political base upon which the interdependent economy has rested.

Thus, some realists, like Gilpin, argue that growing interdependence is more likely in a period of hegemonic stability (since hegemons will tend to opt for liberal economic policies so as to maximise the gains from comparative advantage), whereas in periods where there is hegemonic decline, or no hegemon, the trends towards increased interdependence are reversed.[14] As American hegemony declines more in relative terms, therefore, a move away from an interdependent world economy and more international conflict and instability are to be expected. As such, the prospects for Trilateral co-operation are not good, since a multi-polar world will tend towards economic nationalism, or perhaps even the reemergence of rival economic blocs in the Americas, Western Europe and East Asia.

REALISM AND TRILATERAL CO-OPERATION

According to Gilpin, the concrete forms of postwar co-operation in the Trilateral states have been cemented by American hegemonic leadership, anti-Sovietism and a Keynesian welfarist ideology.[15] For mainstream realists such hegemonic co-operation would be unlikely to persist unless the effects of hegemony were perceived as being especially beneficial by other key states. If hegemonic leadership were perceived in more coercive terms other states would inevitably seek to challenge the hegemon, particularly in a period where the hegemon's economic and military power resources were seen as in relative decline. Gilpin does not equate the decline of American hegemony with the collapse of the international economic order, although he does think that the erosion of American power has greatly weakened the chances of its survival.[16]

From this perspective, Trilateral co-operation is an attempt by the United States to manage its declining hegemony or to have, in David Calleo's phrase, 'hegemony on the cheap'.[17] Under the guise of a more co-operative posture, the United States has attempted to shift burdens to other allied states. Co-operation on this basis is merely tactical and unlikely to lead to a long-term transcendence of national rivalry, identification and interest. The further that the United States drifts towards unilateralism and a short-term view of American interests, the less likely is Trilateral co-operation.

Most realists would be pessimistic also about the possibility of a fully-fledged Trilateralism since, in part, this would require an 'internationalisation' of Japan's domestic structure, a goal pursued by a range of economic liberals and a central aim of the Trilateral Commission. Realists might conclude that the recent attempts by Japan to open its financial markets, as well as to engage in a strategy of increasing foreign direct investment are merely cunning forms of mercantilism. Much of the recent evidence tends to support the scepticism of realists. Whilst Japan is in some respects now attempting to change its culturally isolationist outlook through international

19

education, other developments confirm the growing importance of neo-nationalism.[18] For example, Prime Minister Nakasone sponsored the rewriting of school text-books not just to eradicate the memory of Japanese atrocities in the 1930s and 1940s (which in effect had been done) but to put a more favourable and patriotic gloss on modern Japanese history. The strength of neo-nationalism should be seen in the context of Japan's rising military power: although it only spent about 1 per cent of its GNP on defence it had, by the mid-1980s, the world's seventh largest military force, equipped with very advanced weapons. More pervasively, Japan's economic power has spread throughout the Pacific, into North America, and has threatened to obliterate the so-called 'crisis industries' of Western Europe, whereas foreign capital has traditionally had substantial problems operating in Japanese markets.

In conclusion, realists generally take positions which stress the primacy of politics, the division of the globe into rival nation–states, and the division of identities into different cultures and national traditions: this is an anthropological view which is deeply pessimistic concerning the conditions for the eradication of a state of permanent insecurity. Trilateral co-operation is typically viewed by realists (such as Faoud Adjami and Stanley Hoffman) as a device for the United States to incorporate and perhaps exploit its allies, rather than a manifestation of more co-operative and enlightened policies under new global conditions.[19]

TRANSNATIONAL LIBERALISM

Whilst realism and mercantilism are the oldest approaches in international political economy, liberal political economy dates from Adam Smith's extension of his moral philosophy at the end of the eighteenth century.[20] The main units of analysis in this approach are rational, self-interested actors (individuals, groups, firms), who operate within the constraints of market structure and competition. Each actor attempts to use power resources (wealth, market strength, knowledge) to increase its power, security, affluence and satisfaction, or utility. The concept of the international political economy is similar to that espoused by realists, although inter-state economic interactions can, under appropriate conditions, be viewed as of a positive-sum nature. However, what I call 'transnational' liberals, noting the deepening of global interdependence, sometimes suggest that there has been a transformation in important aspects of international relations, so that realist assumptions of continuity and concepts of inter-state conflict are no longer fully adequate to explain the postwar order.

Following Smith, liberals argue that an effect of such interaction is to increase general economic welfare, provided that political forces do not stifle competition. Such forces may stem from the place of 'special interests' within the state. These can be predominantly political (the weight of bureaucratic, military or party interests), economic (for example, protectionist coalitions), or ideological (such as the force of nationalism). The relative autonomy of the state is determined by the interplay of such forces, which may operate at both the 'domestic' and 'international' levels. Liberal analysis in its classical form, whilst allowing for the role of group dynamics, is ultimately founded on a methodological individualism. Indeed, after Smith, David Ricardo's method of abstract theorising formally separated the 'economy' and the 'polity'. Whereas the economy was in principle constituted by apparently spontaneous individual action, that of the 'polity' was the realm of collective authority.[21]

Liberal theorists argue that economic openness, limitations on the scope of state intervention in the economy, and the primacy of the private sector and private initiative in production and exchange, are most likely to lead to an increase in global economic efficiency, although they concede that the global product is likely to be unequally distributed. If factors of production are allowed a maximum degree of international mobility, however, aggregate global welfare will be maximised. Some liberal theorists also suggest that a key political effect of such interactions is to generate an interdependence based on economic exchange and the global integration of production. This creates transnational webs of interest and the prospect (however distant) of a global community.

Generally speaking, since 1945, there have been two variants to this argument. The first, the corporate liberal-social democratic variant (represented in the Brandt reports) has argued that the market should be regulated for purposes of promoting welfare goals and to sustain growth and economic efficiency. In this view, some global redistribution of income is required to maintain an adequate supply of capital to developing nations, as well as to maintain an appropriate level of global aggregate demand. This is also necessary in order to create the basis for a shared political interest between rich and poor nations, and thus to help sustain global order and stability. This view was partially endorsed in the Trilateral Commission's publications on the North–South relationship during the 1970s and mid-1980s. The second, neo-liberal variant, draws inspiration from Friedrich von Hayek and

Milton Friedman. This is more politically conservative, and argues that too much state intervention undermines, rather than assists the promotion of economic efficiency. In consequence, the best action less-developed countries can take is to rid themselves of their parasitic bureaucracies and let 'market place magic' do its work. In this latter view there is no substitute for possessive individualism and self-help.

As has been noted, both approaches still operate from within the hegemonic economic liberal paradigm, stressing the primary role of the private sector and the need for a world-wide market system. Where they differ is over the degree of state interventionism, the mix of fiscal and monetary policies, and the extent to which international co-ordination of policies is seen as feasible and desirable, in order to sustain the liberal order which each is committed to. The more conservative view stresses market forces as the best means of promoting global structural change and the longer-term movement towards a global community.

Along the lines of Gilpin's arguments, noted above, each of these variants stresses that for appropriate global economic conditions to exist, they must be underpinned by suitable political and military structures. Since most theorists assume that the power of the United States to maintain such conditions has declined, a debate has taken place concerning what concrete form political arrangements should take in order to sustain the liberal international economic order. In common with many realists, some liberal writers suggest that the failure of the Trilateral states to effectively co-operate and maintain international regimes may lead to a world characterised by more aggressive forms of mercantilism, and a breakdown of the liberal order. However, the transnational liberal approach is more optimistic about the prospects for maintaining the liberal order, since it rests upon a consideration of transnational social forces, which in effect create the web of interdependence which helps to sustain the system. The public choice approach provides the method for approaching the practical questions of how international co-operation can be carried out.

First, however, we should note why I have called the perspective 'transnational liberalism'. Richard Falk characterises 'Trilateralism' as the 'geoeconomics of the multinational corporation'.[22] I prefer to use the less familiar term 'transnational' since very few large companies are multinational in the sense of having ownership and managerial control substantially divided amongst citizens of different countries: IBM, whose public relations department actually coined the term 'multinational', is an American-controlled company. Transnational corporate interests are strongly represented within the foreign policy establishments of all the major capitalist nations, and many companies have forged alliances or entered consortia with their foreign counterparts. Transnational liberalism can therefore be defined as the economic doctrine and political ideology primarily associated with the most powerful elements of internationally-mobile capital.

An exemplar of this approach is Robert Keohane and Joseph Nye's ideal-typical concept of 'complex interdependence'.[23] Indeed, this can be said to represent the quintessential metaphor in the ideology of the Trilateral Commission (Nye has been a member of the Commission). In effect what this concept suggests is that the world-wide integration of production, exchange and communication structures has created systematic economic benefits in accord with liberal postulates about positive-sum interactions, whilst simultaneously creating constraints and pressures on individual states. This means that if the benefits of interdependence are to be sustained, collective political action at the international level is necessary, as exemplified by the seven-nation economic summits (involving Britain, Canada, France, Italy, Japan, the United States, and West Germany, and the President of the European Community) which began in the mid-1970s, as well as in organisations such as the International Monetary Fund. This involves maintaining the norms, institutions and rules of the economic order, particularly in the policies of the 'big seven' capitalist nations and the European Community, therefore resisting domestic pressures for state intervention of an economically illiberal nature at home and abroad. All of this institutional and ideological effort at the international level is designed and intended to facilitate co-operative inter-state relations and to maximise the absolute gains to global welfare.

The concept of complex interdependence combines a neo-realist view of inter-state relations with a commitment to liberal international economic arrangements. It is counterposed to an ideal-typical realist concept of the international system as comprising discrete, rival states, with inter-governmental relations as much the most important link between them (via diplomacy). The condition of complex interdependence refers mainly to the intensive and cumulative inter-relationships amongst the major capitalist states. These are *trans-governmental* (such as the interaction between the bureaucracies of different states); *transnational* (involving interaction between private transnational corporations); and *inter-state* (the main channels considered by realists). The agenda of inter-state relations comprises a wide range of 'multiple issues' in which there is no obvious hierarchy and, as such, security issues do not necessarily dominate.[24] Thus,

23

whilst not underestimating the dynamics of inter-state rivalry or the importance of military power, this concept suggests that a complex and extensive range of global linkages has created common problems. Collective action is imperative for their management, especially by those states and transnational interests with the biggest stake in preserving the international economic order.

Societies bound by the condition of complex interdependence (which is most advanced for Trilateral nations) therefore need to maintain and develop methods of collective management such as 'international regimes' (in trade, money, arms control, etc.) which help mediate the relationships between states and also non-state actors. Behind this contestation is the view that the quantitative and qualitative changes in economic and technological forms of inter-dependence create new political problems for the advanced capitalist states, problems which require that their policies are consistent across an ever-wider and more complex range of issue-areas (such as political and economic aspects of space and the oceans). The degree to which such regimes provide stability in the international economic order has been a matter for debate in the literature. Realists are doubtful, arguing that regimes mainly reflect the postwar dominance of the United States, and that they will decay as American relative power declines. Others argue that regimes provide the means for rational co-operation between actors, and as such are a stabilising feature of the system when contrasted with that of the inter-war years. The neorealist John Ruggie has characterised the post-1945 order as a system of 'embedded liberalism', in which a strong 'fit' existed between domestic state-society relations and the international economic order.[25] In other words, domestic welfarism in the 'mixed economy' was congruent with the gradual liberalisation of the inter-national economy under the conditions of the long postwar boom. This allowed international economic regimes to work fairly well in a situation where a range of interests in key states shared similar aims.

The synthesis of neorealism and transnational liberalism in the concept of 'complex interdependence' implies the possibility of a large degree of co-operation between capitalist (and other) states. Such co-operation is based upon rational self-interest, and on the view that the relations between the advanced capitalist states are both competitive and complementary. It is not simply a response to the domination of a preponderant state. In this view, the postwar international economic order can remain stable even if the hegemon is in decline. Although it is conceded that a hegemonic power may be necessary for the creation of a liberal international economic order, hegemony

24

(defined as the dominance of one state over others) is not a necessary condition for its continued existence. Thus this approach gives significant weight to transnational social forces in its explanation of order and change in the global political economy.

Accordingly, theorists of complex interdependence stress the rationality of Trilateral co-operation in a range of issue-areas. Structural changes in the postwar period have eroded the economic sovereignty of all the major capitalist states, including, especially over the last twenty years, the previously relatively self-sufficient American economy. Indeed, the logic of their work suggests that state policy is determined by the interplay between domestic and international interest groups, transnational actors, organisations and bureaucracies in a range of 'issue-areas'. The central concern of their work, in a practical sense, is, therefore, to provide a conceptual apparatus for the 'management of interdependence', a phrase coined by Miriam Camps, Senior Fellow at the Council on Foreign Relations, and an important theorist for the Trilateral Commission.[26]

PUBLIC CHOICE THEORY

A second current of analysis in the transnational liberal perspective is public choice theory, elements of which are found in the work of Mancur Olson and Charles Kindleberger.[27] It is based on neo-classical economics and a liberal pluralist analysis of politics. Each of these approaches had traditionally separated the analysis of politics and economics for methodological reasons. Public choice theory seeks to overcome this separation by clarifying the conditions under which *individuals* see their rational self-interest as being served by participating in groups, and for groups to form coalitions in pursuit of their interests in the 'political marketplace'. This theory, therefore, combines neo-classical economics' methodological individualism with Olson's theory of collective action.[28] When 'interdependence' writers stress the shared interest in collective management of the capitalist world economy by those nations and private actors which have the greatest stake in its smooth functioning, they use public choice concepts to support their arguments.

The public choice approach entails detailed analysis of interest groups within nations. This requires an examination of their formation, strength and tendency to make alliances/coalitions. Such analysis involves unravelling 'the logic of collective action'. Groups act on the basis of a calculus which involves: anticipated costs and benefits; some knowledge about alternative courses of action; ease of communication between individuals and groups (which may depend on the number and geographical spread of actors); and, finally, what Robert Kudrle calls the 'ideological consonance' between individuals and groups (the congruence of their value orientations).[29] Actions take place under conditions of 'bounded rationality', for example, where there is imperfect information.

Public choice theorists generally see co-operation between capital and labour in the same industry as fairly normal, for example, where protection against foreign competition is concerned, or conversely, in a country where export-led economic strategies predominate, in support of liberal economic regimes. Such interaction between groups and coalitions in the public realm (the 'political market'), is seen as the key driving force through which economic and political policies are generated. Foreign economic policies will reflect the balance of forces, crudely speaking, between aggregations of 'internationalist' and 'protectionist' forces. In consequence the idea of a clear cut national interest is seen as problematic. In this sense there is a similarity of view between public choice theorists and those Marxists who emphasise the fractions within capital and labour. In public choice terminology there is a 'politico-economic market' for protection and openness.

Since policy is largely determined by the relative influence of domestic groups and coalitions, there may be substantial differences between the policies each nation pursues. Given the structure of international economic relations, this can produce conflicts between states. Where the dominant domestic coalitions of different nations have congruent interests, co-operation may be facilitated. The variety and extent of international co-operation is conditioned by the pattern of policies pursued by different states, some of which will be more conscious of the international effects of their policies than will others.

All states with a major stake in the preservation of the international economic order must, however, acknowledge that, at a minimum, it requires for its functioning some institutionalisation and collective provision of what liberal economists call 'public goods'. As such, the need for international co-operation is underlined by the failure of the market mechanism to adequately supply such public goods:

> While Liberal economics provides theoretical support for possessive individualism and the market mechanism, this is qualified in various ways, notably in the case of the concept of 'public goods'. Public goods are those goods and services which are jointly supplied and are characterised by an inability to exclude beneficiaries on a selective basis. In this sense, such goods cannot be simply limited to those who are willing and able to pay for them. This implies that left to

26

private enterprise these goods will be under-supplied. As a result they are often supplied by the state, and/or state subsidies are given to the private sector.[30]

Public goods include national security, monetary stability and law and order. At the international level, the supply of such goods (usually financed at the domestic level through taxation) is more problematic, since no world state exists to extract contributions from those who benefit from international public goods such as collective security, stable money and open trade. This gives rise to the so-called 'free-rider' problem, which can be considered as akin to tax evasion at the domestic level. Much of the decision-making concerning the provision of international public goods takes place through international organisations, alliances and *ad hoc* arrangements (such as the Paris Club of bankers). With respect to the practical means for provision of such goods, Bruno Frey argues that it has been shown empirically that the smaller an international organisation is, the more successful it is likely to be in promoting co-operation. This is provided that there is a shared perception of the advantages of membership: thus 'education' and 'propaganda' are important for purposes of developing 'ideological consonance' and sharing information. It is worth mentioning that the 'educational' role of the Trilateral Commission was emphasised in virtually every research interview I conducted with its members, both in terms of developing trust and to enlarge the time-horizons involved in making such cost-benefit calculations.

By implication, as an international organisation expands in size and the scope of its agenda widens, agreement among the parties involved becomes increasingly difficult. In the case of Trilateral co-operation and co-ordination of positions in order to maintain the international public goods of open trade and a stable international monetary system, moving from the 'big seven' of the summits to the OECD (more than twenty nations) adds successively diminishing amounts to the benefits (utility) received by each member, and leads to progressively less co-operation. This argument is based on the application of game theory, where it is assumed that the numbers of votes a country holds in an international organisation determines its power to affect outcomes (decisions). What this argument fails to take account of, however, is the effect of co-ordination of positions, and the importance of agenda-setting procedures which may occur informally, outside of the public decision-making forums. This may have the effect of creating a power bloc of countries with relatively congruent interests and concepts of a particular issue, thus enlarging their collective potential. If this latter point is acknowledged, there is a strong incentive for the 'Trilateral' countries to co-operate, if they are able to identify a collective interest in doing so. From this viewpoint, informal organisations such as the Trilateral Commission may be necessary for co-ordination of positions *vis-à-vis* other groupings. Public choice theorists point out the difficulties of sustained co-operation since a state's foreign economic policies largely depend on the organisation and balance of domestic group interests. Thus the interests of states, expressed in terms of their policy preferences, may only rarely coincide. However, transnational coalitions of interest can influence states to adopt co-ordinated positions.

With respect to the provision of the international public good of security, some nations are more important than others. The super-powers have structural dominance in the security sphere. On the other hand, the larger countries bear disproportionate costs in main-taining their alliance systems. Smaller countries tend to pay a dis-proportionately smaller share of those costs. This is despite the fact that they benefit from the supply of an international public good such as collective defence. This gives rise to the free-rider problem. Frey found that in 1981, for example, the United States spent 5.9 per cent of its GNP on defence, whereas the other NATO countries spent an unweighted average of 3.5 per cent. In the case of the Warsaw Pact the Soviet Union spent 8.8 per cent of its GDP, against an unweighted average of 2.9 per cent for other members:

> The dominating country thus spent 69 per cent more than an 'average' member country in NATO, and 203 per cent more in the Warsaw Pact. In earlier years the tendency towards free-riding was equally strong: in 1973 the dominating country spent 82 per cent more in NATO and 262 per cent more in the Warsaw Pact in terms of the share of military expenditures in GDP.[31]

Of course the American government was well aware of this, and in the 1980s further pressurised its NATO allies to increase their contri-butions and avoid free-riding. Indeed, as Frey's figures show, it had some success in this regard during the 1970s.

TRILATERAL CO-OPERATION AND PUBLIC CHOICE

No *a priori* generalisation about the nature of international conflict or co-operation is possible from this perspective, apart from a pervasive view that a situation where a hegemonic power is in decline may lead to less international co-operation and also to a reduction in the provision of public goods. Thus the Trilateral Commission members see their institution as a forum which would help 'manage the transition' away from a hegemonic to a post-hegemonic order. This requires the collective will to move rationally towards a redistribution of alliance or regime-maintenance costs which reflect national capabilities. This is seen as essential to guarantee the provision of the international public goods from which they most benefit.

However, as Frey points out, domestic producers affected by international competition under relatively liberal economic policies have a greater short-run incentive to fight for protection than the more diffuse groups of interests (including consumers) who benefit from openness. Their short-run losses are more painful and visible, and their complaints can be 'targeted' more effectively, for example at American members of Congress in constituencies where job losses are imminent. Thus in the 'political market' for protection (national) capital and (national) labour may have the same position, and thus lobby persuasively for protection. In consequence of this, during the 1970s and 1980s American internationalists (as well as other trading nations) tended to concentrate efforts in the Executive branch in order to maintain openness, also relying heavily on lobbying in the Senate, and on the presidential veto to counter protectionist legislation coming from 'fair traders' in the House of Representatives. In addition, international co-operation, and the maintenance of a domestic consensus on economic openness is also seen to rest on sufficient economic growth for their competitive interactions to be of a 'positive sum' nature, although there may be conflict over what mix of policies is most likely to produce growth.

Seen from this perspective, the possibilities for effective Trilateral co-operation would rest upon the capacity of enlightened 'internationalist coalitions' to influence their national governments' policies. International co-operation would be seriously impeded by inward-looking and aggressively mercantilist coalitions coming to power in the biggest capitalist states, notably in the United States. How might the Trilateral Commission be viewed in this context? If internationalist coalitions predominate within the making of (especially American) foreign economic policy, the Commission might provide an important forum for promoting certain forms of international co-operation. At a minimum, it might be seen to function as a channel of education, propaganda, and communication and thus some basis for understanding a range of conflicts of interest.

If favourable political conditions hold, the form and effectiveness of co-operation would then be bound up with the size, scope, and decision-making rules of the institution. The latter is illustrated by an

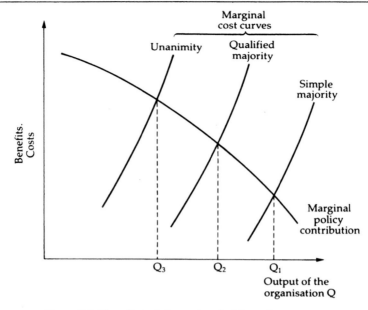

Figure 2.1 The effect of alternative decision rules
Source: B. S. Frey, 'The Public Choice View of International Political Economy',
International Organisation (1984), vol. 38, p. 218

application of the ideas of James Buchanan and Gordon Tullock in *The Calculus of Consent*, shown in Figure 2.1.

Unanimity is the most costly decision-making method since the marginal cost curve shifts upwards and to the left because agreement becomes more difficult as the rules become stricter. With the unanimity rule any country has a veto and all members must take the interests of all others into account. Thus the effort of the Commission to promote consensus, and its general reluctance to publicly commit members to specific policy positions, might be said to be very wise from a public choice viewpoint, given the large number of national members and the variety of political and economic interests they might be said to represent.

There is a further implication for 'Trilateral' co-operation. According to studies cited by Frey, the calculus of costs and benefits to the United States from participation in a range of international organisations has changed as the size of its relative share of world GNP has diminished. Nowadays, the United States has a smaller interest in the public goods produced by international organisations. This also implies that the effectiveness of postwar international organisations has been reduced as the American commitment has been reduced. 'Instead of a "leader" providing international public goods partly in its own interest, the dominant force is now a group of relatively small countries, each of which is relatively unwilling to provide public goods'.[32]

Alongside this tendency towards a declining provision of public goods is the diffusion of international political power as American hegemony declines. This has double-edged consequences for international co-operation. On the one hand, there is less leadership from the dominant power; on the other hand, inter-state authority becomes tendentially internationalised. For example, liberal theorists suggest that international regimes, as configurations of agreed principles, rules and procedures, can act as a stable basis for the interaction of transnational forces. Regimes help to provide order under post-hegemonic conditions. Indeed, John Ruggie has suggested that such regimes constitute the internationalisation of authority in a non-state form.[33]

The Trilateral Commission has made extensive use of the concept of public goods in order to highlight the potential for rational co-operation and regime formation. Examples are its studies of burden-sharing in military alliances, and of conditions for the maintenance of stable regimes for money, trade, security, and global 'commons' (such as the oceans and space). A Commission report also advocated a new regime for co-ordinating macroeconomic policy, mainly as a means of curbing American unilateralism. Indeed, much of the Commission's activity is directed at this latter goal.[34]

Liberal approaches thus produce a less pessimistic (but by no means Panglossian) view of the prospects for international co-operation than is typical of the realist tradition. In this way almost all of the Trilateral studies have concrete proposals to engineer co-operation. Most Commission reports assume that international co-operation is likely to be effective if the numbers of countries (or interests) involved is small. An example of this was a report which cites a quadrilateral study by the directors of French, British, West German and American Institutes of International Relations (all Commission members). This proposed a 'principal nations' approach: only those nations prepared to commit resources to resolve a particular problem should participate in making the decisions concerning it. 'Participation would be linked to the capacity for action'. The nations concerned would vary according to each issue, sometimes including 'non-trilateral countries' and perhaps consultations with third parties. The 'terms of partnership' would be based on 'principles from international commercial practice', in the sense that nations would receive benefits (including decision-making power) in proportion to their contribution.[35]

This suggests of course that the United States would be involved in all issues, with the other 'core' states unevenly involved. The United Nations model of one state, one vote, in the General Assembly is consciously repudiated as inefficient (although not that of the Security Council structure). According to this perspective, in contrast to organisations such as the United Nations, the Trilateral Commission is likely to be more successful at reaching acceptable levels of agreement. Whether this is reflected in the state policies of the 'Trilateral' nations is likely to be more problematic. The Commission report cited above makes this clear. Whereas the 'trilateral partners' share common interests in 'the maintenance of the international political and economic system', it concludes that at a more 'specific level', there are 'a great many differences', in terms of objective interests, perceptions of problems, and their diagnosis.[36]

This indicates considerable realism at the Commission's own efforts in helping to generate 'ideologically consonant' concepts of world order. It also indicates that there might be a greater possibility of a viable consensus between transnationalist interests than one which reflects the full range of domestic interests in each Trilateral state. At a minimum, the Commission has attempted the construction of common concepts, an analytical framework for the Trilateral establishments, and a forum in which American unilateralism might be constrained. As such, in Zbigniew Brzezinski's phrase, it is 'a shock absorber' for intra-Trilateral conflicts.[37]

3 MARXIST PERSPECTIVES: THE QUESTION OF HEGEMONY REDEFINED

Here I criticise two dominant Marxist approaches to the questions of inter-imperialist (inter-capitalist) relations and world order. I argue that they fail adequately to explain the nature of inter-capitalist relations in the 1970s and 1980s. A major reason is because these theories have inadequate conceptualisations of the state and of the internationalisation of postwar capitalism. This is also because their approaches are often determinist and do not sufficiently allow for consciousness and action. To explain these questions, I use a Gramscian, historical materialist approach. This allows us to make better sense of the apparent resilience of the alliance between the major capitalist nations during the period which corresponds to what Ernest Mandel has called the 'second slump'.[1]

CLASSICAL MARXISM

'Classical Marxism' refers here to theories of imperialism originating mainly before and during World War I, as in the work of Hilferding, Bukharin and Lenin.[2] These theorists sought to explain the international relations of the capitalist states in a period when production was organised on a primarily national basis. This was the 'highest' stage of 'monopoly capitalism'. These theories of imperialism were crucial for communist parties' assessments of centripetal and centrifugal forces in international relations. Such international theories predominated within many of the major communist parties, at least until the discovery and espousal of theories of global interdependence by President Gorbachev in the Soviet Union in the mid-1980s.

Let us now briefly sketch the nature of this approach. The main abstraction and unit of analysis within Marxism is a social system defined in terms of a dominant mode of production. This principally refers to the main social forces which organise and control the

33

economy. In the capitalist mode, much of the economic surplus takes the form of interest and profits for capitalists, who exploit labour. In the capitalist system, therefore, there are two basic social classes which have incompatible objective (or 'real') interests. The clash between these interests is captured by the concept of class struggle. In the context of class struggle, whereas the workers of the world are, in theory, potentially able to unite, the formation of an international capitalist class, with common interests and a shared consciousness, is impossible. This is mainly because international competition atomises the interests and collective potential of capitalists. However, at the domestic level, given certain conditions, capitalists can and do co-operate, in order to secure the rule of capital. At the international level, the situation approximates to war. For example, through their control of the state, the interests of monopoly capital are served by mercantilist strategies geared to enhancing profitability on a world scale. Such strategies are often directed at undermining foreign capitalists. In turn, the capitalists of the foreign state will also use mercantilist policies to protect and extend their interests. When general economic conditions deteriorate (as in a prolonged recession), inter-imperialist conflicts intensify.

Notwithstanding a systemic propensity to war, the ultimate constraints on the accumulation of capital and the survival of the system as a whole rest upon the contradictory and divisive class nature of capitalism. Class struggle is manifested, on the one hand, in the alleged tendency for the rate of profit to fall, and, on the other, by the rise of a class-conscious and organised (urban) working class, led by a highly disciplined vanguard group of intellectuals and leaders. The role of left-wing leaders is both political and theoretical (and in fact parallels that of what I call the 'organic intellectuals' of transnational capital). This revolutionary role entails theorising the weaknesses and contradictions of the system in order to help strengthen proletarian parties and accelerate capitalism's downfall.

Within this theory there are two major arguments concerning the nature of imperial rivalry: Leninist and Kautskian. The debate between them focuses upon the conflicts generated by the competition for raw materials, markets and cheap labour, a competition intensified by the tendency of the rate of profit to fall and for class struggle to increase.

The Leninist argument stresses conflicts caused by a collision between the surplus capital of imperialist states as each searches for new markets. Because of national rivalry and economic instability (itself explained by the law of uneven development of capitalism) long-term co-operation between capitalist states was impossible. The internationalisation of capital might appear to be a peaceful process at a particular moment, providing that there was a rough balance of power between the monopoly capitalists of different countries. In the long term, however, uneven development would cause this balance to change. Thereafter, a renewed and warlike struggle along national lines would take the place of any agreement to divide up markets peacefully. Lenin's argument was contradicted by the Social Democrat Kautsky, for whom 'ultra-imperialism' involved a relatively permanent coalition between roughly equal capitalist states at similar levels of development. This could take the narrow form of a cartel or trust, or a wider international oligarchy–oligopoly between imperialist states and national monopoly capitals.[3]

Let us now consider the interpretations of the postwar period which are based on these two arguments. In effect, the issue is the durability of the postwar order among the major capitalist states, in the specific conditions presented by the territorial expansion of communism.[4] In this context there is a neo-Kautskian interpretation of the long peace between the major capitalist powers since 1945, found in the writings of Harry Magdoff, Pierre Jalée and Martin Nicolaus. This view attributes the relative unity of the capitalist powers in this period mainly to a hegemonic 'ultra-imperialism' led by the United States. Acting as a 'super-imperialist', the United States was able to exert its dominance over Japan and Western Europe. This was because of the preeminence of American capital (especially in finance and in advanced sectors of production), and American military primacy. The postwar extension of Soviet communism, and the Chinese revolution provided capitalists and their states with an extra reason for co-operation. This American-led system was rationalised through Cold War ideology and consolidated in military alliances, notably in NATO. Initially, American motivations involved the desire to avoid a return to the depressed conditions of the 1930s and a fall in the rate of profit. This necessitated the international projection of American capital. This meant, in turn, that the global system had to be policed, in order to protect growing and far-flung American interests. In this context, America chose to dominate and impose unity on other imperialist states, but did so under the guise of multilateralism. From a Soviet point of view the Trilateral Commission and similar councils (such as the Bilderberg meetings which originated in 1954) were merely vehicles for this purpose.[5]

By contrast, other Marxists adopt a neo-Leninist interpretation. Whilst acknowledging the role of American dominance as a unifying force, such theorists emphasise that Japanese and West European capital have developed technological prowess and scale economies which, in the longer term, will enable a fundamental challenge to emerge and undercut American supremacy. This prospect is reflected in the fact that the technological and productivity gap between the three poles of advanced or 'late' capitalism has narrowed, to the disadvantage of American capital. As competition intensifies, a likely result will be a return to imperialist conflict. In this interpretation, the consequence is the inevitable end of American hegemony, as other states catch up, in many cases as a result of the injection of American capital and technology. Rival nations take advantage of what Mandel, following Trotsky, calls the 'law of combined and uneven development'.[6] This argument is very similar to that of Robert Gilpin, in *War and Change in World Politics*, where Trotsky's 'law' is also invoked.[7]

For Mandel, hegemonic co-operation was historically specific: it was associated with the *pax americana* and with the unprecedented conditions of the postwar boom. The onset of slump and recession in the 1970s coincided with a substantial relative decline in American economic and military power (many other Marxists assumed that this was clearly evident by 1970). These conditions set the context for a renewed rise in conflict between the imperialist states. America's rivals were becoming competitive equals. When freed from significant American discipline, Western Europe and Japan would shift further towards mercantilist policies. These policies would be either defensive or aggressive, the latter associated with attempts to export inflation and unemployment during the slump. Mandel had expounded the outlines of such a view, as early as 1970, in his influential *Europe versus America*, where a Euro-mercantilism was seen to be emerging to challenge American hegemony.

Other Marxists, however, argue that historical judgements on the decline of American hegemony in the 1970s underestimate the 'internal dynamic, political strength, and global underpinnings which facilitate recovery [from the setbacks of 1969–73] and the reconsolidation of US hegemony in global politics'.[8] Moreover, from this viewpoint, even if one accepts that the three great poles of capitalism are becoming relatively more equal, it does not necessarily imply the forms of rivalry and antagonism predicted by Leninist theory.

Let us now criticise this approach. My first criticism (which also applies to realist interpretations) is that both variants of the classical Marxist approach fail to take full and proper account of the nature and consequences of the internationalisation of economic activity since 1945 and especially since the 1960s. This has involved not only the internationalisation of finance and exchange, but also of production. This has led, among other things, to an interpenetration of capital, creating webs of international material interests. At the same time the rising international mobility and power of (transnational) capital has made control over economic policy more difficult for individual capitalist states. Thus governments may have a strong, indeed growing interest in co-operation and co-ordination of macroeconomic policy with those of other nations: the opportunity costs of non-cooperative economic strategies may appear to be prohibitively high. On the positive side, co-operation may be more likely if government leaders perceive the *absolute* gains from inter-state co-operation to be worthwhile (even where some states appear to gain relatively more than others).

This argument is reinforced by the identification of the sociological corollary of the internationalisation of capital: the emergence of an associated fraction of the capitalist class, whose interests are tied more and more to the world economy. Such a class fraction, whose contours are now emerging, is associated with firms in the *Fortune 500* list of the world's biggest corporations and banks.[9] Each of these giant firms has an interest in a stable international economic order, an interest which helps to mitigate 'inter-imperialist' conflict. This class fraction develops its own transnational networks, partly through its business transactions and its involvement with forums like the Trilateral Commission. It consistently defends liberal economic principles and opposes any significant movement towards mercantilism (see chapter 2).

My second criticism is that the classical Marxist tradition (like realism) has an inadequate conception of the state. Each position in this approach relies heavily on an instrumentalist theory of the capitalist state, seeing it as mainly the implement of the dominant class fraction of finance capitalists (some theorists allow for the possibility that the capitalist state can act as an 'ideal collective capitalist', seeking to secure the best possible short- and long-term conditions for its national capital in general). Even given this type of reductionism, what these theories seem unable to do is to relate changes in the state to the global changes noted above. Changes at the level of the global economy may promote a counterpart, interrelated process at the political level. The association of the government of each major capitalist nation with its own 'national capital' is now more problematic: some fractions of capital seek a nationalist-interventionist state strategy, whereas others seek the extension of free market principles on a world-wide basis. The process of the transnationalisation of the state, that is the modification of its institutional form and its policies by transnational forces, helps to explain why capitalist states had been more-or-less successful in avoiding intense antagonism despite the crises and recessions of the 1970s and 1980s (precisely the conditions where classical Marxist theory would predict severe conflict). I might add that this is one reason why the study of institutions like the Trilateral Commission is important, since it helps to explain the political processes which contain conflicts.

WORLD SYSTEMS THEORY

World systems theory has become very influential on the American left in recent years, much of its support being due to the writings of Immanuel Wallerstein.[10] Allied to this approach is dependency theory, developed in the 1950s and also influential on the left and among nationalist (and some socialist) forces in a number of developing nations, especially in Latin America.

Dependency and world systems writers see the *capitalist world-economy* as part of a single *world system* defining the place of a state within the hierarchy of nations. This hierarchy is divided in terms of *level* (rather than the form) of development into the categories of *core*, *periphery*, and *semi-periphery*. This roughly corresponds to the realist concept of the inter-state system. However, the concept of the capitalist world-economy is based on a quite different appraisal of system dynamics to that of orthodox Marxists. World systems theory stresses the primacy of exchange relations in its conceptualisation of global capitalism. Thus the world is not strictly divided into competing modes of production (feudal, capitalist, socialist) but into categories of states with different levels of development, integrated through the world market. A potent critique of world systems concepts has been made by Robert Brenner, who describes such theories as 'Neo-Smithian Marxism'.[11] As a result of these assumptions and concepts, world systems definitions of imperialism also differ:

> For Frank and Wallerstein, imperialism is a term that covers any use by *core states* of their political strength to impose *price structures* that they find favourable on the world-economy. Sometimes this takes the form of conquest and political overrule; at other times, it takes the form of 'informal imperialism', called by others 'neocolonialism'.[12]

In addition, there are a number of similarities between realism and world systems theory. For example, the dominant interpretation in each approach to the question of international order is roughly the same. Under capitalism, peace between the major powers in the world system is equated with empire or hegemony, and instability with core competition. Both approaches view historical levels of conflict in cyclical terms:

> when power is dispersed (multicentricity) the core appears more unstable and relations between core and periphery tighten up. When one state dominates (hegemony, unicentricity) there appears to be peace among the major powers, and a relaxation of explicit political control of core-periphery relations. That is, during hegemonies there are movements toward decolonisation and free trade.[13]

For world systems theory, the dynamics for these changes are bound up with the uneven and unequal development of the world system. However, there are limits to the scope of development which is possible for states from each category. 'Core' states are those with more advanced technologies, military strength, and a favourable place in the international division of labour (this idea partly corresponds to the Trilateral Commission's concept of a 'vital core' of advanced capitalist states). Less developed states are either 'peripheral' or 'semi-peripheral', the latter being less dependent on the core than is the periphery.[14] The dependence of the periphery is financial, technological and military, and takes various forms at different periods.

Because of the core's economic and cultural dominance, established in the colonial era, a relatively fixed inter-state hierarchy has arisen. Bonds of dependence imply that the autonomy and economic potential of peripheral states is constrained by core states and core capital. Although there is some upward and downward mobility within the world system, a basic structure of extreme inequality persists. This is maintained by either 'formal' (for example by the use of military power) or 'informal' means (as with the indirect application of market power). Core states are assumed to have a high degree of autonomy, whereas peripheral states have relatively little. There is some limitation to the autonomy of the core, particularly its relatively declining states, such as Britain. In the last analysis, all interaction is conditioned by the primordial structure of the world system.

Within this structural context, the forging of transnational class alliances is central to the policies of particular core states. The bourgeoisie and state managers of the core seek to incorporate the *comprador* elements within the elites of peripheral and semi-peripheral states in order to maintain the core's economic domination. This alliance is crucial in the ongoing process of dependency. This process is, however, bound up with a dialectical conflict between transnational capital and 'socialist forces', where the latter will seek to cut the links between *comprador* elements and core capital and force a drastic redistribution of the world product.[15] Seen from this viewpoint, the activities of the Trilateral Commission are equated with working out the contours of a two-fold American-led strategy. The first element is working out an 'ultra-imperialism' of the core to supplement or replace the declining dominance of the United States. A second is what Antonio Gramsci called *trasformismo* or co-optation of elites, particularly of the more powerful semi-peripheral states (including communist states), into the hegemonic structures and processes of the capitalist world economy. A strategy of incorporation would help to guarantee politically the rule of transnational capital.[16] The possibility of the Trilateralists (understood as the controllers and senior executives of transnational capital) successfully agreeing on this strategy is relatively high, because of the shared interest in accumulation and exploitation of labour. However, its chances of success depend on other factors, most importantly, on whether the world economy is expanding, and on whether the contradiction between state and capital which characterises the core capitalist states can be contained.

Like the Marxist, Fred Block, Immanuel Wallerstein sees a conflict within the ruling elements of the core states, which he calls the *janissarization* of the ruling classes (a split between corporate and state managers on the one hand, and the top bourgeois owners on the other, over their respective shares of surplus value) within a broad political grouping which he refers to as the 'party of order'. This 'party' is in effect all the political forces which wish to sustain the dominant capitalist order.[17] Wallerstein claims that transnational corporations and core state apparatuses have grown stronger and their relations more complex and intensive. Nonetheless their possibilities of smooth co-operation are increasingly beset by internecine struggles. The 'cadres' (managerial and middle classes) demand a bigger slice of the pie, whilst the corporations need to make profits, a situation which creates conflicts of interest. Such conflicts can only be contained if there is vigorous economic growth. Moreover, slow growth or recession weakens 'the ability [of the party of order] to stand up against the party of movement' (that is socialist forces).[18] In surveying the prospects for future growth, some of these theorists (notably Wallerstein, but also Marxists like Mandel) argue that the 'world system' entered a long downward 'wave' of relative stagnation around 1970, and suggest that this is likely to persist at least into the 1990s. (Given the time span of Kondratieff 'long waves', which this argument is based on, stagnation might last as long as fifty years.) As such, the prospects for Trilateral co-operation are bleak.

Three further criticisms of these arguments are in order here. The first is that world system theorists simply fail to explain the historical changes which have actually occurred. For example, the recessions of the 1970s and 1980s did not produce the political effects Wallerstein suggests: organised labour was severely weakened on a world scale, and the cadres did not gain the upper hand. Indeed, during the 1970s and 1980s there was a more-or-less successful neo-liberal political offensive geared to rolling back the frontiers of the state in the economy and to reduce its relative share of GNP. This can be explained by our second criticism, which concerns the limitations of the world systems theorisation of contemporary capitalism. What is missing is a careful analysis of the transnational social forces which can serve to maintain the essentials of the global system of capitalism, contain conflict and the emergence of severe antagonisms. Our third criticism relates to the inability of the world systems approach to really get to grips with the problem of international change. This weakness stems from a combination of its state-centric conception of international relations, a basic economism and an essentialism akin to that of realism. Indeed, despite the polemical hope that left-wing forces will triumph, the basic logic of the Wallersteinian approach leads to deeply pessimistic conclusions for socialist forces. His argument implies that any change will occur within a fixed, almost inexorable pattern. Such determinism fails fully to acknowledge that not only does the contemporary stage of capitalism have unique features, but also that historial change is bound up with human agency in complex and often unpredictable ways. What is needed, in other words, is greater methodological openness and analytical flexibility.

GRAMSCIAN HISTORICAL MATERIALISM

The work of Antonio Gramsci, and that of Robert Cox, constitute a fundamentally important development of Marxist theory. Gramsci's contribution is based on a critique of the economism and determinism which he saw as deeply rooted in the Italian labour movement in the early twentieth century. Economism refers here to any doctrine which gives undue primacy to economic and technological forces over political ones in the explanation of historical change. In the Italy of his day, Gramsci argued, economism was associated with mechanical determinism: here politics was treated as either a reflection or mechanical expression of economic developments. The result of this was to encourage fatalism and passivity on the part of workers, and to allow the political initiative to remain with the ruling class. To counteract this tendency, Gramsci sought to develop concepts and theories which related to class struggle, and to the questions of consciousness and political action, in concrete historical circumstances. There is a fluidity and urgency about the development of such concepts and theories. Gramsci's concepts attained their precision when applied to the analysis of particular historical situations.

It is argued here that Gramsci's concept of hegemony and his development and redefinition of other concepts provide a significant critique of, and alternative to, the Marxist approaches discussed above. Indeed, his thought contains the seeds of a new conceptualisation of the relations between social forces and the nature of world order. The Gramscian approach is, however, the least developed of modern Marxist approaches to the study of international relations. One of the tasks of this study is to draw attention to this approach, and to show that it can be further developed. To give a fuller understanding of hegemony it is necessary to elaborate other Gramscian concepts. For our purposes, the most important of these are the state, 'civil' and 'political' society, 'historic bloc' and 'organic intellectual'. These concepts are used in subsequent chapters.[19]

First of all, however, it is worth noting that Gramsci's concepts are dialectical. For example, Gramsci's concept of hegemony is intended to help in the analysis of the relation between social forces at a particular period. It generally refers to a relation between social classes, in which one class fraction or class grouping takes a leading role through gaining the *active consent* of other classes and groups. Hegemony, therefore, is not a relation of coercive force as such (as it is viewed in realist theory), but rather primarily one of consent gained through 'intellectual and moral leadership'.

In Marxism a mode of production is normally conceived of as having three main 'levels' or aspects: economic, political and ideological. Gramsci adds another, 'ethico-political' dimension to the idea of a mode of production through his concept of civil society. To achieve this innovation, Gramsci goes beyond the materialist conception in the *Preface to the Critique of Political Economy*. In the *Critique*, Marx associated civil society with relations entered into for the purposes of production: 'the anatomy of civil society is to be sought in political economy'. By contrast, Gramsci developed Hegel's distinction between 'private' civil society and 'public' political society (that is, the state), although, as Roger Simon points out, the key issue is not the 'private'/'public' dichotomy as such. Rather it is the contrast between consent (which primarily characterises civil society) and coercion (which underpins, but does not constitute exclusively, the power of the state).[20]

Gramsci has both a restricted and an extended ('general') concept of the state. The restricted concept of the state corresponds to the 'political society' which refers to the state's formal governmental apparatus (administrative, legal and coercive). The 'extended' concept sees the state as fused with both 'political' and 'civil' society.[21] In other words, for Gramsci, the separation between state and civil society was purely methodological, and a closer analysis of particular societies often revealed that the public/private distinction made by Hegel failed to reflect actual circumstances. This was because organisations in the civil society often had a public aspect: the leaders of a trade union, employers' association, church, political party, the media, or even a freemasons lodge might be drawn into the state, either directly or indirectly. Some elements of civil society, such as universities or schools, might also be funded by, or be part of, the state. As Gramsci put it:

> What we can do, for the moment, is to fix two major superstructural 'levels': the one that can be called 'civil society', that is the ensemble of organisms commonly called 'private' and that of the 'political society' or 'the state'. These two levels correspond to the functions of hegemony which the dominant group exercises throughout society and on the other hand to that of 'direct domination' or command exercised through the state and 'juridical' government.[22]

Civil society is therefore intertwined, not only with the state, but also with the forces of production. The character of the state, and its engagement in the civil society, varies according to the relation of social forces in any given society. This brings us to the 'extended' notion of the state which arises from political conditions in modern society. The extended concept of the state introduced by Gramsci seems particularly appropriate for analysis in a century in which we have seen the total state, and when the state is so central to the functioning of modern capitalism, as well as Soviet-type societies. Moreover, the state–civil society distinction and the idea of the extended state are particularly useful for the analysis of developed capitalist societies. Gramsci modified the classical Marxist view which defined the central feature of the state as the use of coercion. By contrast, Gramsci argued, for example, that the character of the liberal democratic state should be conceived of in integral terms, as the fusion of consent and coercion for the purpose of rule. In addition, since the relation between state and civil society varied, it was necessary to examine the concrete nature of a given society before arriving at judgements concerning political strategy. For example, whereas in pre-revolutionary Russia the state was everything, with the civil society 'primordial and gelatinous':

in the West, there was a proper relation between the State and civil society, and when the State trembled a sturdy structure of civil society was at once revealed. The State was only an outer ditch, behind which there stood a powerful system of fortresses and earthworks: more or less numerous from one State to the next.[23]

In this particular context, the state was 'the entire complex of theoretical and practical activities with which the ruling class not only maintains its dominance, but manages to win the consent of those over whom it rules'.[24] Therefore, the state is 'political society plus civil society, hegemony armoured by coercion'.[25] This meant that even a major economic crisis would not automatically lead to a serious political crisis, or a challenge to the hegemony of the ruling group:

> It may be ruled out that immediate economic crises of themselves produce fundamental historical events [i.e. revolutions]; they can simply create a terrain more favourable to the dissemination of certain modes of thought, and certain ways of posing and resolving questions involving the entire subsequent development of national life. Moreover, all assertions concerning periods of crisis or of prosperity may give rise to unilateral judgements.[26]

In order that the workers' party could create the conditions to secure state power (and use it effectively) in the West it would necessarily have to involve itself in a long-term and painstaking process of political and cultural education of the masses, institution-building, and the creation of links with potential political allies (for example, with the peasantry of Italy). It would have to be able to demonstrate that it provided a practical and viable alternative to the prevailing political arrangements. Much of its political activity would therefore take place within the civil society. Gramsci called such a strategy a 'war of position'. This was in contrast to an insurrectionary strategy, or 'war of movement'. Whereas the latter strategy had worked for the Bolsheviks in Russia, it could not succeed in the West. In the Western context it meant that the workers' party should forge alliances to form a political bloc of forces able to sustain its political power and, in time, to reshape the social forces in a socialist direction. To explain theoretically how this could be attempted, Gramsci introduced perhaps his most novel and complex concept, that of the 'historic bloc'. This concept was used to analyse constellations of social and political forces.

The concept of the 'historic bloc' refers to those situations when there is a high degree of political congruence between sets of 'relations of force'. Of these, the second type of relation of force is crucial for our discussion of hegemony. The first relation of force was structural or material, for example, the level of the forces of production, the number and location of cities etc. (these had to be largely taken as given). The second was 'political', that is relating to the development of classes and their level of political consciousness; the third was military, including domestic use of military power as well as the geo-political-military forces which configured the development of a particular society.[27]

Within the category of political forces, Gramsci identified three moments in the development of consciousness. The first, the 'economic-corporative' was manifested when a tradesman 'feels *obliged* to stand by another tradesman, a manufacturer by another manufacturer, but the tradesman does not yet feel solidarity with the manufacturer'.[28] This reflected a group solidarity. The second was solidarity of economic interests among members of the same class. This involved posing the question of the state and its reform 'but within existing fundamental structures'.[29] The third, and most political moment was when:

> one becomes aware that one's own corporate interests, in their present and future development, transcend the corporate limits of the purely economic class, and can and must become the interests of other subordinate groups too. This is the most purely political phase, and marks the decisive passage from the structure to the sphere of complex superstructures . . . bringing about not only a unison of economic and political aims, but also intellectual and moral unity, posing all the questions around which the struggle rages not on a corporate but on a 'universal' plane, and thus creating the hegemony of a fundamental social group over a series of subordinate groups.[30]

An attempt to universalise hegemony by politically synthesising a range of class interests lies at the heart of the forging of a historic bloc.[31] The historic bloc is, therefore, an 'organic' link between structure and superstructure.[32] Such a bloc cannot occur spontaneously, nor simply as a result of the force of economic necessity. It needs leadership and action based on a highly developed political consciousness within the dominant social class:

> Undoubtedly the fact of hegemony presupposes that account be taken of the interests and tendencies of the groups over which hegemony is to be exercised, and that a certain compromise equilibrium should be formed – in other words the leading group should make sacrifices of an economic-corporate kind. But there is also no doubt that such sacrifices and such a compromise cannot touch the essential; for though hegemony is ethical-political, it must also be economic, must necessarily be based on the decisive function exer-

cised by the leading group in the decisive nucleus of economic activity.[33]

For a new historic bloc to emerge, therefore, its key elements must engage in 'conscious, planned struggle':

> An appropriate political initiative is always necessary to liberate the economic thrust from the dead weight of traditional policies – i.e. to change the political direction of certain forces which have to be absorbed if a new, homogeneous politico-economic bloc, without internal contradictions, is to be successfully formed.[34]

Since, by definition, Gramsci suggests that the forging of a hegemonic historic bloc entails the dominant social class, the launching of such a political initiative may originate with an enlightened fraction of the bourgeoisie: for example, the establishment of the Trilateral Commission in 1973 might be interpreted as corresponding to an international attempt to launch such an initiative. For Gramsci, the application of the concept of historic bloc was largely specific to a national context, albeit in an international conjuncture, configured by the military relations of force. However, in this book we shall attempt to develop and apply Gramsci's concepts at the international level, so that, at least theoretically, we can speak of historic blocs and the concept of hegemony at the international level. This is the task of the rest of this chapter.

TRANSNATIONAL HISTORICAL MATERIALISM

The neo-Gramscian form of historical materialism, as applied to world orders and transnational labour–capital relations, was pioneered by Robert Cox. This approach, which I will call transnational historical materialism, attempts to explain the dynamics of the contemporary era of global capitalism.

For writers in this tradition, structural changes in the capitalist system require a more flexible analytical approach, one which allows for the possibility of the analysis of transnational social forces, including the interplay between different interests within each state. The key units in Cox's variant are interacting sets of social forces (ideas, institutions, material capabilities), which affect the formation of 'transnational' as well as national class fractions (of labour and capital), and the 'internationalised' (or what I call the 'transnationalised') state. These forces operate at three interrelated (methodological) levels: world orders, state–civil society complexes, and the basic level of production. This enables a reconceptualisation of the question of hegemony. Hegemony occurs when there is a strong congruence between each of these social forces across each level.[35]

Gramsci saw the basic changes in the military-strategic and geo-political balance as originating in more fundamental changes in social relations. This was not to suggest that the state was diminished in importance, it was the basic entity in international relations, and the place where the hegemony of classes or class fractions was built. However, the state was the extended state which included its own social (class) basis within the civil society, rather than the narrower conception typical of realism. In this view, the great powers have the maximum degree of external autonomy, whereas the subordinate powers are penetrated by the former.[36] The most powerful states are those which have undergone a profound internal development, in which the hegemony of a dominant class or class fraction has been built. In time, this revolution becomes internationally expansive. Thus, world hegemony has for its origin the outward expansion of the internal or national hegemony, established by the dominant or ruling class within the most powerful state. In so far as such a state becomes internationally hegemonic, it would have to, in Cox's words, 'found and protect a world order which was universal in conception, that is not an order in which one state directly exploits others but an order which most other states (at least those within reach of the hegemony) would find compatible with their interests'. Moreover: 'The hegemonic concept of world order is founded not only upon the regulation of inter-state conflict but also upon a globally conceived civil society, i.e. a mode of production of global extent which brings about links among social classes encompassed by it.'[37]

Hegemony would be fully achieved when the major institutions and forms of organisation – economic, social, and political – as well as the key values of the dominant state become models for emulation in other subordinate states. In this view of hegemony, the patterns of emulation are most likely in the core or most developed states, rather than in the less-developed periphery. As such, 'hegemony is more intense and consistent at the core, and more laden with contradictions at the periphery'.[38] Bourgeois hegemony, at least in the most developed nations, necessitates a relatively consensual order, with political debates anchored in the acceptance of the agenda and key ideas of the bourgeoisie. This involves a minimum use of illegitimate force and has, for its constitutional expression, a parliamentary or liberal democratic regime. Such hegemony, at the international level, requires more than a simple balance of power or an order between states, since it also involves the complex patterns of social relations which connect social classes in a range of countries:

> World hegemony is describable as a social structure, an economic structure, and a political structure; and it cannot be simply one of these things but must be all three. World hegemony, furthermore, is expressed in universal norms, institutions and mechanisms, which lay down general rules for the behaviour of states, and for those forces of civil society that act across national boundaries – rules which support the dominant mode of production.[39]

For Gramsci, in periods of crisis, the apparatus of hegemony tends to break down, and often political parties fragment, and no single group obtains a broad enough consensus with which to govern. This situation is ripe for a shift in power, the construction or reconstruction of the apparatus of hegemony, and the search for a new basis of consensus takes place.[40] In this sense, the widely perceived crisis in American hegemony of the late 1960s and 1970s, in the context of recession and the apparent breakdown of co-operative action amongst the capitalist powers and the major transnational actors, provoked the need for a new or modified institutional structure. This could promote the search for a new hegemonic consensus on the nature of international arrangements. This consensus would necessarily have to reflect not only the increased weight of Japan and West Germany, but also the growing strength of transnational capital, as well as taking account of the rise of certain newly industrialising nations and the growing international role of the Soviet bloc. This was because rising power centres and the increased mobility of capital meant that the socio-economic and political foundations of the former order were being eroded.

At this stage it is useful to sketch out in more concrete terms what is meant by the concept of a historic bloc at the international level. Following Gramsci, this means a political constellation which reflects an international congruence of objective and subjective forces. At the overt, political level, this would be manifested in an international coalition of interests. As should be evident from our earlier attempts at definition, such a bloc differs from a 'transnational class alliance' (or an 'ultra-imperialism of core capital'). This is because elements of more than one class are involved, under the leadership of a forward-looking and internationally oriented class fraction. Because of its trans-class nature, such a bloc is more organic and rooted in the social structure. It is also embedded in the modes of thought (ways of seeing and understanding the social world) of key individuals in government, and of groups and institutions in various civil societies in strong as well as less powerful nations (for example, the media and trades unions). This means that the alliance of social forces it comprises is seen, to a large extent, as 'natural' and legitimate by most of its members.

From this neo-Gramscian vantage point then, the postwar mix of social democracy, and class compromise in the 'mixed economy' based upon Fordist accumulation (an intensive, growth-oriented regime of accumulation involving mass-production, the physical and psychological subordination of labour through Taylorist scientific management, and a culture and economy of mass-consumption) and growing international trade were key ingredients in an *international historic bloc*. This incorporated a range of class interests which sustained not only the modernisation of the 'mixed economies' of the West, but also the liberal international economic order. Subscribing to this perspective were not only moderates in conservative parties, but also liberals and social democrats, and the leaders of many elements of non-communist organised labour. There was a broad-based political consensus in the Atlantic states which in effect served to generate the ethico-political concepts of civilisation which cemented the bloc. The concepts of liberty, modernity, affluence, welfare and the 'end of ideology' were fused into a concept of 'the West'. These social forces were consolidated into an anti-communist alliance, geared towards the defence of 'the West' from the threat of totalitarianism and, in Koestler's memorable phrase, 'darkness at noon'. The bloc's foundations were forged in a balance between the material forces of national and transnational capital, organised labour and the state. This mainly transatlantic historic bloc was constructed during the late 1940s and 1950s, and lasted until at least the late 1960s.

Which forces served to unravel this bloc? The obvious response to such a question would be that the political and economic distribution of power has changed with the result that the United States and the Atlantic region are in relative decline, whereas new power centres in the Pacific Rim and the communist world mean an inevitable transition towards a more plural world order. This would be a 'crisis of hegemony' as understood by most international relations theorists. A different way to explain this is by posing questions in Gramscian terms. For example, which elements in the postwar international bloc have been weakened, and which strengthened? Which elements are new? What does this mean for the composition and character of a new historic bloc? What are the contours of its dominant ideology?

In the postwar period, and especially since the late 1960s, there has been a rapid internationalisation of production, such that, in the

49

OECD area, about 30 per cent of all manufacturing workers are employed by transnational companies, with many others in the OECD region, and in the Third World, dependent on transnational production and international trade for their livelihoods. At the same time there has been a significant integration of capital and exchange markets on a global basis. In this context, both national governments and organised and non-organised labour are increasingly constrained by the power resources and growing mobility of transnational capital, and by modes of thought which rationalise the rising hegemony of transnational capital. Whilst giant corporations have such power and mobility, labour is relatively immobile and is thus constrained – in terms of the possibility of global solidarity of workers – by nationalism, sectionalism, and specific cultural traditions. In this process, an emerging transnational capitalist class fraction is mobilised by developing its consciousness and solidarity, for example in international organisations, international financial institutions, private international relations councils, and 'philanthropic' institutions, such as the Ford Foundation which sponsor conferences and fund research programmes. Through a series of coalitions based on shared interests and hegemonic concepts about the way in which the world does and should work, a transnational class fraction increasingly occupies the centre of an emerging *transnational historic bloc*, one with a wider leadership basis than in the era of transatlantic hegemony, and one in which the political status of organised labour is diminished.

At the apex of such a bloc are the elements in the state and in capital (drawn from the Trilateral nations) which are linked to dynamic, international production and finance, mainly in the most advanced sectors of each. Certain sections of labour may identify their interests with those of transnational capital, although in a period of recession and higher unemployment, their political weight in the bloc is reduced. By contrast, other sections of labour may combine with 'national capitalists' to form a neo-mercantilist coalition, opposing transnational hegemony. Such coalitions may be mobilised by communist, social democratic, nationalist, populist, or even fascist parties and ideologies. However, the very great differences between each of these tendencies means that a successful counter-hegemonic mobilisation on a world-wide basis is likely to be difficult, if not impossible.

In the current historical conjuncture the tensions involved in moving towards a transnational hegemony can be related to the international spread of 'monetarist' and liberal free-market ideas, and the way they interact and conflict with productive interests and with nationalist and mercantilist modes of thought. In so far as these monetarist-liberal' ideas spread in the advanced capitalist countries, it can be argued that the structural power of internationally mobile capital, particularly financial capital, notably international banks, will tend to increase. Economic policies will come to reflect an international bankers' view of the 'correct' mix (see chapter 5 for a development of this argument).

The emergence of these new conditions, embodying the seeds of substantial intra-class conflict (that is between national and international capital, and associated elements of labour) had earlier called for a political response, from transnational and international elements, which sought to manage a transition to a reconstructed hegemony. Flexible strategies would need to be developed to incorporate new elements effectively into the bloc. The Trilateral Commission can, in this sense, be seen as an institution which was born and develops in the context of the onset of this 'crisis' (in the sense of transition) of postwar hegemony in the advanced capitalist states.

ORGANIC INTELLECTUALS AND TRILATERAL CO-OPERATION

With respect to the question of co-operation within advanced capitalism, we will argue that it is most likely to be successful when there is a close congruence or 'fit' between the dominant social forces and strategies of key states in a given historical conjuncture. However, as has been noted, there is nothing automatic in terms of the correspondence between structural and material conditions and the achievement of a successful, hegemonic strategy. This requires a far-sighted political consciousness on the part of leaders in the dominant groups. The question of conscious action presupposes a group of thinkers and practitioners who can theorise on the nature of global change, and generate concepts which can chart the path towards a reconstructed order. This raises the following questions. How are the concepts which lie at the heart of the hegemonic ideology to be developed? How are the strategies of the hegemonic class fraction to be shaped?

According to Gramsci, any historic bloc requires 'organic intellectuals' to help cement the links between structure and superstructure. These intellectuals are the 'concrete articulators' of the hegemonic ideology which provides cohesion for, and helps to integrate, the historic bloc. Intellectuals are not simply producers of ideology, they are also the 'organisers of hegemony', that is, they theorise the ways in which hegemony can be developed or maintained.[41] Thus intellectuals are a steering force in the political rule of a dominant class fraction in a given historic bloc.

The Gramscian idea of the intellectual is 'the entire social stratum which exercises an organisational function in the wide sense – whether in the field of culture or production or political administration'.[42] Gramsci's notion of the intellectual is a practical one – it is counterposed to the literati and 'traditional' intellectuals. This concept can be used to shed light on the intellectuals and the membership of the Trilateral Commission and other organisations which are involved in the task of the maintenance and reconstruction of global hegemony. The Commission's relevance is illustrated in the following quotation from its first European Chairman, Max Kohnstamm, in a discussion of the Commission's initial research programme:

> This, which must be done by absolutely first-rate intellectuals *will tend to become irrelevant* unless it is done in *constant checking with those who are in power or who have a considerable influence on those in power*. It seems to me that the linkage between the kind of people we must get for our Trilateral Commission and the intellectuals doing the indispensable work of thinking about the *elements for a new system* is of the greatest importance. A Trilateral Commission without the intellectuals will become very soon a second-class negotiating forum. The *intellectuals not being forced to test their ideas constantly with the establishment of our world will tend to become abstract and therefore useless* . . . [It must be] the *joint effort of our very best minds and a group of really influential citizens* in our respective countries.[43]

Gramsci paid special attention to the institutional frameworks in which intellectuals develop, produce and disseminate ideologies and theories. He called these 'ideological apparatuses'. A hegemonic ideology is necessarily produced by, and depends on, a long and difficult, often very contradictory process whereby 'conceptions of the world are created and destroyed, reformulated, and reconstituted through intellectual activity'. To secure its hegemony, therefore, a dominant class or class fraction needs creative intellectuals 'to elaborate, modify and disseminate its class conception of the world'. However, whether the masses adhere to the dominant ideology is a critical test of the 'rationality and historicity' of the 'modes of thinking' of organic intellectuals.[44]

Gramsci noted that the ability to form a historic bloc may be partially accomplished for the bourgeoisie by political parties, with strategies developed by their organic intellectuals. These parties reflect different fractions in the ruling classes and groups. However, this ability may exist outside of parties as a result of the capacity of stronger elements to use cultural institutions, the media, private associations, universities, educational foundations and parts of the state apparatus.[45] This list can be extended to include members of key international organisations.

Seen from this point of view, some of the ideas of Zbigniew Brzezinski, and others associated with the creation of the Trilateral Commission, can be related to the quest for concepts which can form the core of a hegemonic ideology of transnational capital, for example his 'quest for a universal vision' which finds its representation in his idea of a 'community of the developed nations', pursuing a 'planetary humanism' via enlightened co-operation in order to: 'assure a smooth management of interdependence; cooperation not based on coercion and arm-twisting, but on mutuality of interest and indeed on the longer-term interest of mankind'.[46]

As is frequently noted, Gramsci's concept of hegemony is related generally to the national rather than the international level, although Gramsci did believe hegemony was possible, between 'complexes of international and continental civilisations', for example under the leadership of the Communist International. The achievement of a communist hegemony would require a long-run preparation in the advanced capitalist states in a 'war of position', that is, the long-term construction of a viable alternative set of economic, political and cultural arrangements (in which the role of intellectuals would be all-important), and the forging of a new international consensus around them, which would be built, at the world level, on the development of a 'collective national will' at the level of the nation-state.[47]

This type of analysis can also be applied to the hegemony of particular (fractions of) capital, not just at the national but also at the international levels. Seen from this perspective, American organic intellectuals during World War II, notably at the State Department and the New York Council on Foreign Relations, were able to develop a blueprint for the postwar order, and mount long-term strategies for bringing this about, using the tactics of co-optation, compromise and co-operation (with of course some of the 'arm twisting' Brzezinski refers to) to forge a workable international consensus, one that enabled a period of relative peace and prosperity amongst the previously antagonistic allied and axis powers.[48] When such favourable conditions appeared to break down at the end of the postwar boom, new approaches were necessary 'to meet the challenge' of forces which seemed to threaten the rising power of transnational capital.

The Trilateral Commission's initial advocacy of a universalist ideol-

53

ogy of common global interests requiring management by an internationalist technocracy can be seen partly as a means to develop a co-optative response to the strength of labour, and the threat of a disruptive Third World nationalism during the 1970s. This may also have reflected an accommodationist tendency in the governments of the Trilateral states in the early and mid-1970s, whereas the monetarist-militarist offensive of the first Reagan administration and the rise to power of its conservative counterparts in most of the other Trilateral states in the late 1970s and 1980s reflected both a reversal of this earlier defensive posture, and a renewed emphasis on the use of market power as a force to discipline labour and unruly Third World nationalism. Seen in terms of the evolution of the forces of transnational capital these phases can be seen as different tactical strands in a longer-term 'war of position' of transnational capital, *vis-à-vis* nationalism (and national capital) and socialism, corresponding to the political strategy of *trasformismo* (associated with productive capital and the idea of compromise with organised labour) and a more short-term offensive strategy geared to the reassertion of the primacy of international market forces (associated with financial capital and highly capital-intensive production). Also, in the first half of the 1980s, Reagan's willingness to wage the second Cold War was also geared towards the reassertion, not only of American military primacy, but also of the ethico-political core of Western values. The role of the Trilateral Commission, particularly in the 1980s, can be seen in this light as representing a concept of political control over market forces and unrestrained anti-Sovietism, so that they did not destabilise the emerging transnational hegemony, as well as providing the long-term vision to shape the contours of the future.

THE PROBLEM OF HEGEMONY REDEFINED

Thus, in the sphere of international relations the problem of hegemony needs to be redefined to encompass transnational social forces at each level of analysis. The interaction of such social forces can help explain the historical process in a broader, more dialectical way than is possible with realist, world systems and classical Marxist approaches. It is thus possible, using this approach, to differentiate between hegemonic and non-hegemonic forms of world order, and to provide explanations for the origins and the conditions of existence of each. This, in turn, helps to explain under what general conditions and circumstances co-operation between the key interests and states is most likely. This approach also enables us to discuss the postulate of a civil society on a world scale organised around a series of hegemonic principles of political life and economic interaction.

This moves the problematic of hegemony away from the state-centric classical Marxist, realist and world systems concepts, where hegemony is equated with the successful mobilisation of state power by the hegemon, or a condominium of states. In the other perspectives, hegemony is viewed in terms of the Weberian notion of 'power over', that is to say it is largely coercive in character. Indeed, the realist concept is really a concept of dominance and domination, whereas the Gramscian concept fuses the concepts of coercion and consent, and rests upon both normative and material dimensions of power, in its behavioural and structural forms. It therefore helps to reconcile the' 'structure-action' problem in social theory. For world hegemony (and thus peaceful relations between advanced capitalist states) to occur there must be a congruence between major 'social forces' at the domestic and international levels. This implies the need for conscious political action and the pursuit of consent and legitimation as necessary to the development and maintenance of hegemony, since at any point in its evolution, a successful hegemony is one where consensual aspects of the system come to the forefront, although coercion is always potentially in the background.

This approach suggests that forms of political action directed towards the formation of international norms and political consensus – such as the activities of the Trilateral Commission, Bilderberg, the Atlantic Institute, the OECD, the World Bank, the IMF – may all be vitally important ingredients in the development and maintenance of a stable, international order, or in maintaining cohesion among the capitalist states in a period of transition. The argument I put forward in this book is that the role and purpose of the Trilateral Commission is in fact bound up with a 'crisis of hegemony'. In this crisis, there is an increasing primacy for the forces of internationally mobile capital. These forces are serving to unravel the postwar political settlements within and between the advanced capitalist states (that is, the international compromises of corporate or 'embedded' liberalism), at the same time as recession has undermined labour, and the power of the developing nations to create the prospect for a new international economic order. Thus, although it is clear that some rise in mercantilism has taken place, this has been significantly accompanied by continued liberalisation of the capitalist world economy. In this process, despite tensions and considerable conflicts over a range of issues, the cohesion of the advanced capitalist states has been maintained. What is new, however, is the growth in the structural power of internationally mobile, large-scale capital. This power has not yet been fully conceptualised in the literature, and as such the following chapters may be said to have an element of originality.

4 THE DECLINE OF AMERICAN HEGEMONY: MYTH AND REALITY

Here I challenge the widely accepted argument that American global dominance has substantially waned since the 1960s. My criticisms are three-fold: in terms of the conceptualisation of dominance and hegemony, its measurement (with particular reference to military power), and the theorisation of the consequences of changes in the United States position. With respect to the latter issue, is it the case that weakening hegemony and international economic disorder go hand in hand?

Here, therefore, I deal with the outward reach of America as a national system. By a national system is meant more than the usual conception of the American state. What is meant here refers both to the Gramscian conception of the extended state, and to the aspects of American civil society which either have, or may have, the capacity to take on an international dimension: in this respect the internationalisation of the American political economy in the 1970s and 1980s is significant. In chapters 4 and 5 I seek to widen the primarily materialist focus of the debate to take account of the cultural and ideological aspects of hegemony. Understanding the interrelated nature of American and what I call an emerging transnational hegemony is a key to an assessment of the role of the private international relations councils to be discussed in chapters 6–8.

My position in the debate over American hegemony is that the sheer scale of the American political economy and its position in the global system means that the United States continues to gain substantial advantage from its structural dominance: American hegemony is, in the 1980s, far from over. Further, American hegemony has a cumulative and indirect quality. The structural aspects of American hegemony cannot be fully appreciated by using a purely empiricist, or indeed a narrowly materialist, conception of power. Rather, as was noted in chapter 3, we need a synthetic concept of international power which fuses not only direct, behavioural forms of power, but also its structural aspects, in both the 'material' and 'normative' dimensions. These aspects of power are the foundations of the Gramscian concept of hegemony. Let us first of all, however, outline the way in which American hegemony is understood in the bulk of the literature, and then I can proceed with my critique.

THE THESIS OF HEGEMONIC DECLINE

Now I will briefly summarise what I suggest became the accepted wisdom in the international relations literature of the 1970s and 1980s, concerning the decay of American hegemony and its international consequences. Almost perversely, this view was held most tenaciously by academics in the United States, whereas a number of writers from other countries were more circumspect in their assessments.[1] This neo-Spenglerian pessimism concerning the decline of the United States surfaced during the late 1960s and 1970s. This was, of course, partly a response to American engagement and defeat in Vietnam. In American foreign policy, the retreat from globalism was reflected in the policy of detente and in the Nixon Doctrine and, at the ideological level, in President Carter's warnings concerning the 'crisis of confidence' in America's meaning and future. In a more academic vein, the new melancholy, found in the writings of a number of neoconservatives, was exemplified in Daniel Bell's lament that the 'American Century' had ended after only some thirty years (it began after World War II). America was no longer like a sun, providing light and energy to power the international political and economic firmament.[2] Others argued (with a phrase suggestive of *hubris* amid peremptory decline) that the era of extraordinary American power was drawing to a close: America had become more like an 'ordinary country'.[3]

Much of this American gloom was placed, as it were, in suspended animation for most of the Reagan years: the new President, with his belief in American exceptionalism, prowess and possibility, simply did not accept the decadence of hegemony thesis. However, in the later part of the second Reagan administration, and after seven years of renewed American globalism, the neo-isolationist clarion of retreat and retrenchment once more sounded in American consciousness. This was reflected in the fact that, in 1988, Yale historian Paul Kennedy's book, *The Rise and Fall of the Great Powers: Economic Change and Military Conflict From 1500 to 2000*, became an American best-seller (selling over 100,000 copies in its first few months in the bookshops).[4] Kennedy's argument (like that of the realists and world systems theorists discussed in chapters 2 and 3) is that the rise to great power status rests upon economic and technological prowess, whereas the decline of such nations is caused by the fact that they devote ever-growing proportions of their product to the maintenance of national power against the apparent or real 'frontiers of insecurity'. If such powers fail to maintain a balance between consumer demands, military expenditures and the investment required to sustain them, what Kennedy calls 'imperial overstretch' will cause a relative decline in each. In the 1980s this problem afflicted not only the United States but also the Soviet Union, where Gorbachev's *perestroika* reflected a similar crisis of the Soviet political economy, and a potential crisis of hegemony for the Soviet empire. However, unlike many of the theorists discussed in chapters 2 and 3, Kennedy argues that America's decline from hegemony may not be inevitable, although he points out that there is not a single great power in history which has avoided the fate of degeneration: Ming China in 1500, imperial Spain in 1600 (the seventeenth-century Iberian empire), Bourbon and Bonapartist France, the Dutch republic in 1700 (the United Provinces), the British Empire after its zenith in the mid nineteenth century. Thus Kennedy's thesis is in the same vein as Gibbon, Spengler, Toynbee, von Ranke and Lenin, and more recently, Gilpin and Wallerstein.

In this view, as with previous hegemonies and empires, American hegemony has run its course, so that the American leadership needed to find a strategy to withdraw from its over-extended and open-ended global commitments, or risk a further relative demise in its power. The most detailed and elegant of the recent representations of the thesis of American hegemonic decline (tied to a plea for a reconstructed American foreign policy and a wider international commitment from her NATO allies) is found in David Calleo's book, *Beyond American Hegemony*:

> American policy, requiring a supremacy that cannot be sustained, lacks the guiding principles needed to determine priorities. Despite its colossal military means, America feels perpetually threatened and over-extended. It is difficult to exaggerate the dangers of such a condition – either for the world or for democracy in America itself. The United States has become a hegemon in decay, set on a course that points to an ignominious end. If there is a way out, it lies through Europe. History has come full circle: the Old World is needed to restore balance to the New.[5]

The causes of such decadent hegemony are, of course, a matter of debate in the literature, and here I will merely refer to those most frequently mentioned. The most important external factors normally identified are the will and capacity of other states to catch up economically and militarily, so that the hegemon begins to lose its technological, commercial and eventually its financial edge. This is partly because the domestic political power of vested, 'internationalist interests' prevent effective controls on the export of technology and capital.[6] The costs of maintaining international dominance begin to outweigh the benefits, particularly as the productivity gap between the hegemon and its rivals begins to narrow.[7] The hegemon's mature economy reaches a 'climacteric' and it loses its dynamism, partly because military expenditures are an ineffective way to promote long-term economic growth.[8] Attempting to finance vast military expenditures under such conditions provokes fiscal crisis, particularly if the hegemon is unable to prevent free-riding in the security sphere on the part of its allies. Moreover, whereas in the past this process of the loss of primacy could take centuries, in the modern era the quickening pace of technological diffusion has meant that the 'American century' is, in world-historical terms, over soon after it began. The main beneficiaries of the new conditions have been not only the Soviet bloc nations, but also many Third World countries which have begun to industrialise successfully. Perhaps most crucial (and in large part because of America's postwar efforts) Western Europe and Japan have risen from the ashes of World War II to become the major economic rivals of the United States. These changes have occurred at the same time as the United States has suffered a major military defeat in Vietnam, its leadership has lost its sense of direction (reflected in Calleo's comments quoted above) and suffered massive blows to its prestige, most recently in Iran. This means that where there was once a workable consensus within the establishment, by the mid-1970s a variety of different conflicts divided the American leadership, producing what was in effect a deep ideological crisis concerning the direction and purposes of American foreign policy.[9] Moreover, the long period of internal political turmoil and cultural hedonism in the United States was, in part, the domestic side of this loss of international power.[10]

In addition, it is argued, a deeper transformation in America's international position occurred, particularly after 1970, with the result that America's international autonomy was significantly constrained by global interdependence. This new condition applied to the United States at precisely the moment when its economic and military power was in substantial relative decline, with significant political consequences for the global order. As Bruno Frey argues (along with Trilateral Commissioners like Graham Allison and Nobuhiko Ushiba) one significant repercussion of these changes is that there is less and less an effective 'leader' in the global political economy, which means that important international public goods which serve to maintain the global order may be under-supplied. Some American realists, such as Stephen Krasner and Robert Gilpin, have even gone as far as to suggest that because global interdependence requires strong (that is hegemonic) political foundations, the trends towards growing interdependence may well be reversed. As such, the longer term consequence of American decline is likely to be a distintegration of the postwar international economic order. For these thinkers declining hegemony is associated with the outbreak of, and rise in, economic nationalism and a tendency towards the formation of mercantilist blocs. Gilpin concludes that the 1980s was a period of transition, increasingly characterised by a 'mixed system' of mercantilist competition between states, a move towards economic regionalism and the onset of 'sectoral protectionism':

> In the mid-1980s, the liberal international economy established at the end of the Second World War has been significantly transformed. The trend towards the liberalization of trade has been reversed and the Bretton Woods principles of multilateralism . . . are being displaced . . . The displacement of the United States by Japan as the dominant financial power and the global debt problem have raised troubling questions about the leadership and stability of the world financial system.
>
> [I] believe these changes are responses to hegemonic decline and are caused by diverging national interests among the advanced countries. As a consequence of profound changes in the international distribution of power, in supply conditions, and in the effectiveness of demand management, the liberal international order is rapidly receding.[11]

Many of Gilpin's conclusions were widely held by many political leaders in the United States in the mid-1980s (where Gilpin became one of the new Cassandras). These views were also represented in a vast and ethnocentric American literature which sprouted in the academic journals during the 1970s and 1980s, elaborating the theory of hegemonic stability.[12] By contrast, the more nuanced realist theoretician Calleo acknowledged that many West Europeans interpreted such changes not so much in terms of weakening American hegemony, but rather as a manifestation of its unilateralist reassertion. In this assessment, the United States was manipulating the world economy during the 1970s and 1980s in order to compensate for its own internal economic disorder, and as such was exporting disequilibrium to the rest of the world. As such, American economic policy began to pose a greater threat to Western solidarity than did the Soviet Union itself. This reading suggests that the cause of international economic disorder and stagnation of the 1970s and 1980s was to be found substantially in United States macroeconomic policies (rather than in the tendency of allied states to break ranks based on a *sauve qui peut* mentality).

A less gloomy variant of the 'end of the liberal order' thesis was that of Robert Keohane, whose widely acclaimed book, *After Hegemony*, suggested that the international order could be maintained and managed by rational state actors if they were able to identify and act upon enlightened self-interest. Noteworthy about this book was that its central premise (reflected in Gilpin's arguments also), namely that American hegemony had 'ended', was not fully challenged in the literature.[13] Keohane's argument was similar to that of important intellectuals in the Trilateral Commission and the major international relations institutes of Britain, France, the United States and West Germany.[14] The quintessence of this broad argument is that after hegemony there may well be more conflict and disorder in the world political economy. To avert threats to international economic stability, state and non-state actors should collectively act to strengthen and extend international institutions, regimes and public goods. Through such institutionalisation of international bargaining and other forms of political interaction, a more favourable environment for international co-operation is likely to be fostered, enhancing communication and the perceived pay-off structures for different actors. This lengthens the 'shadow of the future' and a collective rational interest in sustaining political co-operation. In this context, during the 1980s there was a growth in the international relations literature applying game theoretic approaches to the question of international co-operation, some of it along the lines discussed in chapter 2 in the section on public choice theory.[15]

Perhaps the best synthesis of the prevailing American arguments is that of Calleo, who, in this analysis of the future of the Western alliance (including Japan), carefully balances centrifugal forces (such as mercantilism, regionalism, cut-throat competition) against centripetal ones (for example the globalisation of production, investment habits and expectations) before concluding that:

> In the long run, neither America, Europe, nor Japan seems likely to have the economic weight and political power to dominate the world economy that appears to be developing. In the economic spheres, as in the political and military spheres the world system will become increasingly plural – with a proliferation of important actors, includ-

ing states determined to safeguard their national prosperity. Taken altogether, these conditions and trends point, if anything, toward a new age of cartels – a web of agreements that permits competition but limits the damage. Some such organised competition would be the most rational and humane outcome and perhaps the only way to preserve the fabric of an open world economy in the face of so many destabilising changes.[16]

AMERICAN HEGEMONIC DECLINE: A CRITIQUE

Now I will criticise the conceptualisations which underpin the above arguments. In particular, I will argue that we should avoid reductionist concepts of power and hegemony and theorisations which pay insufficient attention to changes in ideas, identification and interest between nations.

The prevailing concept of hegemony in the literature is a realist one. However, similar conceptualisations are also to be found in neo-liberalism and some types of Marxism. The realist concept, in fact, lies at the very heart of the theorisation associated with the 'pessimistic' view of American hegemony.

Like world systems theorists, realists define hegemony in terms of the preponderance of one state in the inter-state system, equating hegemony with domination anchored in an unequal distribution of military and economic capabilities. The concept of power which underpins this concept of hegemony is a Weberian notion of power over, *macht* or domination. This can be either overt or covert and is usually associated with intentional action. The realist concept of hegemony therefore tends to be primarily associated with *behavioural* forms of power which may be perceived and measured by an empiricist methodology. Where this concept of hegemony is linked to more structural forms of power it often rests upon material aggregates: the states with a disproportionately high share of economic power resources and military might exercise structural domination, in the same way as a monopolist dominates the market behaviour of smaller firms. In today's global political economy, a more accurate analogy for the relations among the metropolitan capitalist states might be that of a price-leader (the biggest firm: the United States) in an oligopoly, with the leader's behaviour exerting an asymmetrical influence on the other major firms (for example, Japan, West Germany, Britain, France, Italy). In other words, the concept of structure is, as in neo-classical economics, an individualist one.

In this context the hegemon is *primus inter pares*, using its power to control international outcomes. The standard American interpretation

63

suggests that the relative decline of the United States means that its control over such outcomes has diminished. My argument is that such a view is exaggerated and erroneous, largely because it fails to acknowledge sufficiently the fact that not only can the United States develop conscious policies to exercise its *structural domination*, it can also, by virtue of its political, economic and military centrality within the non-communist world, exercise considerable *structural power*. Moreover, since the United States possesses a unique *structural dominance* within the global political economy, other nations' potential actions, welfare and prospects may be constrained or affected by the United States, irrespective of any conscious design by American policy-makers. In other words, the very size and weight of the United States within the international system substantially affects the conditions under which all other states and interests must operate. The policies of other states matter a great deal, but, like the price-leader oligopolist, none has a comparable impact to those of the United States.[17] This argument is in fact implicit even in a realist conceptualisation. Here states calculate the costs and benefits which stem from the pay-off structure (or international economic environment) and compute their utility functions relative to those of other states. This means they will generally avoid policies which antagonise the dominant power (which is assumed to have the power to retaliate and discipline others). In this way, the hegemonic system is, in some respects, self-policing and needs to be defined in terms of expectations and anticipations, by what does not happen, as well as by overt political action.

Returning to the question of how we conceive of the structures within which different states and interests interract at the global level, in the early postwar period the world economy could be conceptualised and understood as a series of *national* political economies, with their major economic agents interacting at the international level, mainly through trade. Seen from this perspective, as Table 4.1 suggests, the United States relative share of international economic activity would appear to have substantially declined (measured in terms of the share in trade). This was also the case in terms of its share of the world product (see Table 4.3).

However, an aggregated view, particularly if heavily premised of trade, is, in important respects, misleading. There are a number of reasons for this. The first is that aggregated views often fail to take account of the quantitative and qualitative transformations in the American and global political economies. As is frequently noted, such changes involve the fact that America is much more interdependent

Table 4.1A. *Exports, FOB, billions of current $US*

	1950	1960	1970	1980
Trilateral	34.0	81.0	214.0	1,224.3
United States	10.1	20.4	42.6	220.7
Japan	0.8	4.1	19.3	130.5
W. Europe[a]	20.1	51.0	136.0	806.1
W. Europe[b]	n.a.	25.6	44.1	256.1
West Germany	2.0	11.4	34.2	192.9
United Kingdom	6.3	10.6	19.3	115.2
World total	60.8	128.3	313.9	1,855.7

B. *Exports*

	as % of GNP				as % of world exports	
	1950	1960	1970	1980	1950	1980
Trilateral	7.3	8.8	10.5	17.2	55.9	66.0
United States	3.5	4.0	4.3	8.4	16.7	11.9
Japan	5.6	9.4	9.5	12.5	1.3	7.0
W. Europe[a]	13.8	15.5	17.8	25.1	33.1	43.4
W. Europe[b]	n.a.	7.8	5.8	8.0	n.a.	13.8
West Germany	8.5	15.8	18.4	23.5	3.3	10.4
United Kingdom	17.0	14.7	15.6	22.2	10.4	6.2
World total	11.7	11.3	12.6	21.2	100.0	100.0

Notes: Trilateral=USA, Canada, EEC and Japan. [a]Western Europe: including intra-European trade. [b]Western Europe, excluding intra-European trade. 'World' total excludes inter-trade amongst the following: China, Mongolia, North Korea, and North Vietnam (from 1976, Vietnam).
Source: N. Ushiba et al., *Sharing International Responsibilities* (New York, Trilateral Commission, 1983), pp. 81, 93, based on UN and Eurostat statistics.

Table 4.2. *World GNP, in constant 1975 dollars (% of total)*

1950 (total $2 trillion)		1980 (total $8 trillion)	
North America	36.6	North America	25.6
W. Europe	28.6	W. Europe	25.9
Japan	3.0	Japan	8.0
Rest of the world	32.1	Rest of the world	40.5

Source: adapted from Ushiba et al., *Sharing International Responsibilities*, p. 5

Table 4.3. *Relative decline of American power**

	1950	1980
Military position		
military expenditures	50	23[a]
US nuclear position	monopoly/invulnerability	parity/proliferation
Economic strength		
GNP[b]	34	23
manufactures	60	30[c]
monetary reserves	50	6
Political centrality		
	Reconstructs Japan & WE; unchallenged leadership	US now a 'key ally' of Japan & WE; multipolar world system

Notes: *numbers refer to US percentage of global totals; [a]1977; [b]expressed as a percentage of total world GNP converted into $US at official exchange rates; [c]1975. WE=Western Europe.
Source: adapted from N. Ushiba *et al.*, *Sharing International Responsibilities*, p. 8.

with the world political economy. Since 1945 there has been an incremental, if uneven process of global economic integration, much of it carried out by virtue of the activities of transnational firms. In the 1950s and 1960s this involved American capital emanating outward, with American firms investing heavily in Europe under the Bretton Woods system of fixed exchange rates and a gold-dollar standard. Since the early 1970s there has been, however, a rapid transnationalisation of the previously relatively self-sufficient American political economy. America has become much more dependent on imports of raw materials, notably oil. Federal Reserve economists have found that there was a seven-fold growth in the nominal value of American international activity in the period 1970–85, so that by the mid-1980s international transactions accounted for roughly a quarter of total United States GNP. The pace of internationalisation was significantly faster than the growth in United States GNP. In the 1970–85 period nominal GNP growth was 9.5 per cent per annum, whereas international economic activity grew by 14 per cent per year.[18]

This internationalisation process partly reflects the fact that foreign investors increasingly came to view a significant direct investment stake in the American economy as an essential prerequisite for their global strategy. This was because of the need to develop economies of scale which would enable firms to survive the competitive battles of the future; and, of course, to secure access to the vast American

Table 4.4. *Annual real growth in GNP per employed person, 1960–78* (percentage change)

	1960–73	1974–8
Japan	8.9	3.2
Italy	5.4	1.1
West Germany	4.7	3.0
France	4.5	3.0
United Kingdom	3.2	0.8
United States	1.8	0.1

Note: between 1970–9, the real median family income of Americans increased only 6.7 per cent. This compared to an increase of 37.6 per cent in the 1950s and 33.9 per cent in the 1960s.
Source: J. Agnew, *The United States in the World-Economy* (Cambridge, Cambridge University Press, 1987), p. 131.

market by 'domesticising' their operations. It also implies that the United States economy may now need significant injections of foreign capital to sustain its level of productivity growth, as well as, especially during the 1980s, huge inflows of portfolio capital to finance its fiscal deficits. The need for injections of foreign capital into the United States is underlined by evidence on American productivity growth. Trends became less favourable in the 1970s and 1980s, although the United States still had a clear overall lead in productivity. The annual rate of growth of American manufacturing productivity was well below that of most other industrialised countries in the 1977–83 period. Output per man hour of work in 1984 was lower than that of West Germany and only slightly better than Japan's. The narrowing of America's technological lead in some sectors (for example, electronics) and its loss in others (for example, some types of motor vehicles) has been widely interpreted as a threat to some of the basis of American state power. Thus continuing foreign direct investment into the United States may be vital in maintaining American productivity growth, and the growth of the economy more generally (see Tables 4.4 and 4.5 for the situation which prevailed in the 1960s and 1970s.)[19]

Moreover, the United States seems to have undergone a wide-ranging decrease in its relative share of exports of manufactures, including high-technology products, a sphere which is generally seen as vital for the material basis of hegemony (see Table 4.6). The United States is now more likely to import newer technologies from its competitors than was previously the case.[20] This contributed to the fact that American trade in high technology in 1986 was in deficit for

Table 4.5. *Comparative productivity improvements for 11 capitalist countries, 1960–79*

	1960–73	1973–9
Italy	6.6	2.4
United Kingdom	4.0	0.1
Canada	4.4	2.5
France	5.9	4.8
United States	2.8	0.9
West Germany	5.4	5.0
Japan	9.9	3.8
Netherlands	7.6	4.2
Belgium	7.0	4.9
Sweden	6.7	1.8
Denmark	7.2	4.1

Source: Agnew, *The United States in the World-Economy*, p. 139.

the first time since 1945. American imports of high-technology products grew six times faster than exports in the 1980s. However, much of the deficit in high-technology trade was because American corporations increasingly produce abroad for competitive reasons, notably in electronics and in high-volume products such as personal computers.[21] By the late 1980s, however, there were signs of a return to American production in these industries, as new technologies and lower labour costs as well as new consumer requirements made production close to final markets a more attractive business tactic. One important element here was the growing use of just-in-time (JIT) technologies, pioneered by Japanese auto producers. These technologies allow final products to be customised so that, in effect, vehicles are built to individual specifications in one to three days and sold immediately. JIT depends on a network of highly responsive local suppliers. New methods of working, new technologies and changing organisational techniques may well combine and possibly help improve the productivity position of the American economy in the 1990s. Finally, it is also worth noting that for most of the postwar era Japan was a net importer of high technology, so a short-term reversal for the United States position needs to be set against its longer-term position.

Partly with the latter in mind, the United States government began to develop a two-fold strategy of encouraging foreign direct investment, as well as rethinking its industrial policy. By 1987, it was contemplating the creation of a Federal Department of Science and

Table 4.6. *American shares in industrial country exports to world market*

	1970	1980
High-technology product groups		
Aircraft	71%	62%
Computers and office machines	42	36
Scientific, medical and control equipment	32	29
Telecommunications equipment	19	13
Medical and pharmaceutical products	18	16
Selected other products		
Agricultural machinery, tractors	32	31
Heating and cooling equipment	24	22
Machine tools	17	13
Pumps and compressors	29	21
Construction and mining machinery	39	39

Sources: US Department of Labor, *Trends in Technology-Intensive Trade (1980)*; OECD, *Foreign Trade*, series C. Cited in L. A. Fox and S. Cooney, 'Protectionism Returns', *Foreign Policy* (1983–4), no. 53, p. 83.

Technology (suggested by the Presidential Commission on Competitiveness in 1985). This might serve to refocus American high-technology expenditures away from the military sector into more commercially viable areas. A shift in American military-industrial strategy could yield significant productivity and commercial gains. As I have argued elsewhere with David Law:

> What should be emphasised, therefore, is that a reorientation of American military-industrial strategy, given the gigantic sums of Federal funds involved, could produce impressive commercial gains for the United States economy. American automobile producers have also shown that through re-constructing their managerial and production systems, building a 'world car' and rationalising their global production, they can still compete with Japanese and South Korean producers. American capitalists are now more willing to learn management and production techniques from their Japanese counterparts, and where necessary to forge alliances with them, and other foreign firms.[22]

In addition, it is important to note that in some areas giant American corporations are still very much at the cutting edge of technological developments. In telecommunications and informatics American companies are at the forefront, with only Japanese firms posing a serious threat. The market in this area was one of the fastest growing in the 1980s, but industry analysts claim it has hardly even begun to touch its full potential.[23] Finally, the United States, while more dependent on imported raw materials and oil than it was twenty years ago, is still much more self-sufficient in energy than any of its major competitors, and has still not even begun to use this energy as efficiently as the Japanese or West Europeans. If it does, then this advantage could be enhanced. Moreover, the 1988 United States–Canada Free Trade Agreement gives American raw materials companies privileged access to the mineral riches of the world's second largest national territory. Mexico's massive economic problems and foreign indebtedness manifested during the 1980s also suggest that American access to oil south of the Rio Grande will continue to be provided, perhaps indefinitely.

Most American commentators suggest that the 'internationalisation of Uncle Sam' reflects increasingly ubiquitous constraints for American policy-makers. The end product of postwar economic developments is that America's foreign economic relations are now less one-sided than was the case in the 1950s when the country was, so to speak, comfortably supreme. However, it is my contestation that the economic metamorphosis of America's and the world political economy means that its structural dominance in the world economy has probably increased. The continued dominant position of the United States is underlined by the transformation of the monetary system into a pure dollar standard after 1971 and by the growing integration of American and global capital and exchange markets. This is a point which has been frequently stressed by the noted monetary economist, Susan Strange, although her arguments have usually fallen on deaf ears, at least in the American academic community.[24] In consequence of the internationalisation process, changes in American monetary and fiscal policy take on a wider and more global aspect. Thus, when the United States opted for a very tight money policy in 1979 (in the context of rising oil prices and a high level of inflation in the world economy), Federal Reserve policies effectively precipitated the deepest global recession experienced since the 1930s. This aspect of American structural dominance was, however, retrospectively noted, in 1985, by Henry Nau, a former economic adviser to Reagan's first National Security Council. Nau then advocated the conscious mobilisation of America's 'structural power in the market-place' in order to set the economic terms for United States co-operation and interaction with its major allies and with the Third World nations.[25]

The Weberian view of power which informs the prevailing conceptualisations of American hegemony is, of course, useful for explaining some aspects of inter-state relations (especially the use of military power or economic coercion). However, it is weak in explaining much of the social basis of power, including the power of ideas, which are more-or-less seen as epiphenomena or as legitimations of a system of domination. This means that not only is the concept of power reduced, but there is a tendency within the major approaches (notably economic liberalism, classical Marxism and world systems theory) to reduce the concept of civil society to the narrowly materialistic, and to perhaps over-emphasise the military and economic aspects of American hegemony. By contrast, the Gramscian concept of civil society involves the wider political culture, including the questions of identity and ideology. The best recent American example of the forces of the domestic political culture and the global impact of their remobilisation is the nationalist-populist appeal of Ronald Reagan, who, it should be reemphasised, simply did not accept the prevalent declining hegemony thesis. It is important to stress here that Reagan was the first postwar President to be elected on the basis of a wide-ranging populist constituency (which he had assiduously cultivated since the 1960s). Reagan's domestic appeal was primarily to 'traditional' American values of possessive individualism, anti-communism and Manifest Destiny. Such rhetoric was a powerful catalyst in attempts to remobilise American strategic power in the military sphere, as well as (perhaps more unconsciously) American structural dominance in the international marketplace.

Reagan attempted to create a renewed sense of American identity and geopolitical purpose, at the same time as holding out the promise of a world free of nuclear weapons. The Reagan offensive, carried out with widespread domestic support (Reagan was by far the most popular modern President) involved a series of domestic and international initiatives, including the revitalisation of a Cold War posture towards the Soviet Union. Along with his macroeconomic policies, this offensive managed to reassert American prerogatives in its allied relations and to place the Soviet Union on the defensive. Reagan's rise to power can also be partly explained by revanchist forces in the political culture which reacted against the threats to American primacy, and in particular to the humiliations of Vietnam and the 444-day Iran hostage crisis. The mood of revanchism and the yearning for America to reassert its right to be number one was, of course, crucial in Carter's election defeat in 1980.

This mood had fairly deep roots. It was in sympathy with that which prevailed in the early 1970s when the so-called new economic policy and Nixon shocks of August 1971 were greeted with widespread domestic approval. The 'shocks' included the imposition of a unilateral 10 per cent import surcharge on goods and services of foreign producers, the suspension of the convertibility of the American dollar into gold (thereby establishing a pure dollar standard) and an attempt to deny the Japanese access to supplies of their most important sources of foreign protein, American soybeans. Not surprisingly, America's allies interpreted these moves as blatant nationalism, a repudiation of American obligation to its allies, as well as the signal of the possible end of the United States commitment to economic universalism.

Beyond the neglect of domestic politics and political culture in discussion of American hegemony in the international relations literature, a neglect which calls into question any attempt to analyse American foreign policy solely in terms of a 'rational actor' model, we can make two much more fundamental criticisms of the dominant conception of hegemony. These refer, first, to what might be called an underlying 'inevitability thesis' concerning the decline of hegemony. The second, an issue which I have alluded to above, is the economic reductionism at the heart of many of the theorisations of hegemonic decline, such that normative elements are undervalued and the possibilities of significant changes in national identification and interest are ignored.

As has been observed in chapters 2 and 3, the first of these problems stems from the essentialist concept of underlying historical continuity which informs the prevalent theorisations of hegemonic decline. This generates a view of repetitive (although shortening) cycles of hegemonic decline and fall. It neglects a number of historically unprecedented qualitative changes in the world political economy (in which I have called the transnational stage of capitalism), as well as the specific ways in which American centrality in the world economy has been transfigured and extended. Moreover, and to a greater extent, the prevailing view eclipses the postwar passage through which American power has taken on a more universal aspect. This universalisation emerged partly by virtue of the early postwar spread of New Deal ideology and later by the extension of possessive individualism (which Reagan's rhetoric and policies sought to encourage); the globalisation of production and exchange; the emergence and later re-emergence of Cold War politics and superpower rivalry; and what might be termed the Americanisation of Western civilisation (there has also been a significant Americanisation of the cultures of the Pacific and other parts of the non-communist world).

In this latter context it is important to note that the United States has historically acted as a pole of attraction for peoples of all races from the rest of the world. America's rise to hegemony was not only partly caused by a relativly efficient economic system capable of absorbing foreign investment during the nineteenth century, but also occurred because of its unique ability to attract large quantities of skilled and unskilled labour. The waves of immigrants were attracted to the land where there appeared to be boundless opportunity and the prospect of real social and geographical mobility. These relative economic and social advantages may be rather less today than was the case in the nineteenth century, but they are still very significant, particularly if they are contrasted with the cultural xenophobia of America's major economic contender, Japan, and its major adversary, the Soviet Union. Whereas the movement of people and capital in the nineteenth and early twentieth century was predominantly one-way (for example from Europe to the United States), since 1945 this has taken on a wider aspect: the United States still is able to attract skilled and unskilled labour from overseas (much of the latter as 'wetbacks' who have crossed the Rio Grande), while other nations have incorporated American ideas and institutions, not least its brand of consumer culture.

As has been mentioned earlier, the system of thought which accompanied the rise to globalism of the United States has had two effects: it has helped to provide a cultural context for the postwar era in the West, and its mainly liberal economic principles have acted as organising concepts for the debates between, and practices of, important political decision-makers from a range of countries. Hence elements of legitimation and ideology interact with a deeper epistemological level creating a global synergy of ideas beneficial to the outward extension or maintenance of American power. The agendas, questions and solutions of the problems of the non-communist postwar order have generally been posed in major international organisations and inter-state negotiations in, and on, American terms.

In this light it is important to reiterate that the economic and political framework for the relations between the three major poles of developed capitalism in the postwar world was created by American power and the basic foundations of this are still very much intact. In essence, the global economic order still takes a mainly liberal (and American) form. This framework has permitted the rise of giant transnational corporations, and most of the largest of these are American. Such giant firms, while not directly representative of the outward emanation of American national power, are still representative of American influence. These companies, *par excellence*, represent the age of transnationalisation and global economic integration.

Indeed, with respect to the forces of global economic integration, it is my argument that these have developed to such a point that the possibility of a dramatic return to neo-mercantilist economic blocs is unlikely, although there has been some tendency towards this, particularly in the European Community, where intra-European trade has grown rapidly, and a single integrated European market was planned for 1992. Nonetheless, political integration and a shared sense of European identity have lagged far behind this economic trend. At the same time, international investment flows have continued to multiply, and, in contrast to the 1960s, there has now emerged a two-way tendency in direct foreign investment, not just from the United States, but increasingly into the United States from other countries (see chapter 5 for evidence). This has resulted in a progressive interpenetration of capital, itself partly necessitated by the importance for modern corporations of developing vast economies of scale. As Keichi Ohmae has demonstrated, such investments mean that companies require a politically secure stake in, and continued access to, the three largest non-communist markets of the globe: North America, Western Europe and Japan.[26]

Second, a major difficulty in explaining the resilience of the economic order arises partly because of the realist and world systems' focus on the state as the primordial actor, coupled with the assumption of fixed and relatively unchanging allegiances and political identities. This means that the connections between the integrative forces mentioned above (which also include alliances, co-production ventures in the military and industrial fields and the habits and expectations of consumers and of the electorate) and the normative questions of political identification are often missed in the mainstream approaches. Partly because of its almost pathological focus on nationalism, this problem is a central weakness of realist theory. Here political identity and interests are seen as fixed along national lines so that any hegemonic state is likely to be met with the inevitable challenge of potential rival states, whose interests and identities are, in the long term, not compatible with those of the dominant power. This will mean that any alliance with the hegemon is seen as tactical and contingent and when the time is ripe (that is in a situation of hegemonic decline) any such alliance may easily be broken. The potential for this will serve to erode the hegemon's position since it will require ever more resources by the dominant power to maintain and to stabilise its global position. In Sartrian terms, realists anticipate that the United States will ultimately face its own existential hell as it realises, like the incompatible characters of *Huis Clos* (No Exit) that it cannot control the will of others.

74

In consequence, the state-centric assumptions of realists and some Marxists may lead to a neglect of the prospect of changes in identification and interest in ways that might effectively augment the power resources of the hegemon, sustain co-operation, and mitigate conflicts. Such assumptions lead to an underestimation of the importance, not only of American civilisational models and the pro-capitalist and liberal democratic values associated with Americanism, but also to a systematic misunderstanding of the role of liberal economic ideas and associated international institutions in the development of American hegemony. This of course undervalues the place of consciousness and action in the historical process, as well as the role of the American state after 1945 in penetrating and rebuilding the political systems of its major opponents of World War II, nurturing American political and economic interests in allied countries, and in establishing permanent military installations in many countries. In sum, since 1945, the United States has strengthened its political centrality in this postwar civilisational project by means of a series of multilateral institutions, and perhaps most importantly, through a number of bilateral relationships, so that, beyond the Americas (where American dominance was already established by 1945), the power of the United States has stretched outward into the Atlantic, the Middle East, and the Pacific. Rather like iron filings clustered round the ends of a huge magnet, each state in the two regions was drawn politically and economically to the United States. For example, the United States forged special bilateral relationships with Mexico, Canada, Britain, Israel, West Germany and Japan. These facilitated the spread of American influence, and have underpinned its hegemony. Of these, the most important in the long term is probably that between America and Japan.

As I suggested in chapter 3, the type of 'nation-state reductionism' which is at the heart of the fashionable judgements on American hegemony also leads to an underestimation of the long-term potential of institutions such as Bilderberg and the Trilateral Commission which serve to generate common concepts of civilisation and of strategy, as well as specific forms of elite interaction and identification. Taken together, and in the wider context of the globalisation of communications and the improvement in transportation, this means that the conception of 'national interests' held by the ruling elites in a given member country may tend to both 'Americanise' and 'internationalise', that is, be re-cast in a wider set of horizons (including time-horizons), at least when contrasted with previous historical epochs. (See chapters 6 to 8 for detailed discussion of private international

75

relations councils.) An interesting aspect of this process is that, at least with respect to the Bilderberg meetings, it would appear that in the immediate years after World War II, it was the outlook of American leaders which needed to be 'internationalised'. Many Americans were still wedded to isolationist concepts of American interests, whereas others with a more internationalist outlook had little knowledge of foreign affairs (beyond the Americas and parts of the Pacific) and of their counterparts in reconstructed Western Europe. Thus the process of changes in identification must be seen in dialectical terms, as the leaders of the shattered powers of the non-communist world came to terms with the contours of a new international system after 1945. This is consistent with the proposition made in chapter 3 where it was noted that international hegemony has for its origins the outward expansion of the hegemony of the dominant group in the leading state, so that other states will tend towards the emulation of the hegemonic state's major institutions and models of political and economic life. In the postwar period, at least in the Trilateral nations, this has been accomplished through the outward spread of American economic, military, political, and cultural power, fused into a concept of Western civilisation (Japan is, of course, more problematic in this regard). This outward extension of American civilisation built upon an earlier European hegemony, and the spread of English as the major international language (itself partly a legacy of the British Empire).

However, the process of internationalisation of political and cultural outlook of elites still would appear, by the late 1980s, to lag behind the process of global economic integration. In some countries it was fairly advanced, whereas in many others it was either embryonic or in its relative infancy (as in Japan). This suggests that institutions such as the Trilateral Commission may have a significant long-term role to play, at least as incubators in this process at the elite level. This process has both a positive and negative aspect in that it simultaneously involves the promotion of values and practices which are 'internationalist' whilst restraining unilateralist and nationalist tendencies both within and between member nations. For example, within the membership of the Trilateral Commission, leaders in Western Europe and Japan, as well as internationalists within the United States foreign policy establishment, saw a central purpose of their activity to continue the process of the internationalisation of the outlook of the American public and its leaders, so that their operative concepts of the international system would not be major obstacles to comprehensive attempts at greater international co-operation, understood in liberal terms.

76

To return to the theme of theorisations of hegemonic decline, it can be stated that the dominant thesis concerning the decline of hegemony might be more plausible if the rate of economic and military change (which in turn is related to the pace of technological change) was much greater than the rate at which the cultural power and political appeal of the hegemon were developed and extended (this also involves the organisation and use of military power). In previous eras the pace of technological change and diffusion was very slow, whereas today it is rapid. However, one aspect of changing technology in the twentieth century has been a dramatic improvement in transport and communications, which facilitate the activities of transnational corporations and the attempts of the American government to organise, co-ordinate and develop its world-wide alliances. Since for the period since the 1950s the United States has had a significant lead in global communications, it has been able to take advantage of the international use of English in a way which was impossible for Japan and a large number of other states. The spread of the use of English, allied to more powerful international channels of communication and cultural interaction (for example, through tourism, educational exchanges and business contacts) may serve, in time, to globalise national political cultures. Important in the long term will be the twin processes of the internationalisation of education, especially higher education, and the transnationalisation of mass communications, notably television. This process might therefore have the effect of internationalising the relatively parochial outlook of many Americans, as they communicate with larger and more diverse groups of foreign peoples. Further, the influx of Hispanic and Asian immigrants into the United States in the last twenty years is serving to increase the capacity of Americans to communicate with regions beyond the traditional postwar Atlantic axis. Again, however, this is a dialectical process, since other countries are also acquiring such capacities.

Above and beyond these criticisms, virtually all theorists (and all Soviet leaders since Lenin) agree that dominance in the security structure is the most fundamental to the maintenance of hegemony, since military primacy confers an authority and prerogative across a range of other questions. Thus, whilst it may be possible to speak of Western Europe and Japan as major economic rivals, their dependence on the United States for their security means that necessarily they remain in subordinate positions. In the late 1980s there is little sign that this situation would change. Moreover, when the wider strategic position of the United States is compared with that of the Soviet Union, it is clear that America is still globally dominant in the military-security sphere. It is to this question that we now turn, since it relates once again to one of our initial issues: the question of the measurement of hegemonic decline.

THE SECURITY STRUCTURE AND AMERICAN MILITARY DOMINANCE

As is shown in Tables 4.2 and 4.3, aggregative measures of national power resources (such as GNP, number of military bases and size of armed forces) show a significant relative decline in American capabilities. However, these aggregates may be misleading. In addition, what is not reflected in these tables is the fact that since the mid-1970s, United States dominance in the security structure has been reconstituted. This has occurred in two ways: through increases in American and allied military expenditures, and in terms of strategic developments since the mid-1970s which have favoured the United States relative to its Soviet rival. I now will examine these changes and some of their effects.

Theorists of hegemonic decline tend to overestimate the loss of the American military power, which has declined much less than its share of world GNP would suggest. Of course, the Pentagon's propaganda machine consistently overestimates such decline in order to obtain higher military appropriations, and to force allies to contribute more for defence.[27] Measuring American military power with reference simply to American forces also fails to take account of allied expenditures which supplement the United States security posture, as well as the stance of non-aligned countries like China. When taken as a whole, Western supremacy *vis-à-vis* the Soviet bloc becomes more obvious. The United States can, of course, never regain its territorial invulnerability unless it is able to secure the elimination of strategic nuclear and chemical weapons.

It perhaps should be emphasised that what makes the United States different from previous hegemons in apparent decline is its continuing ability to maintain a vast and global military capacity.[28] Despite arguments suggesting the contrary, the United States is still at the apex of the global security structure. By contrast, when Britain's economic power relatively declined, its global military power declined. However, Britain sustained its naval might for some considerable time in the twentieth century. One of other reasons why the United States is able to sustain such an impressive global military capacity is because of the sheer size of its GNP, which is able to finance the continued provision of the 'public good' of international security

Table 4.7. *World military expenditure, 1975–84 (selected years)* in $ billion at 1980 prices and exchange rates)

	1975	1981	1982	1983	1984	World share (%)
IMEs	257,534	290,278	307,827	324,230	348,697	53.7
NMEs	171,972	185,448	189,757	191,671	196,133	30.2
MOECs	33,352	45,143	48,598	44,874	44,988	6.9
RoW	43,452	54,238	61,862	60,018	57,419	8.8
World	507,480	576,860	609,900	622,800	649,070	100.0

Notes: Industrial market economies=IMEs; Non-market economies=NMEs; Major oil-exporting countries=MOECs; Rest of the world=RoW.
Source: R. Luckham, 'Disarmament and Development', *IDS Bulletin* (October 1985), vol. 16, p. 3.

even through its proportionate share of world GNP has fallen. After all, its 1980 share of world GNP was 25.6 per cent of $8 trillion, as opposed to 36.3 per cent of only $2 trillion in 1950, at constant 1975 prices. The United States GNP in 1980, before the Reagan boom, was greater than the *entire* global total thirty years previously (see Table 4.3).

The 1978–86 United States rearmament originated in the Carter administration (where Zbigniew Brzezinski, the former Director of the Trilateral Commission, was National Security Advisor). Carter initiated the arms build-up by creating the Rapid Deployment Force, decided on the deployment of the MX missile, and attempted to create a new strategic framework for the Persian Gulf.[29] The economic consequences of this were enormous since, for example, American expenditures between 1980 and 1985 rose in real terms by 51 per cent.[30] The Western lead in military terms is partly reflected in the massive allied expenditures on weapons relative to the Warsaw Pact countries and the rest of the world. This is shown in Table 4.7. Furthermore, many independent military specialists suggest that on the whole the West has vastly superior weapons systems, although there are massive problems in comparing different sets of forces and the contexts they can be used in. We would only know if NATO forces were superior if there was an actual military exchange since the perceptions, tactics, and mobilisation capabilities of each side are part of any military equation.[31]

According to its own estimates, American military expenditures were roughly 25 per cent of the world total by the mid-1980s, and were thus just under half of the total for all industrial market economies

Table 4.8. *Soviet and American military expenditures 1970–80* (selected years, in $US billion, at constant 1978 prices and exchange rates, figures rounded)

	1971	1973	1975	1977	1978	1979	1980
United States	120.7	115.0	110.2	108.6	109.2	109.9	111.2
Soviet Union	93.9	96.9	99.8	102.7	104.2	105.7	107.3

Source: F. Halliday, *The Making of The Second Cold War* (London, New Left Books, 1986), p. 57.

combined. Fred Halliday suggests that it was possible that in fact American expenditures were potentially 200 per cent higher than official figures revealed since these omitted a range of military and military-related items in, for example, the Department of Energy (nuclear warheads), NASA, and military aid to Third World allies.[32] Halliday relies on figures from the independent Stockholm International Peace Research Institute. SIPRI figures are usually more reliable than official government figures. The general level of American expenditures can be adduced from Table 4.8. It will be noted that in 1978 the exchange value of the dollar was relatively low when compared to the 'rise of the superdollar' after 1979.

According to Halliday, the total for NATO (at constant 1978 prices) in 1980 was $193.9 billion, whereas the Warsaw Pact spent $120 billion. If NATO and Japan were added then the allied total became about $203 billion, with Chinese expenditures around $40 billion.[33]

Let us now turn to the distribution of costs and benefits among the members of the NATO alliance, and the question of burden sharing.[34] Each of course receives the benefit of collective defence, although the proportionate costs to each national economy are not what they would appear to be simply with reference to aggregate statistics. For example, there are national variations in the pattern of arms expenditures, with the United States spending virtually all of its military budget on domestic goods, services, veterans' benefits, etc. (thus mainly benefiting home suppliers and the domestic economy). This contrasts with the situation of smaller NATO countries, whose military imports (often from the United States) are proportionately higher:

> Roughly 95% of the US defence budget was spent domestically, whereas only 80% of the defence budgets of the smaller NATO countries were spent inside their countries. The obvious implication is that the same percentage increase in military expenditures is costlier for the smaller countries than for the larger countries.[35]

80

Moreover, the West European share in NATO expenditure rose consistently through the 1970s, partly because of substantial American pressure and threats to withdraw American troops from Europe ('bring the boys back home' Mansfieldism continued in the 1980s: all the presidential candidates in the 1988 election committed themselves to force Western Europe to meet a greater proportion of NATO costs). According to one estimate, the West European share was 22.7 per cent in 1969, and 41.6 per cent in 1979.[36] This reflects American success in redistributing alliance military burdens and points to a long-term resolution of the so-called 'free rider' problem with little threat to American dominance within the NATO alliance system.

In addition, during the 1980s there was a potentially very significant change in the economic strategy of the Pentagon, which became more willing to inject an element of competition into the process of arms procurement. This created new opportunities for foreign investors. To add to this equation, the high and rising costs of arms imports during the 1970s and 1980s created strong pressures for transnational arms production, for example through joint ventures and technical collaboration, licensing and investment. The American pressure for more equitable burden sharing was an added political impetus to this process. European producers, for example, could not hope to match the economies of scale available to the giant American military-industrial sector. A striking example of this economic imbalance was the unprecedented offer of collaboration made on 7 March 1988 by Pentagon officials to the countries engaged in the consortium developing the European Fighter Aircraft (EFA). If the Europeans (West Germany, Britain, Spain and Italy) had accepted the offer of a co-production venture based upon the upgrading of the American Hornet 2000 in exchange for scrapping the EFA, they would have saved an estimated US$ 8.5 billion.[37] The Europeans, in fact, opted for the production of the EFA for reasons of political and technological independence. None the less, as the example demonstrates, the economic forces which make for transnational strategies of arms production and accumulation are considerable and would appear to favour the United States and its giant military-industrial corporations, at least compared to those in Western Europe. An increase in transatlantic collaboration, along with the probability of similar transpacific collaboration with Japan, would further serve to cement the centrality of the United States in the non-communist security system. This would increase the domestic weight of political and economic forces supporting the alliances.

The main challenge to the United States comes, of course, from the

Soviet Union. This challenge, however, is conditioned by the general problems both of maintaining the range and quality of military-industrial technological innovation and of preventing its diffusion to rival states (even allies) whilst seeking access to the technology of others. This is dramatised if the absolute cost of maintaining American military dominance is contrasted with Britain's costs in the nineteenth century.[38] By the 1980s it is possible that these costs to the United States may be about one hundred times greater than those for Britain in the heyday of its international power in the mid-nineteenth century, even allowing for increasing allied contributions. However, such cost increases affect all military powers, and would appear to be particularly acute for the Soviet Union as arms technology becomes more expensive and sophisticated. Military power is more wide-ranging today, which helps the United States relative to rivals who have less across-the-board research, development and production capabilities. This is of some considerable importance to the Soviet Union, which cannot hope to match the United States across a widening range of technologies. To be competitive in many high technology industries scale economies are necessary and, if the home market is not large enough, exports are vital in order to generate the revenue to finance further research and development. As has been noted, although the United States has been very successful in creating such markets overseas, it needs them far less for the development of such scale economies than do its allies (this is reflected in the EFA example, above). This fact enables the United States to operate what is in effect a policy of purloining allied technology whilst simultaneously tightly controlling its use (for example in the SDI, and the 1988 agreement on use of the allied space station project, where the United States alone was permitted secret military experiments, in contrast to other nations involved).

The continuing American lead in military high technology (with the exception of parts of the space programme) is surprising given the very high proportion of Soviet net national product devoted to the military, and because the Soviet Union has the apparent advantage of long-term planning in its military-industrial policy. This is reinforced by the fact that there is much more continuity in Soviet military expenditures than in those of the United States, which have shown some tendency to fall in the aftermath of wars. Nonetheless, as the evidence from the late 1970s and 1980s shows, domestic forces in the United States are able to rapidly mobilise significant increases in military expenditures. Thus, against the political backdrop of growing tensions between the superpowers, United States military expenditures rose from 5.5 per cent of GNP in 1976, to almost 8 per cent in 1986. This was occurring at a time when Soviet economic growth was faltering, and the Soviet Union seemed increasingly unable to innovate, absorb or effectively diffuse high technology within its highly bureaucratic, centrally planned economy, despite Gorbachev's limited attempts at reform. Thus although technology may be diffusing more rapidly than ever before, high technology appears to diffuse more slowly within centrally planned economies, in contrast to the situation for most advanced capitalist states. The paradox here is that whereas the central planning mode of military-industrial development was useful in allowing the Soviet Union to catch up militarily with the United States, this system would appear inadequate to provide the levels of innovation required to compete in the technologies of the twenty-first century. This explains Gorbachev's comments about the Soviet industrial system being in a pre-crisis situation in the mid-1980s, with substantial reform needed to reinvigorate the economy. In this analysis, *perestroika* and the new look in Soviet foreign policy reflects not so much a more enlightened view of economic questions and a heightened sense of a common global condition: rather it represents a growing alarm at the prospect of long-term Soviet weakness.

The United States had hoped that its higher military expenditures would stimulate its lead in high-technology industries (although it is challenged in some by the Japanese). Although research and development expenditures in the United States have not grown as fast as those in Japan in the last twenty years, as a percentage of GNP, United States spending in the 1980s was greater than in Japan or Germany by a ratio of more than 3:1. This was a renewal of the early postwar role of the Pentagon as the major agency in American 'military-industrial' policy.[39] As was noted earlier, the key worry for the United States was whether this policy was the most efficient way to raise its rate of productivity growth which had been declining relative to that of its major economic competitors during the 1970s.[40] In the hope that it was, the Reagan administration poured enormous funds into scientific education and basic research, as well as creating tax incentives for research and development which spurred investment in technological enterprise. The success of these measures within the American scientific community was shown in a *New Scientist* report which stated that by 1985 many academics had been 'converted to Reaganomics'. In 1985, 70 per cent of Federal expenditures on research and development were allotted to defence. At the same time, the United States strengthened its embargo on many technological exports through the

1979 Export Administration Act, as well as using its muscle in the COCOM to lengthen the list of restricted items. These practices caused severe transatlantic tensions, particularly since many West European leaders became convinced that SDI technologies would not be made available to Europe, even if European research led to their development.[41] The Hornet 200–EFA joint production offer, can be seen partly as a response to European grievances, particularly since the offer contained the promise of 60 per cent of the work for European manufacturers.

The second point to be made in this section is that the remobilisation of United States military power should also be seen against the wider strategic and political background. Again, changes in strategic alignments have worked to reconstitute American military dominance relative to its Soviet rival.

For example, the unity of the communist world has been undermined since the Sino-Soviet split, and, since the early 1970s, China has moved gradually towards the United States and Japan, and further away from the Soviet Union. The Soviet 'loss' of China, once its foremost ally, more than outweighs any 'gains' it may have made in Afghanistan, Vietnam, and parts of Africa.[42] Indeed, the Soviet engagement in Afghanistan may well turn out to be more a long-term 'loss' than a 'gain'. Of course, the United States has a strong interest in China's progress (up to a point) as an economic and military power. The United States needs to be involved in the promotion of Chinese development, not only to balance Soviet military power in the region, but also partially to offset Japan's economic power in the Pacific Rim (and to obviate the long-term possibility of a 'Confucian bloc' emerging). At the economic level the American interest is of course to enable American firms to make profits in a rapidly growing country with the world's largest population.

Perhaps in recognition of this, after 1982 China took a more 'independent' stand towards the United States, in contrast to its more pro-American position before then. There was no sign that China was willing to have either the United States or the Soviet Union play the 'China card' against the other, having recognised that its pro-American and anti-Soviet stance of the 1970s actually narrowed its option of playing the superpowers off against each other. Nevertheless in the 1980s China had much closer relations with America and other Trilateral states than it did with the Soviet Union. Moreover, the success of the pragmatists' economic reform programme was shifting China in a market-oriented direction, and even further away from the Soviet model of development. After the successful negotiations with

Britain over control of Hong Kong, under the slogan of 'one nation, two systems', there loomed the prospect of a more rapid reintroduction of capitalism into China, although this was being resisted amongst the 'reds' in the leadership, and in the bureaucracy, as was clear from the reaction to the student protests of 1986–7. In the late 1980s it seems a remote possibility that the Chinese would move substantially back towards a much closer relationship with the Soviet Union at the expense of its growing contacts with the West and Japan. These moves should also be related to the increased willingness of Japan to be involved as a partner in the security activities of the West, or at least alongside the United States. Finally, it was also the case that the wider balance of military power in Asia had moved in favour of America and its allies during the 1980s. Beyond Asia, the United States remained largely unchallenged by the Soviet Union in Latin America and throughout the Pacific, although Soviet influence in the region has been growing slowly.

Again, with respect to wider strategic considerations (as well as to SDI and defence technology transfer), American–Japanese bilateral links may prove to be the most significant in the long term, particularly since the climate of public opinion concerning Japanese defence has shifted in the direction of backing Nakasone's policies, which endorsed the development of 'dual-use technologies'. Many of these technologies are useful for the SDI. As Professor Masashi Nishihara of the Japan Defence Academy noted in 1985:

> It is this high technology, competitive with American counterparts, plus Japan's new stance towards positive defence that make Japan–US security relations *stronger than ever before*. Japan and the United States, whose leaders have similar views on East Asia and the Pacific and whose combined gross national products comprise 32 per cent of the world's GNP, are in a position to be the core for other types of trans-Pacific security co-operation.[43]

As Nishihara also mentioned, the huge bilateral trade imbalances between the United States and Japan in the 1970s and more so in the 1980s became a major political 'hindrance' to such security co-operation. This imbalance was US $36.8 billion in 1984.[44] The Japanese in fact were subjected to a double offensive by the Reagan administration, that is, to open Japanese markets and boost domestic demand. However, some of Nakasone's efforts at liberalisation were blocked or delayed by industrial and agricultural lobbies, as well as within the all-powerful Japanese bureaucracy (although domestic demand was expanded). Nonetheless it can be observed that, with strong anti-Japanese feeling in the Congress, American leaders can consistently use the threat against Japan of denial of access to the United States market although such threats need to be seen in the context of the American need for a steady supply of Japanese savings to help finance its huge budget deficits in the 1980s. (Japan may have been funding as much as 40 per cent of the deficit in the mid-1980s.)

CONCLUSION: DECLINE OR CONTINUITY?

Even when material power resources are used to assess the changes in American hegemony, it is easy to underestimate the absolute scale of its national power when compared to previous hegemonies. It seems more plausible to argue that the basic structural continuities in the American neo-imperial system have remained intact. Duncan Snidal suggests that it is not just the proportionate relationship between the hegemon and other powers which is significant in evaluating structural dominance and domination. In a period of consistent, if uneven, growth the *absolute* gap may in fact be as great, if not greater than before. In this context it may well be the case that the hegemon's capacity and willingness to supply a range of public goods may not necessarily decline.[45] This argument would indicate that much of the literature is too narrowly focused on relativities, rather than on the surplus available for international purposes. This may mean that American control over international outcomes has not fundamentally deteriorated. This argument is reinforced if America's structural centrality in the world economy is taken into consideration. A more detailed examination of the nature of the internationalisation of Uncle Sam suggests that, in some senses, American control over certain outcomes may have increased. This argument is taken further in chapter 5.

In addition, because much of the literature is state-centric in nature, it does not allow for the extensions of American political and cultural influence which effectively 'Americanises' the civil societies of a range of other states, making them more congruent with that of the United States. This process, involving American cultural imperialism, is not without its contradictions, although when it succeeds, it represents a significant imperial 'gain' for the United States. This outward expansion of the United States has also served to foster the values of consumerism and possessive individualism, so that increasing proportions of the populations of, for example, Third World states have come to identify with American cultural values. Such developments benefit not only American, but also transnational, capital in general. In the immediate postwar period it was, however, mainly American capital which was most able to take advantage of this process.

On a wider plane, I agree with Bruce Russett, who argues that the major economic and political achievements of the United States were historically unprecedented, in that, while it was not so overwhelmingly powerful as to be able to set all the rules for the postwar economic order, it was able to establish the basic principles of a renovated capitalist system which involved more than four-fifths of the world economy, as well as organising a system of collective security to maintain political and economic control over large parts of the globe.[46] With the decolonisation of much of the Third World, the United States was able (or more accurately its corporations and banks were able) to enter previously closed markets and assure supplies of raw materials and flows of profit income. In a recent essay, Susan Strange has concluded that the United States and its corporations still predominate in what she calls the four basic structures of the world economy: the security, production, monetary and knowledge structures. Using the analogy of the four sides of a pyramid, Strange argues that each represents an interdependent face of the American colossus on the world stage. She therefore suggests that the idea of America's 'lost hegemony' is a myth which ought to be of interest to students of the sociology of knowledge, as well as international relations scholars.[47]

The analyses which stress the continuity of American dominance and of the postwar order rest partly upon the claim that this order is historically unique, and qualitatively different from previous hegemonies. Thus, like the Romans, the United States built its hegemony with a combination of tactical alliances. By contrast with the Roman empire, however, American outward expansiveness is more global, and more comprehensive, in the range of linkages it has promoted. Thus a cyclical interpretation of the rise and decline of hegemonies may lead to an erroneous set of conclusions concerning the American case. The Gramscian metaphor of an organic alliance (one which is relatively permanent and structural) can be contrasted with the tactical United States/Soviet/British alliance during World War II. This alliance was short term and easily broken. By comparison, the opportunity costs of breaking the American–Japanese and American–West European alliance systems would be very high for the junior partners, especially since the available alternatives are de-alignment, neutrality or re-alignment with other nations in a new power bloc. This is one reason why I think the metaphor of an 'organic alliance' helps to capture the quality of America's relations with Western Europe and Japan. This metaphor also implies that United States postwar policies, despite inconsistencies and failures, have none the less helped to foster a significant change in postwar international relations. These developments have been underpinned by continuing American military and geopolitical dominance.

The prospects for American hegemony are therefore not as bleak as suggested in the prevailing American interpretations. My argument, extended in chapter 5, proposes that the more crucial issue is the change in the relationship between the American and the world political economy. What has been developing in the 1970s and 1980s is a shift away from an *international economic order* of economically sovereign states and *national* political economies, linked together primarily by trade flows, towards what I call a *transnational liberal economic order*.[48] In this ascending order, capital flows and interpenetrating investments are fusing the world political economy into a more integrated whole. In this emerging scenario, which I would suggest will continue to unfold into the twenty-first century, America will continue to play a leading and central role. The class forces which will be at the vanguard of many of the changes in the economic structure will be those associated with highly mobile and large-scale transnational capital. Thus the question is not so much that of the future of American hegemony (which will persist partly because of pre-eminence in the security sphere). Rather it is the movement towards a necessarily incomplete and contradictory *hegemony of transnational capital*.

5 TOWARDS AN AMERICAN-CENTRED TRANSNATIONAL HEGEMONY?

CLASS FRACTIONS AND HISTORIC BLOCS

Here my focus is on the class nature of global hegemony. From a Gramscian perspective the question of 'hegemony for whom?' requires class analysis which pays attention to the political coalitions central to historic blocs. While the Marxist tradition stresses the concept of a ruling class, it also allows for divisions between capitalists and the possibility that elements of one fraction of capital may become dominant or hegemonic.

The term class is used here in a specifically Marxist, rather than Weberian sense, although the term 'establishment' is also employed to encompass associated elites within a wider social process aimed at securing the hegemony of a fraction of transnational capital. The Marxist tradition stresses conflict between groups which arises from their position in the social relations of production. Within each of the two basic classes there may be competing fractions, associated with different material interests and levels of consciousness. The latter refers to the ability of classes or fractions to conceptualise and politically advance their interests relative to other groups and classes. A given class or fraction's organic intellectuals may resort to claims of a universal type, suggesting that their leadership is in a general interest, an interest which may be posed at the national or international level.

The subsequent discussion focuses mainly on a transnational fraction of capital, developing its hegemony. Leading elements of this fraction have a highly developed consciousness, shared institutions and complementary, although sometimes conflicting, material interests. This transnational class fraction has foundations in North America, Western Europe and Japan, extends to some parts of the Third World, and is forging some, although as yet minimal links with the elites of some communist states.

Such a class formation in the North Atlantic context was first identified by Kees van der Pijl. He traced its Anglo-American roots back to a transatlantic financial community which emerged before World War I.[1] By contrast, the material basis for such a class formation in the postwar world lies mainly in the internationalisation of global production under the auspices of transnational corporations. By the late 1980s, it may be suggested that this class fraction forms the apex of an emerging *transnational historic bloc* based in the key capitalist states. The contours of this bloc will become clearer in our discussion of the Trilateral Commission in chapters 6 to 8. This bloc has begun to supersede what I call the *international historic bloc* which cemented the postwar international economic order.

TRILATERALISM AND TRANSNATIONAL CAPITALISM

Initially it is worth noting three points with respect to transnational companies. First, the growth in transnationals' investment has been faster than the postwar growth of the global product. Second, overseas production by transnationals has grown faster than world trade. Third, the geographical spread of the activity of transnationals has widened (that is in terms of control over operations in larger numbers of countries) at the same time as links between different companies have intensified. Transnationals have been forming consortia and co-operative ventures with increasing rapidity during the 1980s, creating what the United Nations Centre on Transnational Corporations has called 'corporate clusters or galaxies'. Control over production has been facilitated by rapid developments in transport, communications, data processing and by changes in company organisation and in the labour process.[2] In other words there has been a cumulative transnationalisation of the world political economy since 1945, a process still far from complete, but one which has accelerated in the recessionary years of the 1970s and, especially, the 1980s.

The transnationalisation process is at its most developed form in the wealthiest capitalist nations, especially the 'Trilateral' countries. For example, in 1987, 30 million of the 90 million manufacturing workers of the member countries of the Organisation for Economic Co-operation and Development (OECD) were directly employed by transnational companies, with many millions of others indirectly dependent on the activities and production of transnationals for their jobs.[3] However, as debates on the 'new international division of labour' reveal, the process is a global one, although in manufacturing it is concentrated, outside the OECD, in a limited number of 'newly-industrialising' nations, such as South Korea and Taiwan.

A number of factors have been adduced to explain the growth of transnational activity, but the one least frequently mentioned is the growth in the number of formally sovereign states, each pursuing competitive and mercantilist policies. Such policies include competition to attract foreign capital through investment incentives, low and stable inflation rates, the provision of suitable intrastructure, and weakening the power of organised labour. These are aspects of the creation of a suitable business climate to attract foreign investment. The growth in the number of sovereign states pursuing different types of mercantilist policies is a political counterpart to the internationalisation of capital. This internationalisation in turn depended initially upon American military and political dominance in the non-communist world, a dominance which meant that some liberalisation of capital was permitted.

As the Reading school on the multinational enterprise, led by John Dunning, has pointed out, the division of the globe into national economic units has also been a force in the 'internalisation' of transnational operations. Firms cut down on the transaction costs which would occur through the operations of two separate firms by integrating activity in one firm, thereby tendentially internalising the 'world market for commodities, finished products and finance'.[4] A further advantage for transnationals is their ability, through transfer pricing and intra-firm trade, to minimise tax liabilities and maximise global profits, implying a narrower tax base for governments than would be the case if production were organised along national lines. (This would appear to be the only really novel way in which transnational capital is able to increase the extraction of the social surplus.) Ankie Hoogvelt estimates that by the late 1980s perhaps 40 per cent of total world trade was in the form of intra-firm trade by transnationals, although the 1988 United Nations survey puts the figure closer to 30 per cent. The globalisation of production has also been facilitated by technological developments, for example, enabling the breaking down of production into discrete and increasingly unskilled tasks.

Over the last fifteen years there have been a number of unprecedented developments in the financial sphere, and in the relations between money and productive fractions of capital, with a number of destabilising consequences (discussed later in this chapter). For most of the postwar period the transnational phenomenon was mainly confined to extractive industries and manufactures, with most firms financing expansion through internal sources of capital. Since the late 1960s this situation has changed, with productive companies becoming more dependent on banks and the burgeoning offshore financial (Eurodollar) markets for supplies of finance. In addition, many productive corporations have been internally restructured in ways which given their financial divisions more influence over corporate strategy. An important variable in this equation was the internationalisation of American banks, and the development of innovations in financial services designed to circumvent national banking regulatory systems. Partly as a result of such developments, banks have become increasingly important in influencing (and in some cases controlling) the operations of transnationals in mineral extraction and manufactures.

What the trends noted above suggest is that transnational companies are playing a growing role in the world economy. Let us now discuss these developments with respect to trade, production and finance. World trade since World War II has grown rapidly, both in absolute terms and as a percentage of world GNP, as Table 4.1 shows. From this table we can see the predominance in world trade of the Trilateral countries, whose share rose as a percentage of world exports, from 55.9 per cent in 1950 to 66.0 per cent in 1980, with the substantial increase between 1970 and 1980 mainly due to the oil price rises. The larger shares for Japan and West Germany more than compensated for the declining shares of the United States and Britain. World trade also grew rapidly and faster than the growth in output. Growth in output stopped during the recession of 1979–82, and no growth in trade in real terms occurred in 1981. From 1982 trade grew again, and reached 9 per cent p.a. in 1984, falling to about 3 per cent in 1985.[5] Trade may have had an accelerationist effect on growth in output.[6] Such developments were accompanied by the increasing interpenetration of capital, initially mainly in the form of direct investment from America to the other Trilateral countries, and then later, and particularly in the 1980s, from these countries to the United States. During the 1970s and 1980s there was also an increase in portfolio investment. This has served to intensify the transnationalisation of capital, and to raise the mutual stakes invested in each of the Trilateral countries.[7]

The recent pattern of overseas direct investment is interesting for this study because it reveals, first, the underdeveloped nature of the process of transnationalisation in Japan when compared with other Trilateral countries, and second the magnetism of the American economy since the late 1970s for investors from other countries.[8] Overall, however, four countries predominate as recipients of foreign direct investment: the United States, Canada, Britain and West Germany. In the 1980s they accounted for nearly half of the global total of cumulative overseas investment, with the total share for Third World countries falling from a maximum of 30 per cent in 1967 to about

25 per cent in the late 1970s.[9] The major source of foreign direct investment has been the United States. American dominance in this regard was established during the 1960s, with Canada and Western Europe its main target areas. United States overseas direct investment changed gradually over the decade and gravitated more towards other parts of Europe, and to a much lesser extent the Pacific, and away from the Americas.[10] Japanese foreign direct investment, still small by United States and British standards, none the less has risen quickly in Western Europe and Latin America.[11] However, Japanese companies, measured in terms of the numbers of employees abroad, were still not very transnational when compared with their American and West European counterparts in the late 1980s.[12]

The transnationalisation process was initially mainly the result of an outflow of investment from the United States to Western Europe (1945 to the mid-1970s); then increasingly from Western Europe and Japan into the United States (especially in the 1980s). What has failed to occur is a comparably significant amount of overseas direct investment into Japan. By the mid-1980s Japan was awash with available capital to invest, and there was a surge in Japanese foreign direct investment. This is likely to continue in the 1990s (assuming the yen stays at its high levels relative to the dollar). Nevertheless, the transnational phenomenon is still very much dominated by the United States, although the massive revaluation of the yen against the dollar since mid-1985 (by perhaps 50 per cent up to March 1987) propelled Japanese transnational companies up the table of the top 100 companies very rapidly indeed. Japan had seven of the top ten banks in the world by the end of 1985.[13]

Irrespective of country of origin, what is clear is that transnational firms have become dominant forces in the transfer of capital, production, and technology in the global political economy. Robert Kudrle summarises some of the implications:

> The [transnational company] exemplifies the era of transnationalism and the increasingly complex problems *nearly all* governments face in devising effective, coherent international economic policies. From 1960 until the late 1970s, annual foreign production of [transnationals] grew at over 10 per cent, while world trade grew at 9.5 per cent and world production at about 8 per cent . . . Moreover, the enormous growth in world trade has taken place in large part under the aegis of the [transnationals]. Over half of US exports are now accounted for by [transnational] activity.[14]

Is there a relationship between these changes in the material structures of the global political economy and changes in class formations and state structures? How are such changes related to prevailing ideas in political economy in the non-communist world?

First, evidence indicates there is indeed a developing transnational capitalist class fraction within a wider 'Trilateral establishment'. The elite within this class fraction can be said to be at the zenith of an emerging transnational historic bloc, whose material interests and key ideas (within a broader political consciousness) are bound up with the progressive transnationalisation and liberalisation of the global political economy. Thus its key members include top owners and key executives of transnationals, central and other international bankers, many, though not all, leading politicians and civil servants in most advanced capitalist countries, and those in some developing nations. Although not members of a capitalist class in the strict Marxist sense of the term, some of the elites of communist states can, for these purposes, be considered as members of a wider international establishment. In this context it is significant that in 1987 the Soviet Union announced measures designed to accelerate inflows of foreign direct investment, and China's 'four modernisations' were well under way. As was noted in chapter 4, the growth of this class fraction has been facilitated by improved transport and communications, and increasingly by 'private' as well as 'public' institutions fostering dialogue and interaction between elites. Such dialogue and interaction may serve to promote a transnational 'identity' and a shared consciousness which may foster a closer identification of interests. This promotes conditions where this fraction becomes, to use Marx's phrase, more a class 'for itself' as opposed to merely a grouping of disorganised material forces. This issue is central to our considerations in chapters 6 to 8.

Second, the strengthening of some of these links and associated networks has gone with the 'transnationalisation' of the state.[15] By this I mean a process whereby state policies and institutional arrangements are conditioned and changed by the power and mobility of transnational fractions of capital. In the 1970s and 1980s this gave increased weight to certain parts of government, notably finance and economics ministries relative to foreign and defence ministries, as well as the private offices of Prime Ministers or Presidents. (For example, the 'sherpas' who plan and co-ordinate the seven-nation economic summits are drawn from the staff of the heads of government.) More crucially, state agencies linked to industry, employment and welfare tended to be downgraded as the competition for foreign capital intensified amid recessionary conditions. The corporatist agencies identified with the postwar Keynesian consensus were increasingly marginalised, the political role of organised labour declined and smaller scale 'national' manufacturing industry was put under pressure from international competition. Key individuals within the financial and economics ministries were linked to networks of international organisations and international interests represented in institutions such as the Trilateral Commission, and thus were part of an informal structure of international influence. Apart from the fact that a large number of Trilateral Commissioners were significant figures in the political establishments of their own countries, of the world's largest 100 companies in 1985, at least 60 had key executives who were Commission members. Commission members were associated with major productive transnationals, with banks and firms dominating the world's rapidly growing financial services markets as well as with giant media corporations.[16]

Third and, of course linked to our first two points, crucial to hegemony of a transnational class fraction, is acceptance of ideas and policies conducive to transnational forces within major government bureaucracies and international organisations. This would in fact appear to have occurred. Both the International Monetary Fund and the World Bank came to adopt liberal economic discourses and policies over the last twenty years. Here it is worth noting that in 1987, in the World Bank, the United States controlled 20.1 per cent of the votes, Japan 6 per cent, Britain 5.7 per cent, France 5.4 per cent, and West Germany 5 per cent, that is, over 42 per cent of the voting power was concentrated in the hands of just five Trilateral countries. (A similar situation existed in the Fund, where the United States had the voting power to block any major constitutional or policy changes, and again, where Japan's position failed to reflect its economic power.) Such liberal ideas and practices are intended to promote market efficiency; the virtues of free trade and investment; flexible exchange markets; the control of inflation and public expenditure; the private sector relative to the public; and labour market flexibility (and the dangers of trade union monopoly power which may obstruct the introduction of new technology and hold up real wages at a level incompatible with full employment). Given that these ideas became more widely accepted during the late 1970s and 1980s, they also served to restrict the ability of subordinate classes to analyse the nature of the political economy, and construct alternatives. A dramatic instance of this was Prime Minister Thatcher's claim, made in the context of her aim of eradicating socialism from Britain, that there was 'no alternative' to her supply-side monetarist policies. Thus this structure of thought manifests the positive and negative aspects of class ideology.

THE CRISIS OF POSTWAR HEGEMONY

The questions here are first, what have these ascendant class forces meant for the coherence of the postwar international historic bloc? What do these imply for the nature of international economic order? We can approach these questions by initially recapitulating the main social forces in the liberal international economic order which prevailed during the 1950s and 1960s.

The forces of transnational capital developed in the postwar context of the compromise of 'embedded' or 'corporate' liberalism.[17] This international political settlement accorded with ideas associated with the New Deal: it was a negotiated formula between the various fractions of capital and labour in a range of capitalist states. This matched the structural properties of the postwar capitalist system to American initiatives and American-dominated international institutions. Central to this arrangement were notions of the domestic 'mixed economy' and a liberalising international economy. These were, at the time, relatively compatible. They allowed for a range of national policies to be practised in a relatively expansionist, stable international structure. Keynesian and mercantilist frameworks of thought (premised on the idea that the market had been discredited as an autonomous economic steering mechanism) existed alongside the American government's desire to move towards the vision inspired by FDR's Secretary of State Cordell Hull: global free trade and an extension of the long-standing American policy of the 'open door' to foreign investment. These expansionist and 'internationalist' goals were developed, however, in an international economic system which consisted of identifiably separate 'national capitals', and national political economies. At the level of production, the ascendant and internationalising forces were associated with what Gramsci called a 'Fordist' pattern of accumulation, namely a mass-production and mass-consumption system which controlled, rewarded and incorporated (organised) labour, in many cases through corporatism and social democracy. Binding this together was an American-centred security structure with its ideology of anti-communism and the defence of the free world. Together, these political arrangements and associated social forces would, in the long term, unleash a global national-international dialectic.

This international set of ideas, institutions, and material forces which were synthesised in the postwar political settlement remained largely compatible during the 1950s and 1960s, when economic conditions were especially stable and propitious. The Cold War and other

96

political concerns helped to catalyse the formation of strong alliances between the United States, the major powers in Western Europe and Japan. In Gramscian terms, this meant that class forces of labour and capital from a range of countries were associated in an *international historic bloc*, with America at its core. This historic bloc also reflected the rise to prominence of a Fordist, intensive regime of accumulation, as production became more capital-intensive and more global in reach. This historic bloc cemented the postwar *international economic order*. In so far as it is possible to speak of a 'crisis of hegemony', it is because forces of transnationalisation and recession (and perhaps also the eclipse of the Cold War) have served to increasingly undermine the coherence of this historically specific politico-economic constellation. In this context, during the 1970s and 1980s there has been a movement towards a *transnational liberal economic order*, partly because national regulatory and economic intervention systems have begun to give way to powerful transnational forces: the dialectical balance between 'national' and 'transnational' forces appears to have tilted in favour of the latter.

In a recent paper, van der Pijl has argued that the 1970s saw the end of a 'long wave' of corporate liberal class formation, and the emergence of a new wave, linked to a 'neo-liberal' tendency within the transnational class fraction I have mentioned. He states that the initial stages of the development of the Trilateral Commission (which he incorrectly attributes to the defence of the old, corporate liberal order) coincided with the final instance of the long postwar wave of corporate liberal class formation (involving industrial capitalists, workers and financiers in the OECD countries). This helped to cement the hegemonic American-centred international historic bloc. As the forces of some parts of industrial capital and industrial labour (particularly in traditional 'smokestack' industries) were put on the defensive in the late 1970s and 1980s, a challenge to the order was sustained by the rise of a new class formation, organised around banking and the promotion of high-technology, capital-intensive industries. During the 1970s and especially from the end of the decade onwards, banking and financial services claimed a higher share in the profit distribution process, as well as a more prominent role in control over industrial investment.[18] Such investment, mainly relating to the so-called 'third wave' of the technological-industrial revolution, increased significantly in many OECD countries in the 1970s. Thus a:

> Neoliberal class formation, from the late 1960s on, developed through the reemergence of bank capital, including the reintegration of investment banking and securities departments with commercial

banks; a breakdown of corporatist state/capital/labour collusion; and, significantly, the growth of rentier incomes warranting Jacob Morris's qualification of a 'Revenge of the Rentier' contradicting Keynes's prescription of his euthanasia.[19]

Thus this adjustment towards neo-liberalism involved a movement away from the Fordist pattern of accumulation in many of the major capitalist states. There was also a shift away from the older forms of mass industrial employment, and towards more efficient, high-tech and capital-intensive industrial production and towards services. Neo-liberalism, while consistently stressing the virtues of the market, also involves the idea of strengthening some aspects of the state, notably the role of finance ministries, in order to roll back other parts of its operation. This accords with the concept of the transnationalisation of the state. For example, in accord with the new monetarist doctrines which became influential during the 1970s, the transnationalisation of the state went with arguments and policies which stressed the need to respond to the imperatives of international competition. Thus, such proposals would take away from the state the responsibility for bailing out lame ducks and give it the capacity to concentrate on industrial 'winners' and mobilising markets. In this process, organised labour, at least in the declining industrial sectors, became more politically marginalised.

One source of neo-liberal thinking can be traced to neo-conservative think-tanks in the United States, whilst another source is the influential international body, the Mont Pèlèrin Society, created in 1944, whose luminaries include its founder, F. A. von Hayek, and Milton Friedman. Many influential Western politicians are members of this society which champions 'free market conservatism'. For example, in the late 1960s Theodore Lowi described the American system as a 'state of permanent receivership', with the state effectively propping up worthless enterprises at the taxpayers' expense, a system bound to help generate long-term fiscal crisis. Thus the state had to choose between what he termed 'creeping socialism' and economic decline, or a reinvigorated neo-liberalism which would confront vested interests ('interest group' liberalism) and dismantle their privileges. In effect, this would unleash the creativity of the market and revitalise American capitalism, simultaneously creating the conditions for a relegitimation of the state apparatus in the United States, since it would be seen to act in accordance with and to preserve American anti-statist traditions. A neo-liberal offensive would help to resolve the 'crisis of public authority' which was said to be paralysing the United States government and the political apparatus in the 1970s.[20] Noteworthy here is the fact that the theme of market-centred change is central to the Trilateral Commission's economic studies (the Commission's North American Director, Charles Heck, is a great admirer of Lowi's *The End of Liberalism*). In the Trilateral studies, deviations from the principles of market rationality are only accepted if they are directed towards the promotion of market principles at some point in the future. This can even be said to apply to policies towards the low-income developing countries where most of the exceptions to free-market policies are tolerated. A Trilateral Commission report on OECD industrial policy written in 1978–9 sought to devise guidelines for policies which would promote 'an economy that is more skill-intensive, science-based, innovative, and high in value-added', and which recognised that 'the enterprise sector is the prime mover in the economy'. The report's premise was 'market forces and entrepreneurship are the foundation of our economic system'.[21]

The report argued that the proper aims and criteria for industrial policy were: (i) efficiency; (ii) freedom and health of the market system; (iii) 'social aims'; (iv) security; (v) international co-operation. Following guidelines drawn from the public choice approach, the report suggested that measures should be general rather than specific, be long term in orientation and should rely on a 'properly functioning market'; policies should be 'transparent', and if possible involve co-operation between government, business and labour. They should be developed in a wider co-ordinated framework through an international organisation such as the OECD.[22] The report was produced in the context of what had become a new policy orthodoxy in the mid-1970s, the central slogan of which was the 'war on inflation'. This consensus was also represented in an OECD report, *Toward Full Employment and Price Stability*, prepared by a committee of top economists chaired by Trilateral Commissioner Paul McCracken.[23] The McCracken Report stressed the need for tight control of national money supplies, cuts or restraint in government expenditures, and attempts to stop the rise in real wages. This would serve to reverse the downward trend in profits (and upward trend in real wages) which had taken place between 1968 and 1974, as well as to attack inflation. As with the Trilateral Commission report, McCracken and his associates stressed the need for markets to steer change, and, in contrast to some of the European Trilateral Commissioners at the time, generally ruled out corporatist solutions. The report also acknowledged that the costs of such a set of policies would be much higher, potentially permanent, levels of unemployment, and therefore the major capitalist states (mainly those in Europe) would have to jettison commitment to one of the central pillars of the postwar welfarist consensus. The changes involved an attack on wage indexation, and a general offensive designed to 'liberalise' labour markets. This report, in other words, contained the essentials of the neo-liberal orthodoxy. The first major sign that this orthodoxy had been put into practice in the Trilateral countries was in Britain in 1976, when the Labour government under Prime Minister James Callaghan and Chancellor Denis Healy (both subsequently became Trilateral Commissioners after the fall of the Labour government in 1979) went to the IMF for a loan, and introduced monetarist policies in compliance with loan conditions. The people's party thus set the scene for Mrs Thatcher's 'there is no alternative' slogan and policies.

THE RECESSIONS OF THE 1970S AND 1980S AND THEIR EFFECTS

My argument here is contrary to that of Gilpin and Wallerstein who associate slowing growth and recessionary conditions with a movement towards mercantilist policies of economic closure (see chapters 2 and 3). For such policies to succeed would imply a strong identity of interest between labour, national capital and the state. This possibility has been made more unlikely because of the internationalisation of production, the weakening of organised labour and what I have called the process of the transnationalisation of the state.

I contend that the forms of mercantilism generated by recession in the 1970s and 1980s are designed to increase the attractiveness of national economies for foreign capital, rather than to shut such capital out. This also involves the competition to attract highly skilled labour (or human capital), through competitive income tax cuts. The most recent example of the latter was the British 1988 budget, which cut the top level of income tax from 60 to 40 per cent (it stood at 83 per cent in 1979) in a move justified as an attempt to reverse the 'brain drain'. In sum, the 1970s and 1980s were characterised not only by a long-term crisis of the old postwar hegemony, but also a series of recessions and rising unemployment in a range of countries. It can be argued that these recessions catalysed the demise of the former order and provoked increasing liberalisation of important aspects of the global political economy. Such liberalisation is a key characteristic of 'the crisis of hegemony'.

The scale of recession in the 1970s and 1980s is revealed in Figure 5.1. This shows severe recessions in 1974–5 and 1980–2, the latter much the deepest. The trend was a slowdown in the growth of output

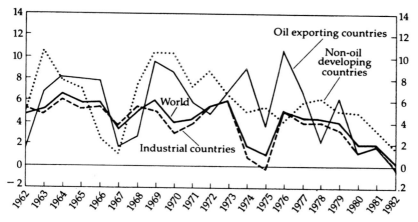

Figure 5.1 Real gross domestic product by region, 1962–82 (per cent change over previous year)
Source: International Monetary Fund, *International Financial Statistics,* supplement on output statistics (Washington DC, International Monetary Fund, 1984), p. x

among all groups of countries for 1963–72 and 1973–82. The growth in per capital output of industrial countries between 1973 and 1982 was 1.7 per cent per annum, in contrast to 3.7 per cent in the former period, and that of the oil exporting countries fell from 5.6 to 3.8 per cent in the two periods. The non-oil developing countries' per capita growth rates fell from 3.6 to 2.7 per cent in the two periods. In the Western hemisphere, the growth in per capita output in 1973–82 was 2 per cent, compared with 3.3 per cent in the previous decade. In the United States, the 1979–82 recession was the worst since the 1930s and it saw, in the summer of 1981, a prime rate of interest of 20.4 per cent, which broke the usury laws of some of the American states. The effects of the slowdown were particularly severe for less-developed and indebted nations, especially in Latin America (see Table 5.1). This was also the case for Africa.

What was crucial, at least in ideological terms, was that recession helped activate the reappraisal concerning the role of the public sector and the appropriate 'mix' of intervention and market in a capitalist economy. These recessions also led to changes in expectations about international relations, for example, the likelihood of concessions by the developed countries to less-developed countries and the viability of commodity agreements and cartels such as OPEC. The pressure of recession, an acceleration in the fall of real prices of commodity exports (see Figure 5.2) coupled with very high real interest rates in the

101

Table 5.1. *Developing countries' real rates of growth, GDP per capita, 1968–85*

	1968–77	1977–81	1981–5
15 heavily indebted nations	3.9	1.4	−1.7
Latin America	3.6	1.7	−1.5

Source: International Monetary Fund, *World Economic Outlook, 1986* (Washington DC, International Monetary Fund, 1986).

late 1970s and early 1980s (see Figure 5.3) forced many indebted nations to turn to the IMF, which in turn pressed these countries to liberalise their economies and cut the size and growth of the public sector. In addition, since 1981, the Soviet Union was weakened relative to the major capitalist states because of the rapid fall in the price of oil, its major source of foreign exchange.[24]

These recessions had obvious short-term purgative effects associated with a downswing in the business cycle. This promoted a general restructuring of capital and of capital-labour relations. For example, during 1979–82 there were record numbers of bankruptcies, and the decline of older, less-competitive industries was accelerated.

Thus, noteworthy links between different aspects of global restructuring in the late 1970s and early 1980s were discernible. In many ways the recession of the early 1980s can be seen as facilitating the material and ideological renovation of American hegemony. This might appear unexpected since recession was more severe in the United States than it was among its main economic competitors and its main military rival, the Soviet Union. Moreover, the Federal Reserve virtually initiated and deepened the recession with tight monetary policy (1979–82) at the same time as real oil prices rose following the fall of the Shah of Iran. However, in 1982 the Reagan 'boom' took off, with a combination of fiscal stimulus (involving vastly increased military expenditures entailing a spiralling budget deficit) and supply-side, tax-cutting measures (designed to stimulate investment and improve productivity and the competitiveness of certain sectors of the American economy).

America's capacity to expand out of recession in this way contrasted with the other major capitalist states which exercised strict controls on growth of public spending. This was an aspect of America's continuing economic exceptionalism. A second element of exceptionalism, that is Reaganite populism, provided much of the justification for

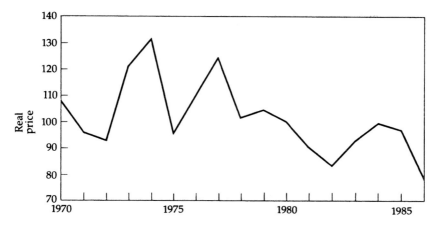

Figure 5.2 Real prices of developing country commodity exports, 1970–85 (1980=100)
Source: Feldstein *et al.*, *Restoring Growth in the Debt-Laden Third World* (New York, Trilateral Commission, 1987), discussion draft, p. 13A. Based on OECD and IMF statistics

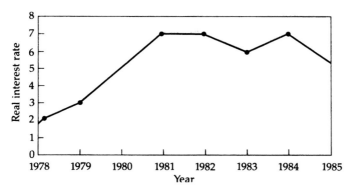

Figure 5.3 Real interest rates, 1978–85 (Eurodollar rate minus US GNP deflator)
Source: Feldstein *et al.*, *Restoring Growth in the Debt-Laden Third World*, p. 13B

the policies which helped generate the post-1982 boom. Reaganism was in tune with, as well as a catalyst for, the resurgence of possessive individualism and hostility towards statist paternalism. Along with the Reaganite stress on the need for a 'strong America' these themes served to vindicate tax cuts, the deregulation of industry and banking, an attack on union power (for example, firing all striking members of the American civil air traffic controllers' union, Patco), and provided part of the context for the spread of a get-rich-quick, speculative and

103

increasingly short-term mentality in the United States (and to a certain extent elsewhere).

From the vantage point of the late 1980s the United States appeared much more successful in restructuring major sectors of its economy than Western Europe, at least with respect to job creation, investment and profit growth, although less so with respect to improving its rate of productivity growth. In this context, foreign-based transnationals were becoming much more dependent upon the American market at the same time as American manufacturing capital shifted many of its assets towards high-profit sectors like energy reserves, financial services, real-estate, emergent technology, and defence.

With respect to labour, the 1980s witnessed a substantial shift in the balance of power between organised labour and capital. This was true in most major capitalist states and was reflected in lower wage claims, falling union membership, lower resistance to technical change and attempts by capitalists to eliminate overmanning and, partly as a consequence, in 1983–5, higher profit rates (American corporations had their highest profit rates for a decade in the mid-1980s). A particularly noteworthy statistic was that in 1986, the real average weekly earnings of American workers were 8.5 per cent lower than they were in 1970:

> American wage and salary earners have enjoyed no real improve-
> ments in living standards for 20 years now – a misfortune which can
> be found in almost no other country outside Africa and Latin
> America. Most of the fall in US earnings occurred from 1979 to
> 1982.[25]

Since 1983, important sectors of organised labour in the United States accepted real wage cuts, with much lower pay levels for new employees than for established workers. This created a two-tier wages structure. American labour unions jeopardised their long-term solidarity and strength, whilst union membership continued to decline:[26]

> While inflation has been slowing, so has the escalation in pay
> settlements [in the US]. As a result, there are now millions of US
> workers for whom an annual pay cut – in actual money wages, not
> just in 'real terms' – is a fact of life.[27]

Key reasons for this trend were both an increase in foreign competition and, of much greater significance, the impact of more and more American producers operating with non-unionised labour. Perverse though it may seem, non-unionised American workers actually enjoyed consistently higher pay rises than their unionised counterparts after 1982.[28] These developments should be seen in a context where there was no strong socialist movement, in contrast to Western Europe, and to a lesser extent Japan. Capitalist hegemony appeared more firmly embedded in the United States, and to have strengthened in the last decade, despite the Reverend Jesse Jackson's attempts to organise a Democratic coalition of the disadvantaged during the decade, along left-liberal principles.

A similar story can be recounted for Japan. Here the once powerful Japanese trade union movement rapidly lost influence, and its membership declined. In the 1940s, over half the workforce in Japan was unionised, whilst in 1986 only 28.9 per cent were unionised. In 1985 the number of working days lost through strikes (already very low by American and West European standards) fell to its lowest level since the war. Between 1980 and 1986 manufacturing sector efficiency rose by 30 per cent, whilst wages increased only 10 per cent.[29] Japanese corporations began to lay off workers, cut overtime and reduce traditional twice-yearly bonuses, and large-scale redundancies became commonplace. Not only blue-collar but also white-collar employees took pay cuts. For example, in April 1986 Nissan Motors' 2,300 middle managers took a 5 per cent cut and its 48 top managers a 10 per cent cut.[30]

REAGANOMICS: ITS IMPACT, ITS LIMITS

Let us now return to the debate over the impact and importance of the policies of the Reagan administration with reference to the tendencies towards a transnational hegemony. Beyond this issue, the case of the Reagan administration is important for our study of Trilateralism since the Californian Reagan, as candidate and President, voiced his suspicions of the Trilateralists and their policy prescriptions. Indeed, Reaganism was widely interpreted as antithetical to Trilateralism as a concept of international action and to the Trilateralists as a social grouping of East Coast establishmentarians. Controversies over Reagan's policies can be related to the debate concerning structural and behavioural forms of international power. Our discussion of the debates also sheds light on the question of organic intellectuals and the issue of an oversight mechanism for global capitalism.

In contrast to the Carter administration's avowed goals of overhauling Trilateral relations and moving towards 'world order politics' through co-ordinating economic policies with its allies and with Third World regional influentials such as Saudi Arabia and Brazil, the Reagan administration initially pursued a different, and some claimed incoherent, economic strategy, lecturing the representatives of these states at the 1981 Cancun North–South conference on the need for more 'market place magic'. For example, critics of Reaganomics included the Director of the Institute for International Economics, Fred Bergsten (whose views found resonance with many American Trilateral Commissioners). Bergsten reproached Reaganomics for jeopardising the long-run health of the United States economy. Reagan (like his Californian predecessor as President, Richard Nixon) has failed to understand 'the international consequences of U.S. actions'.[31] By contrast, according to Georgetown's more conservative former Reagan staff member, Henry Nau, Reagan's policies were quite cognisant of international forces. Nau argued that Reagan's moves were designed to project America's structural economic power and set the conditions for its economic relations with other states.[32] Nau was keen to differentiate the Reagan administration from its predecessors:

> The Reagan Administration based policy on a new appreciation of U.S. economic power in the international market-place, a power that its predecessors perceived to be declining and therefore less and less able to influence world economic developments. By renewing incentives to disinflate and enhance market incentives at home, the administration used U.S. power not as an end in itself, but as a means of encouraging these reforms abroad. Simultaneously it urged new international negotiations to maintain open markets, recognising that U.S. economic policies could not shape international behaviour if markets closed.[33]

In support of his argument, Nau added, perhaps with a trace of euphemism, that Reagan's policies 'sparked world-wide interest in the market approach', and their flexibility 'permitted the administration to initiate through the relatively autonomous marketplace a necessary, politically difficult, and temporarily painful struggle to restore sound domestic priorities'.[34]

Nau's argument dissents significantly from neo-realist and liberal wisdom concerning hegemonic decline. Nau suggests that at least since World War II, and probably since the 1930s, the United States has been structurally dominant in the world economy. Indeed, I would go further than Nau and suggest that American economic power, while showing relative decline in aggregate terms, is in fact enormous when compared to that of any other country, and has an international aspect which gives the United States government an unparalleled prerogative *vis-à-vis* the rest of the world. What seemed to be at issue was the question of whether American leaders were able to perceive the implications of such structural dominance and harness it in their policies.

Reagan's policies, particularly in his first administration, corresponded graphically to a realist concept of unilateralism in that they showed a willingness by the United States government to reorient the policies of other states so that they became more open to American economic penetration. In Giovanni Arrighi's terminology, this reflected a long-term transformation in United States' strategy away from a formal (political, military) to an informal (market-based) system of control.[35] As has been indicated, this process was much more painful for other countries than for the United States, since Reagan policies siphoned capital from abroad, raised the dependence of other states on the American market, and globalised the financing of American military programmes. Premised initially on domestic remobilisation, Reaganomics had the effect of strengthening transnational forces, through promoting the further interpenetration of capital, the liberalisation of markets, and deepening the interdependence between American and other states' macroeconomic policy-making conditions.

Reaganomics, whilst being in some ways a nationalist strategy, therefore acknowledged and harnessed the higher degree of integration of the United States into the global political economy. By contrast, Nixon's 'domesticist' strategy of August 1971 was adopted when the American political economy was really just entering a stage of internationalisation. Moreover, whereas Nixon's apparently defensive tactics partly sought to protect American national capital, and to an extent American workers, from the effects of international competition, Reagan's policies were more offensive, more market-based, and involved an attack on organised labour. Reagan's policies also facilitated a growth in concentration within certain sectors of the American economy, so that its bigger corporations were better able to compete internationally.[36] Thus, although perhaps not consciously intended, Reagan's policies none the less reinforced the tendency towards transnational hegemony. In a more liberal world marketplace, the largest and most mobile forms of capital will tend to become stronger.

The Achilles heel of Reaganomics was, of course, the contradiction between growing military expenditures and the relative narrowing of the American fiscal base. Reaganomics has proven to be a perfect recipe for long-term fiscal crisis. This meant that, in order to finance the budget deficit, the United States had to offer relatively high yields on Treasury bonds, which kept interest rates high, not only in the

United States, but world wide. Apart from aggravating the debt servicing problems of the developing nations, this also tended to depress world investment, while simultaneously the United States attracted a vast influx of capital. Although this may have appeared to make domestic sense to American policy-makers, it had serious global macroeconomic consequences, at least if one took a long-term view. If world-wide growth rates continue to be depressed, the international marketplace Reaganomics was so concerned with might actually stagnate, even though the United States experienced a boom. This would have acute repercussions for American transnationals, which drew increasing proportions of their profits from overseas operations in the 1970s and 1980s. At a secondary level, the Reagan boom was accompanied by a massive surge in imports, causing the United States trade deficit to rise to unprecedented levels (partly because world demand was depressed elsewhere, and also because of the high level of the dollar). This generated substantial protectionist pressure in Congress. However, fears of protectionism gave an added impetus to foreign companies to locate production facilities in the United States.

Recognising some of the dangers and contradictions inherent in this mix of policies, some American leaders began to perceive limits to Reaganomics. Elements within the second Reagan administration began to pay more attention to international economic co-operation. The major figure behind this thinking was the new Treasury Secretary, James Baker III, the former White House Chief of Staff, who changed jobs with the former Secretary, Donald Regan. Regan, the ex-chief executive at financial services giant Merrill-Lynch, was a believer in the relatively unfettered market. Baker's view suggested that intervention of some kind, co-ordinated with the other major economic powers, was needed to save the market from itself. In September 1985, Baker launched the first of his 'initiatives' in a meeting with the Group of Five finance ministers, resulting in the so-called Plaza Agreement. This was followed up in 1987 with a second initiative, resulting in the Louvre Accord.[37]

The initiatives reflected a new American perception of the need for international co-ordination and co-operation in the sphere of macroeconomic management. Specifically, the first initiative involved measures to reduce the overvaluation of the dollar (and thus to help reduce the trade deficit and defuse protectionist pressures in Congress), to find a way out of a potential world-wide deflationary spiral and regenerate global economic growth and to get to grips with the 'debt crisis'. The major domestic stumbling block continued to be United States fiscal policy, which was having depressive economic effects outside the United States. The Pentagon initially resisted cuts in military expenditures, whilst there was also strong resistance to further reductions in domestic welfare expenditures. Outside the United States, the strategy involved attempts to force a demand stimulus in other major economies.

To keep the American side of the bargain required curbing the Pentagon's ceaseless appetite for vast expenditures. In the longer term, it meant some internationalisation of the perspective of the American military-industrial complex, such that its leaders redefined their concepts of security to include international economic co-operation and stability. In the late 1980s there was some sign of movement on this, since the Pentagon launched its system of competitive tendering, cutting procurement costs, and embarking on transnational co-production ventures to extend scale economies.[38] The growth in American military expenditures in fact stopped in 1986, and there developed a widespread political consensus not to increase its levels. An important nail in the coffin for Pentagon big spenders appeared to be the resignation of Caspar Weinberger as Secretary of Defense in 1987, to be replaced by Frank Carlucci, who set about making spending cuts *before* Congress applied the axe.

In addition, by early 1988, there was substantial evidence that Japan had attempted to boost domestic demand, as had Britain, although this was less true for West Germany. Moreover, the value of the dollar fell dramatically against a range of major currencies, by something in the region of 40 per cent in the nine months following the 1985 Plaza Agreement, partly as a result of the co-ordinated actions of the Group of Five. The United States backed a shift in IMF policies, away from harsh conditionality, towards policies which were more likely to promote some long-term economic expansion in recipient countries. Overall, these changes represented substantial movement towards policies favoured by most Trilateral Commissioners.

With respect to United States' security policies *vis-à-vis* its major alliance partners, the Reagan administration, much like its predecessor, trod a thin line between exploiting their allegiance and destroying European confidence in, and loyalty to, the United States by doing so. A good example of this was the way the United States used a large number of inducements to gain allied participation in the launch of the Strategic Defence Initiative whilst simultaneously intensifying the wide variety of methods the Americans have used to restrict transatlantic technology transfer. It was widely believed in European leadership circles that these methods, as well as specific clauses in research contracts, would be deployed to deny European producers valuable spin-off benefits from SDI research and development. In other words, the United States seemed to want control over non-American technological breakthroughs.

The risks of undermining alliance consensus were also highlighted in the sphere of nuclear weapons negotiations when, at the Reykjavik summit in 1986, the United States effectively proposed massive cuts in strategic arsenals, and endorsed the prospect of a nuclear-free Europe (and by implication a willingness to bargain away the nuclear weapons of the French and British without prior consultation). Such proposals created a political crisis in the NATO alliance, since, between 1979 and 1983, European member governments attempted to convince their publics of the need for *more* not less nuclear weapons to counter Soviet potential. This position was, in fact, consistent with the longstanding strategic policy of the major West European members of NATO: to strengthen the coupling of American and European nuclear forces, hence the push to install cruise and Pershing II missiles. In other words, the real reason for the cruise/Pershing deployment was political, that is, to reinforce the impression in the minds of the Soviet leadership that transatlantic alliance solidarity had been reinforced.[39]

However, it may be asserted that these moves, whilst significant, did little to fundamentally undermine the forces which create the common interests which sustain alliance unity over most basic principles. In the last analysis, this may indicate a strong sense of confidence on the part of the United States based on the knowledge that neither Western Europe nor Japan could provide a real alternative to United States military leadership. Nonetheless, for all Reagan's increases in expenditures, it may be doubted whether they have resulted or will result in a really significant change in the United States relative military capabilities. They may have more (perhaps marginal) impact on the performance and profitability of certain American industries.

The same was not true, however, of United States economic policies during the late 1970s and 1980s which had far-reaching effects. The recession of the early 1980s debilitated the power of labour, both inside and outside the United States. It contributed to a deterioration in the terms of trade for developing nations, and to a weakening of OPEC's influence on oil prices. Shortage of foreign exchange led many countries to establish export processing zones, and adopt a more 'welcoming' attitude to foreign enterprises. Shortage of tax revenue, with which to sustain government spending, made governments more willing to consider privatisation of public sector assets. Privatisation programmes emerged not only in Britain, somewhat of a pioneer in this regard, but also in many developed and developing countries, and even in the United States. Doubtless many of these tendencies reflected other factors than United States economic policy, but the latter was clearly influential. These developments were in contrast to the defensiveness towards OPEC and the Third World which prevailed for much of the early and mid-1970s, and which was reflected in a number of Trilateral Commission and Council on Foreign Relations publications, arguing for 'partnership' and 'accommodation' with Third World countries, the strongest of which had begun to use their resource and commodity power to substantial effect.[40]

Reagan's policy can thus be interpreted as an intensification of the push towards the postwar United States goal of liberalising the more dynamic sectors of the international economy, as well as liberalising labour and capital markets within the United States, in ways which benefited the strongest American corporations. A range of countries have moved in these directions, although a great deal of statist mercantilism still persists. The 'liberalisation' of the Chinese economy is but one example, although the Chinese had other reasons for their changes in policy (the Soviet Union and Vietnam also opened the door to foreign direct investment, the latter offering 100 per cent repatriation of profits from 1987). The traditionally mercantilist Japanese also moved, albeit slowly, towards the liberalisation of their capital markets. Moreover, the fact that such 'liberal' policies were still being pursued by the United States, while calls for protectionism were mounting in Congress, reflected the influence of American transnational fractions of capital in the determination of American foreign economic policy. Notwithstanding rhetoric concerning the 'threat' or 'virulence' of protectionism expressed consistently in Trilateral Commission literature, it can be argued that protectionism in certain sectors (or its threat) may promote an increase in foreign direct investment and greater transnationalisation of production. Some American and European protectionism may, for example, help to undermine Japanese insularity, and reduce the comparatively 'national' and corporatist orientation of Japanese enterprises, making them more transnational.

It can be argued therefore that Reaganomics involved a reconstruction of the postwar hegemonic settlement, with the United States at the centre of structural changes liberalising important aspects of the global political economy.

THEORISING THE RISING POWER OF
INTERNATIONALLY MOBILE CAPITAL

What message can be drawn from our analysis of changes in American hegemony and transnational capitalism in the 1970s and 1980s? A key feature of the period was the rising power of internationally mobile fractions of capital relative to labour, national capital, and many states. This change was part of the transformation of the postwar international economic order. I would like to advance a synthetic concept of the 'power of capital' to help explain these changes.[41] The power of capital operates along two dimensions associated with behavioural and structural forms of power. The first corresponds to the sociological concept of agency, the second to the concept of structure. By the power of transnational capital I have in mind the cumulative capacity of internationally mobile capital to impose constraints, partly through the operation of market forces, on national governments and labour organisations. This notion of structural power draws attention not just to constraints, but also to structure as a power resource.[42]

For my argument then, the power of internationally mobile or transnational capital varies, depending upon:

(i)   its size and scale relative to states and to labour;

(ii) its relative mobility and fungibility (the facility with which it can be used for different purposes and in different locations – money capital being generally more mobile and fungible than industrial capital);

(iii) its relative scarcity (that is, its supply relative to demand – there was a relative glut of capital on the international markets in the mid-1970s because of petro-dollars, whereas it was relatively scarce and costly in the late 1970s and 1980s);

(iv) the extensiveness of the process of the transnationalisation of the state, as has been defined earlier in this chapter. This would imply a rise in:

(a)   the extent to which sets of ideas (such as economic liberalism and the doctrine of sovereignty) which encourage transnationalisation spread and become prevalent, perhaps through informal networks and in governments, international organisations, and to other agents;

(b)   the degree to which 'organic intellectuals' who are associated with such frameworks of thought come to have influence over state policies, notably in the United States, to a lesser extent in other capitalist states, and in key international economic

112

institutions, especially the IMF, the World Bank, and to a perhaps lesser extent, the OECD.

The first aspect of the power of capital is the conscious, organised, exertion of political pressure by various sections or fractions of capital, so as to secure rules, policies and resource commitments favourable to profit-making and the accumulation of capital. This also applies to elements in state bureaucracies, political parties, and international organisations supportive of such policy changes. This face of the power of capital is congruent with the concept of agency. This operates at both domestic and international levels, and can be overt or covert in nature. The Trilateral Commission might be seen, therefore, as a (private and partly confidential) forum within which, and from which, this type of political pressure can be exerted. The activity of the Commission is related to the generation and promotion of patterns of thinking compatible with a shift in the focus and organisation of state action towards what I have called the transnationalisation of the state. The Commission and its kindred private organisations represent a means by which a transnational 'strategic consciousness' can be developed, and in which power resources may be mobilised.

The second face concerns forms of international structural power which, under certain conditions, create sets of constraints on national fractions of capital, certain states, and labour, as opposed to trans-national fractions of capital, for whom they can be viewed as a positive power resource.[43] The structural forces I have in mind make the adoption of policies favoured by transnational capital more likely. What are the forms of structural power which tend to benefit the interests of transnational capital? The major one is the extension of the geographical and economic dimensions of the market.

The movement of large amounts of capital between countries, in the form of direct foreign investment, short-term capital flows and long-term portfolio investment, in response to economic and political conditions, acts to condition, for example, the behaviour of govern-ments, firms, trade unions and other groups. Through the market such structural power is premised upon the greater mobility of transnational capital than its 'national' counterpart. By large, I mean relative to the size of any potentially countervailing elements. Thus, these capital flows are now vast relative to the size of trade flows, the foreign exchange reserves of central banks, and the potentially countervailing resources of national capital and labour organisations. The growth of such mobility and scale intensifies the need for governments, competing to attract foreign capital under recessionary conditions, to provide an appropriate business climate for overseas

113

investors. A state will be judged in terms of its comparative hospitality to foreign capital. Thus the policies of the state towards the market, towards labour-capital relations, towards the provision of an appropriate social and economic infrastructure, are incrementally recast in an international framework. These changes are, in large part, responses to the cumulative process of transnationalisation. This process is akin to that of a snowball rolling down a mountain side, gathering pace and size. In consequence, the policies of deregulation of financial markets which arose in the United States in the 1970s and 1980s provoked similar changes overseas, the net effect of which was to liberalise the financial structure of the system as a whole.[44]

Both behavioural and structural dimensions of the power of capital may be linked as ideas and institutions change. For example, the unprecedented co-operation between banks from various countries under the aegis of the IMF in the early 1980s with regard to the debt crisis represented a higher level of consciousness and co-ordination than existed previously. This stands in dramatic contrast to the ability of labour to combine its forces across nations in any comparable way. The degree to which such changes were reflected in a growing international consensus on the direction of state economic policies was revealed in a speech given to the Trilateral Commission by Paul Volcker, Chairman of the Federal Reserve Board between 1979 and 1987. Volcker was for many years a senior banker at Chase Manhattan, and a former member of the Commission and the Council on Foreign Relations:

> there is an economic strategy . . . maybe not well coordinated, maybe not implemented as smoothly as it could have been . . . that is internationally shared, for almost the entire time I've been in this office . . . We had to create stability in a price sense, in a monetary sense, if we were going to have a foundation for progress in other directions. You can raise questions about how it has been implemented . . . but there is a remarkable reduction in inflationary pressures around the world . . . and there has also been a very considerable convergence, so even the highest inflation countries . . . are much closer to the pack than . . . five years ago.
>
> There is another element of common strategy too that's been persistent for some years. It's a harder one to describe: more emphasis on market orientation in economic policies, more concern and effort to reduce the proportion of government in GNP, more emphasis on private initiative. Obviously that matches a lot of rhetoric and oratory in the United States. But what is really startling is the rhetoric and oratory in France that parallels this kind of broad orientation of policies. It is even true in much of the developing world.[45]

Nonetheless, there may be conflicting as well as complementary interests between different fractions of transnational capital. For example, energy corporations prefer a high oil price, whereas most other transnational corporations prefer a low oil price. The example of the oil price also illustrates the interdependence between different fractions of capital in that some leading banks made loans to oil-exporting nations like Mexico, Venezuela and Nigeria, who, of course, needed buoyant oil revenues to service their debts to the banks. Also, the very distinction between national and transnational fractions of capital is a matter of degree, that is, as to the proportion of investment and sales outside the parent country. Firms whose assets are heavily concentrated in one country will be more vulnerable to an appreciation of that country's exchange rate than will be the case for firms who have a small proportion of their assets invested in that country. Another important distinction is that between financial and industrial fractions of capital, the former being less concerned about a rising exchange rate or high interest rates. The high liquidity and mobility of most financial capital contrasts with the higher opportunity costs for, and the constraints on, industrial transnationals when relocating production.[46] Moreover, the time horizons of financial and productive fractions of capital are often different, the former usually being shorter than those of manufacturing companies.

Despite the qualifying comments made above, in a broad sense, it can be argued that transnational capital has increased its structural power relative to labour since the 1960s. This has occurred, in some measure, because of changing economic conditions (and political response to these changes): the end of the postwar boom and the emergence of recession and slower growth rates. As I have argued, these changes have led to substantial economic, political and ideological restructuring.

It is important to emphasise, therefore, that the structural power of capital inheres within the operation of the capitalist system itself, although its scope and intensity will vary according to political and economic conditions. Nevertheless, its systemic character implies that co-operation of an active, conscious type between fractions of capital (for example, to lobby for subsidies or other kinds of protection, or conversely for liberalisation and deregulation of a sector) may be less important than the general way in which it places constraints on other agents within the global political economy.

This point can clarified with respect to transnational finance capital (strongly represented in the Trilateral Commission). Although it can be analysed in terms of a transnational coalition of forces which actively seeks to shape a range of state policies, such capital can also be analysed in terms of a set of social forces which include the extension of the power of market discipline. In practice this is partly based on the liberalisation of foreign exchange and capital markets, a process fostered by the lobbying of transnational fractions of capital, especially financial capital. This process was propelled by the competition between different national financial centres, especially that between New York, Tokyo and London. What do these developments mean for the overall thrust of our argument? In modern financial markets, the relatively high degree of international mobility of capital is bound up, at the institutional level, with the nature of local financial markets and the opportunities afforded across a range of states for freedom of capital flows. Such flows can have dramatic effects, not just on the foreign exchange markets, but also on commodity and stock markets. In the 1980s, financial experts were predicting a 'brave new world' for the international banking industry.[47] The globalisation of markets means that decisions to shift capital do not need to be co-ordinated in order to have dramatic effects. Apart from the potential constraints these shifts create on the actions of government and labour, they can also have unintended consequences, for example, the large loans by banks to certain less-developed countries in the 1970s helped create the conditions for the emergence of the debt crisis of the early 1980s, and a major threat to the solvency of many of the self-same lenders. Indeed, apart from ethical questions, many commentators have noted the destabilising effects of these rapid, and sometimes highly volatile, flows of financial capital.[48]

More generally, this suggests that the process by which the structural power of financial fractions of capital has been extended has not been a stable one. Susan Strange warned that the growing uncertainty, volatility and speculation in the markets might undermine the respect for 'ethical values . . . upon which a free democratic society relies'. Her arguments also anticipated the October 1987 stock market crash, which started in New York and spread rapidly to markets elsewhere (at one point the People's Republic Bank of China stepped in to bail out the commodity futures market in Hong Kong). Strange traces the origins of this new situation to 1973, when coincidentally, the Trilateral Commission held its first meetings. 'The year 1973 stands out as a benchmark, a turning point when the snowball of change from the leisurely 1960s to the hectic yo-yo years of the 1970s and 1980s began to gather momentum.'[49]

As Strange points out, the new banking fraternity resemble less and less the stereotypical image of cautious, conservative, sober-suited patricians. Today's bankers are increasingly risk-takers, gamblers in a global financial casino, whose waking moments are dictated by distant time-zones. Computer monitors and modems are the most obvious links between these individuals and firms. Are there deeper links? From the point of view of a transnational coalition of forces, some writers have commented on the existence of a 'banking complex', in the major capitalist states, centred in the United States. This complex, analogous to an internationalised military-industrial complex, comprises a network of private and central banks, other financial institutions, policy-oriented academics in certain think-tanks and prestigious universities, as well as influential members of the (financial) media.[50] It can be viewed as part of a wider, 'transnational network' identified in chapters 6–8.

The interests of financial fractions of capital are especially well provided for in terms of (organic) policy intellectuals, since they have access to massive data bases, droves of political risk analysts, many publications of their own, and have endowed elite universities with well-paid posts and large research funds to generate a wider basis for the practical forms of knowledge needed to understand the political economy and, of course, to make profits. These intellectuals, and their banker counterparts, are often the best brains that money can buy. They are a subgroup of the more wide-ranging types of thinkers alluded to by David Rockefeller in his speech proposing the establishment of the Trilateral Commission in 1972: the Commission would be 'bringing the best brains in the world to bear on the problems of the future . . . to collect and synthesize the knowledge that would enable a new generation to rebuild the conceptual framework of foreign and domestic policies.'[51]

Such thinkers try to maintain a long-term political vision which goes beyond the short-term outlook and apparent anarchy of the financial casino. Thus these organic intellectuals may operate either inside, on the fringes of, or outside the banking complex. Most importantly, however, they must develop the capacity to theorise the conditions of existence for capitalist hegemony as a whole, as well as for the leadership of a particular fraction of capital. In many cases this requires the technical expertise to master often difficult (for example, financial) issues. For Gramsci, the degree of 'organicity' in this respect related to the relative proximity of the intellectual to the organisation of the forces of production and exchange, and to the occupation of senior positions in state bureaucracies which relate to the maintenance of stable political conditions within which such forces operate. With respect to the banking complex, the most organic intellectuals are the leaders of transnational financial corporations (rather than the major shareholders), key financial institutions such as the IMF, central banks and economics and finance ministries, especially the United States Treasury and Federal Reserve. The Trilateral Commission involves a wider and more diverse group of intellectuals with expertise in political matters more generally.

The degree to which such a transnational complex of interests moves towards an increased degree of co-operation rests, in part, not only on congruence of material and institutional forces, but also on the extent to which its key intellectuals share a common outlook. It also rests upon the degree to which such shared ways of seeing and interpreting the world are diffused and shared amongst personnel at lower levels within the organisations in question, and, to an extent, within the population at large. As is indicated in public choice theory, the wider the sets of issues and problems, the more difficult this will be.

Nonetheless, the moment of hegemony occurs if and when there is a widespread acceptance of the key principles and political ideas of a leading class fraction or constellation of interests. If the principles of a class or class fraction become hegemonic it means that the policies which embody them will appear more natural and legitimate to broad elements within the society. Such hegemony therefore implies that the alternatives to such principles and policies are lacking appeal or are politically discredited. Here it is crucial to note that hegemony is not simply a form of direct ideological domination. Hegemony is won in the context of a political struggle and its central goal is to obtain political legitimacy for the arrangements preferred by the dominant class. Simultaneously, however, the achievement of hegemony in the realm of social and political ideas may come to constitute a structural force which conditions and constrains the potential for development of alternative social forces. If the leading capitalist class fraction in such a hegemony is one which is internationally oriented, then its key principles typically would include the view that the market mechanism is the most efficient form of global economic organisation, capital mobility and free trade to increase global welfare, and that the long-term improvement of the condition of the planet and its inhabitants would be best served by strengthening the capitalist states *vis-à-vis* communism.

The quality of the organic intellectuals of transnational capital relates to the accuracy of their interpretation of the nature of global structural forces and the potential contradictions they contain. The substance of co-operation within transnational networks rests partly

118

on the *practical effectiveness* of such intellectuals in their analysis, that is, how far they share a similar diagnosis of problems and have a congruent policy outlook, which optimises the conditions for their co-operation.[52] It also rests upon the extent to which such intellectuals are, at least with respect to government policy, to put it simply, 'in the right place at the right time' (for example, in strategic positions in different governments, especially that of the United States). An excellent example of this was the move of James Baker III from the White House staff to the Treasury, which was soon followed by initiatives on the debt crisis and exchange rates.[53] This contrasted with the policy pursued by Donald Regan at the Treasury which was more in tune with Strange's casino image of financial capitalism, based on a free-market orientation not disposed to international economic co-operation. The policies of 'benign neglect' (called by Robert Gilpin, 'malign neglect') of the dollar, and the *laissez-faire* orientation to the debt crisis embodied in Regan's Treasury policies can, on one level, be interpreted as promoting both liberalisation and transnationalisation in the world political economy. However, these policies also under-mined some of the political cohesion of the Trilateral nations, partly because of their long-term implications for global macroeconomic conditions. As such they threatened to unravel some of the political fabric required for the management of the transnationalisation process.

Seen from this point of view, the Baker initiatives reflected a need for co-operation to minimise some of the unintended consequences of the structural power of capital, and an attempt to begin to safeguard the long-term stability of global capitalism. Reagan's Secretary of State, George Shultz, was also influential in this respect. The moves also signalled a shift towards a more mainstream transnationalist perspective in American foreign economic policy, with its emphasis on the 'management of interdependence', in for example, the Baker initiatives and the US–Canada Free Trade Agreement negotiations of 1987–8 (and the possibility of extending this to Mexico, thus counter-vailing the negotiating power of the EEC countries acting as a bloc). Of potential future importance here is the fact that James Baker is a very close friend, political associate and, not least, was the 1988 campaign manager of George Bush's bid for the American presidency. Pre-sumably on Baker's advice, Bush's first public act on winning the election was to distance himself from his particularly distasteful and malicious campaign and hold out an olive branch to the defeated Democrats. Bush's catch phrase was a 'kinder, gentler nation'.

It is noteworthy, in this regard, that Bush's Democratic opponent,

Michael Dukakis, had, late in the campaign, successfully espoused a populist-nationalist position on foreign economic policy, stressing the need for protectionist policies. This eleventh-hour change of position came fairly close to winning the election for Dukakis: many commentators observed that if the campaigning period had lasted a further week, the Democrat might well have won, particularly since Bush's negative tactics were increasingly perceived as illegitimate. At times Bush's political commercials and speeches concerning Dukakis bordered on racist smears and implications of a lack of patriotism.

Bush's second act as President-elect was to announce this first and most crucial appointment to the new Cabinet: Jim Baker as Secretary of State, a nomination which was greeted with widespread acclaim in Congress, in the press and in the all-important Senate confirmation hearings, where Baker outlined a set of pragmatic Trilateralist aims for the new administration's foreign policy. Baker, it is important to remember, had distanced himself from the nomination of Senator J. Danforth Quayle as Bush's vice-presidential running mate, a decision at the insistence of Bush's media managers who thought that a Robert Redford lookalike would help to close what was thought to be a 'gender gap' in the pattern of Bush's electoral support: the idea was that middle-class housewives might be more willing to vote for Bush with a pin-up on the ticket. Earlier, on Baker's departure for the campaign trail, Nicolas Brady, the main author of the Presidential Commission of Inquiry report into the global stock market collapse of October 1987, was appointed to the Reagan Treasury post, and was renominated to the Bush administration. Brady's report criticised not only the use of computer programs to control the buying and selling of securities (which tended to amplify market fluctuations) but more fundamentally, the greedy, short-term outlook in the financial and securities markets. This mood was captured in the 1988 box-office movie success starring Michael Douglas as the ruthless deal-maker in New York's financial district: the anti-hero of *Wall Street* personified the new creed of neo-liberal possessive individualism. Drawing lessons from the way disaster was actually averted at the time of the crash (the United States Federal Reserve intervened to supply extra liquidity to the markets), Brady's report suggested the consolidation of stronger powers of Federal surveillance and intervention in the marketplace: another instance of 'saving the market from itself'.

Bush's major appointments, therefore, can be interpreted as important signs that the pragmatic and more co-operative trend in United States foreign and foreign economic policy is likely to continue into the 1990s, one focused more on key allies, especially Japan, a fact symbolised by President Bush's attendance at Hirohito's funeral in early 1989 (despite world-wide condemnation of the Emperor–God's role in promoting the rise of Japanese militarism before and during World War II). In James Baker's nomination hearings he suggested a more cautious and careful approach to American–Soviet relations and the need to guard against 'Gorbymania': the prioritisation of the super-power relationship at the expense of those with America's key allies. Finally, on virtually his first full day in office, Bush's Cabinet held a domestic summit with major figures from the Congress on a budget deficit reduction programme. According to press reports, both sides pronounced themselves very pleased with the general approach taken towards tackling the problem, although no specific measures were discussed. What appeared important here was the attempt to find agreement on basic principles, that is, the foundations of a 'practical consensus' were being explored. These examples illustrate the way organic intellectuals (particularly those in key positions in the United States) may, under certain conditions, be crucial to the process of constructing a potential steering mechanism for financial markets in particular and internationally mobile capital more generally. The wider context for such efforts is the attempt to sustain stable and legitimate political relationships between the governments of key economic powers in the capitalist world.

To conclude, further remarks made by Volcker illustrate a little of what I have in mind, as well as outlining the agenda for action from this perspective, as it was perceived in late 1985:

> When one looks at that G5 meeting in September – a very limited and short meeting, although it had some advance preparation – it does seem to me an exceptionally clear recognition of the fact that we are in a stage where, if we are to take advantage of what has already been achieved on the *stability front* and in *general philosophical orientation*, we are going to have to move to much closer *coordination* and *cooperation* in the *areas that have been neglected* [we need to] . . . resist protec-tionism . . . [reduce] the US deficit . . . [put more emphasis on] the need for growth . . . [improve and stabilise] exchange rate perform-ance.[54]

6 PRIVATE INTERNATIONAL RELATIONS COUNCILS

This chapter discusses the development of private initiatives relating to the international relations of the major capitalist states and locates the origins of the Trilateral Commission.

Contrary to the claims of right-wing conspiratorialists, these private international relations councils are not shadow governments of plutocrats manipulating international relations. Rather, they are consciousness-raising forums where individuals representing elements of the state and civil society in affiliated countries can come to know and influence each other. This process continues to be important for American leaders, as well as for the Japanese.

Private councils are part of a much wider international process of elite familiarisation and fraternisation, mutual education and, broadly speaking, networking. This process involves both consciousness-raising and social intercourse. It is relatively indirect with respect to the precise contours of policy but it is nonetheless significant. Private councils provide forums for developing or reinforcing concepts of international relations and foreign policy which may diffuse within the nations represented. The following quotation from Gramsci helps to capture the process I have in mind:

> it is not true . . . that numbers decide everything, nor that the opinions of all electors are of 'exactly equal' weight. Numbers . . . are simply an instrumental value, giving a measure and a relation and nothing more. And what then is measured? What is measured is precisely the effectiveness, and the expansive and persuasive capacity, of the opinions of a few individuals, the active minorities, the elites, the avant-gardes, etc. Ideas and opinions are not spontaneously 'born' in each individual brain: they have a centre of formation, of irradiation, of dissemination, of persuasion – a group of men, or a single individual even, which has developed them in the political form of current reality. The counting of 'votes' is the final ceremony in a long process . . .[1]

PRIVATE INTERNATIONAL RELATIONS COUNCILS

The Trilateral Commission was formed in 1972, and first convened in 1973. It is the most recent in a series of private international relations councils in the twentieth century. Chronologically, these developed roughly as follows:

  (i)   *The Anglo-Saxon context* originating in the late nineteenth century and continuing during the inter-war years: for example, the Round Tables.

 (ii)   *The Atlantic context* emerging after 1918 and more pervasively after 1945, as in Bilderberg.

(iii)   *The Pacific context* after 1945: for example, the United States–Japan Shimoda Conferences in the late 1960s, and in the 1980s, the 'Wise Men's Groups'. These forums widened in the 1980s to include other Pacific nations.

 (iv)   *The Trilateral context* post-1973: with the establishment of the Trilateral Commission, and the broadening of the Atlantic Institute to include the Japanese.

  (v)   *The Euro-Pacific context* following 1976: with the 'Hakone' meetings which are a product of the Trilateral Commission.

The Commission went beyond the Atlantic axis and created a wider framework for the internationalisation of outlook of the postwar Japanese elite, one which went farther than the Pacific focus of the Shimoda meetings. This anticipated the move away from export-led growth to more comprehensive Japanese engagement in the world political economy in the late 1970s and 1980s. These councils emerged because individuals with some weight in international circles had the motivation to bring together diverse individuals and interests for common purposes. For example, in the case of Bilderberg, the ideas of the Polish *éminence grise* Joseph Retinger and Prince Bernhard of the Netherlands, found resonance with corporate liberals in the United States and in Western Europe in the 1950s. In the case of the Trilateral Commission those of David Rockefeller and others found resonance with similar currents of opinion in both the Atlantic region and in Japan.

The forging of diverse interests for a common civilisational purpose is the positive side of the elite process at the heart of these councils. On the negative side, these councils are said to act to absorb political frictions between constituent elements. Thus, at a minimum, the Commission's proponents argue that while it is unable in itself to resolve international conflicts, it can act as an 'early warning system', as well as a channel of communication at the private level, particularly when governmental relations are under strain. Taken together, these positive and negative aspects also suggest the metaphor of a gyroscope, asserting equilibrium in allied relations. One way in which this is advanced, within the Commission, is by bringing together different, but commensurable academic traditions (heretofore drawn from transnational liberalism and functionalism) in the study of international relations, in a unique way.[2] These efforts combine the work of scholars and policy experts from the Trilateral nations. Endeavours are aimed at creating a 'common vision' of how the politico-economic world works, what its key problems are, why these problems exist, how they might be collectively approached, and perhaps solved.

The existence of such forums prompts the question: which interests seek to develop such links and why? Generally speaking, at least in the twentieth century, these interests have been associated with internationally expansive economic forces, as well as those concerned to promote political integration within the Atlantic and West European frameworks. With the rise of Japan, these efforts came to embrace the three centres of economic power in advanced capitalism. Let us now examine some of the precursors of the Commission.

THE DEVELOPMENT OF ATLANTICISM

'Atlanticism' first emerged as an Anglo-American idea, in the late nineteenth century, as Britain turned to the United States for finance and support during the Boer War. In this context, an influential 'Round Table' was formed by Cecil Rhodes and others who had advocated an association of the English speaking peoples, partly as a means for Britain to counteract its continental European rivals. Later a range of political and economic interests in the United States (notably in Wall Street, led by the House of Morgan) gave their support to Woodrow Wilson's policy of entering World War I on the side of the Allies.

After 1918, the Atlantic union concept of the Anglo-Americans gave way to a new concept of Atlantic partnership, a concept which gave more weight to continental European interests, downgrading the Anglo-Saxon chauvinism implicit in the Round Tables. However, as Kees van der Pijl notes, the idea of Atlantic partnership only became viable for centrist political parties and associated internationalist fractions of capital within the continental powers after their East European interests were undermined, first by the Russian Revolution of 1917 and, more crucially, after 1945, when communist expropriation and economic blockade of the East made them turn more towards the United States.[3]

124

Between the wars, interests advocating Atlantic union – what Polanyi referred to as *haute finance*, associated with London, Amsterdam and New York – were, however, out of tune with the growing spirit of militant nationalism and state interventionism in the economic crisis of the 1930s. This remained the case until a new 'synthesis' between money and industrial capital and organised labour was worked out in the United States during the New Deal and World War II.[4] The eclipse of influence of financial capitalist interests in the crisis of the 1930s, in the context of the 'great transformation' away from the concept that the market should be the central organising principle of social life, also meant the demise in the influence of international forums such as the Round Table.[5] It was not until the 1950s that such transnational groups would regain influence, in the Atlantic context in the shape of the Bilderberg meetings, and in the framework of West European unity in the European Movement and Jean Monnet's Action Committee for a United States of Europe (ACUSE).[6]

Let us now examine the place of American forces in these transatlantic constellations. Until the 1930s, United States foreign economic policy, particularly in trade, had been mainly protectionist. This reflected the dominance of the Republican isolationist coalition since the late nineteenth century. However, as both Thomas Ferguson and Theda Skocpol argue, long-term structural factors in the United States were working against the Republican coalition, and in favour of the Democratic Party which gradually came to advocate New Dealism.[7] Peter Gourevitch has indicated that this was also the case (although much less so) in other industrialised countries where, gradually, forces were emerging which would tend to support the postwar consensus, which John Ruggie sees underpinning the postwar liberal international economic order. This permitted the United States to institutionalise its hegemony over the major capitalist states in a relatively consensual way.[8]

Kees van der Pijl describes the 'corporate liberal' synthesis which came together in the United States in the late 1930s and early 1940s. This became the driving force for postwar American globalism, and for postwar 'Atlanticism'. This synthesis, or coalition, included not only international finance, but also high-technology industries (notably automobile manufacture), and sections of organised labour. It was expressed in the postwar period in terms of Keynesian interventionism, corporatist capital-labour relations, and welfarism. This grouping of forces began to press during the early 1940s for a neo-Wilsonian universalism, based on the idea of an integrated world capitalist economy and the establishment of liberal democratic regimes in the largest possible number of developed countries. This also involved the decolonisation of the West European empires. Task forces were drawn from Cordell Hull's State Department, and the prestigious Council on Foreign Relations (CFR) to help concretise these objectives into postwar plans. The CFR was conceived in Paris in 1919, founded in 1921 by a group including Herbert Hoover, General Tasker Bliss, Christian Herter and Yale President Charles Seymour.

The realisation of what the CFR task forces designated as the 'Grand Area' concept of an integrated liberal world economy as a necessary economic 'living space' for the United States required not only the defeat of the Axis powers, but also the breakup of the British Empire, and the end of the old-style colonialism in order to dismantle autarkic economic blocs.[9] Grand Area strategy envisaged an open door for American foreign direct investment, a liberalisation of trade, and an internationalisation of the New Deal under Fordist accumulation conditions, primarily within the Atlantic economies and, to a lesser extent, in Japan. This strategy found resonance with centrist political elements from the continent, some of whom were temporarily exiled in London during the war. The viewpoint and programme was opposed by more domestically oriented and isolationist elements within the United States and by those who adhered to the old, sphere-of-interest forms of imperialism in France and Great Britain after the war.[10]

Postwar American strategy, largely shaped along the lines of the New Deal synthesis, was firmly opposed by the Soviet Union. American globalism was restricted to encompass only the capitalist nations of the world. Central to United States plans became, therefore, the shaping of West European economic and political development in a direction complementary to that of America. This took concrete form in the Marshall Plan, NATO and the international organisations and regimes of the Bretton Woods system and the United Nations. To the extent that this strategy was successful after 1945, it began to mobilise forces within Europe and the United States, represented in the Bilderberg meetings and the European Movement. Bilderberg brought together a comprehensive array of major figures from all politically significant fields. Its participants included military leaders and strategists, senior centrist politicians, international business people, some trades unionists, civic and cultural leaders, media and academic opinion leaders. These individuals, and the institutional and material forces they symbolised and indeed represented, were politically aligned with the notion of an 'Atlantic partnership'. In order to cement the concept of partnership, the purpose of these meetings was to promote open and confidential dialogue and an airing of differences, whilst simultaneously encouraging an ever-growing density of economic, political, military and cultural links between the Atlantic nations. This was seen as the means by which a modernised and prosperous liberal democratic capitalism could be consolidated and protected from communism, as well as creating a web of economic and political interests which would underpin the Atlantic Alliance in the long term.

The notion of the New Deal or 'corporate liberal' synthesis is not meant to suggest that the emerging globalist strategy, nor the domestic form of the New Deal itself, was simply the product of far-sighted members of the 'ruling class'. Rather, it was a result of a large number of political forces within the United States, including popular interests (notably industrial workers in the Democratic Party), urban-liberal elites and some (but certainly not all) capitalist interests. Moreover, the New Deal was very limited in scope, partly because of inertia in the state and civil society, and opposition from the Supreme Court and from within the main political parties. It was the war and its aftermath which helped fully to mobilise New Dealism.[11] Nonetheless, postwar American strategy presupposed the extrapolation of these forces on an Atlantic, and indeed, potentially global basis.

What were these forces? Ferguson uses the concept of a 'multinational bloc' to describe part of the constellation of forces behind the New Deal and its subsequent internationalisation. Support for the Democratic Party from the 1930s to the 1970s was based upon a coalition between most organised labour and those industries with relatively low wage shares in total value-added in production, and which were relatively invulnerable to foreign competition. Firms with these characteristics, notably in the automobile industry, tended to become more important and influential during the 1930s. This coalition was reinforced by the trade-offs and compromises made among its constituent interests: increased welfare spending was conceded by business in exchange for labour's support for certain liberal measures at the international level. Among the most internationalist elements in this coalition were Wall Street financial circles, who began to perceive the potential for a greater international role for the dollar:

> The multinational bloc included many of the largest, most rapidly growing corporations in the economy. Recognised industry leaders with the most sophisticated managements, they embodied the norm of professionalism and scientific advance that in this period fired the

imagination of large parts of American society. The largest of them also dominated major American foundations, which were coming to exercise major influence not only on the climate of opinion but on the specific content of American public policy.[12]

This bloc became a part of the nucleus of postwar Atlantic hegemony (in the Gramscian sense). This fused corporate liberalism, Fordism, Keynesianism, welfarism and a permanent arms economy rationalised through Cold War ideology. By 1952, the governments of Western Europe were largely controlled by forces sympathetic to this perspective, although this is not to suggest that it was unchallenged. Indeed, many Europeans were dissatisfied with the United States occupation, and the way that the United States was undermining their colonial interests, creating the conditions for a development of what van der Pijl and Soviet theorists call a 'centrifugal tendency of imperialism'. This tendency served to make Atlantic unity more problematic, at least until the 'Kennedy Offensive' of the 1960s attempted to politically reunite the West.[13]

Thus, in the early 1950s Atlantic rivalry reemerged. Domestic pressures within the United States for continuing internationalisation receded, at the same time as obstacles to American investment in Europe developed. Liberal internationalists became worried at the prospects of a contraction of American involvement in Europe. Moreover, liberals in the United States came under attack in the McCarthyite wave of hysteria, and indeed, Harry Dexter White, the American architect with Keynes of Bretton Woods, was accused of being a communist spy and summoned before the House Committee on Un-American Activities. White then suffered a heart attack from which he died.[14] The effects of the witch-hunt caused many socialists and social democrats in Europe to worry about the long-term implications for their positions relative to the United States, particularly if Washington were to become further dominated by the hysterical anti-communist right. According to Alfred Grosser, these pressures were felt most acutely in Germany, while in France, General de Gaulle began to mobilise nationalist sentiment designed to maximise French autonomy. Thus the Cold War was coming to have a rather contradictory affect on the unity of the West: on the one hand, it tended to forge a closer identity of interest between the Atlantic states in the face of the Soviet threat, while on the other, it tended to place many of the major liberal and social democratic advocates of Atlantic unity in severe political jeopardy. Their sense of insecurity had earlier been amplified by the news that the Soviet Union had exploded its first atom bomb on 14 July 1949, and later, by its announcement on 8 August 1953 that it had made a hydrogen bomb.[15] Not all of the proponents of European integration were convinced of the wisdom of Atlantic partnership or continued United States leadership, although the latter was made virtually inevitable by the failure of Western European governments to agree to set up the European Defence Community and by the admission to NATO of West Germany in 1954. As George Lichtheim puts it, since the Atlantic Alliance was imposed upon the European countries largely by factors out of their control, leaders of nations recently 'masters of their own destiny' were bound to view the United States as a 'temporary overlord'.[16]

BILDERBERG

In this context, in 1952, a private initiative was undertaken by Europeans concerned at a potential waning of American commitment to Western Europe, as well as at hostility towards the United States on the part of a large number of European business and political leaders of both left and right.[17]

This initiative, which came to be known as the Bilderberg meetings, became an unofficial, private counterpart to the formal institutions of the Atlantic Alliance. In many key respects, it was the prototype for the Trilateral Commission, involving similar types of politicians, diplomats, corporate and banking chiefs, academics from prestigious universities and think-tanks, media interests, some trades unionists, and, of course, the ubiquitous American law firms.[18] Bilderberg also had military officials and heads of government in attendance, including senior members of the Central Intelligence Agency (CIA), which provided funding for the first meeting.[19] The key differences between the forums are that Bilderberg is almost completely secretive (whereas the Trilateral Commission is more open) and, much more importantly, Bilderberg never included Japanese. Also, Bilderberg had a higher proportion of social democrats and trades unionists. Most Bilderberg attendees have been from the United States, Canada, Britain, West Germany, France, Italy, Holland and Belgium, although individuals from Spain, Portugal, Ireland, Switzerland, Turkey, Australia, Norway, Denmark, Sweden, Finland, Iceland and Australia have sometimes attended the gatherings (the European flank of the Trilateral Commission has been restricted to members from European Community countries, or countries about to join such as Portugal and Spain). Politicians are almost entirely drawn from the centrist political parties and, in particular, the modernising and forward-looking internationalist tendencies within those parties. Other key elements are

129

individuals associated with important Atlantic and international institutions (such as NATO; the European Community; the Organisation for European Economic Co-operation (OEEC); its successor, the OECD; the International Monetary Fund; and the World Bank). In all, more than 900 men (spouses were not invited), and about a dozen women attended these meetings between 1954 and 1978.

American leaders were able, through their participation, to better understand and assign proper weight and consideration to different sectional, national and international interests in the formulation of American policies. This was achieved by bringing together powerful and influential individuals, and allowing them to interact in private with theorists and intellectuals who had broadly sympathetic aims and perspectives, and who took a long-term view. The first conference was held in 1954 when 'the United States was at an all-time nadir of popularity in Europe'.[20] The meeting allowed a new generation of European leaders and *protégés* to associate privately with their American counterparts. The meetings served the added purposes of helping to contain Franco-German and other intra-European rivalries and promoting a more cosmopolitan viewpoint. The forum was seen by Europeans as providing a means to constrain United States unilateralism and to encourage the American leadership to pursue policies which would ensure the continuing development of the Atlantic Community. Bilderberg documents refer to its aims as the search for a 'highest common denominator of mutual understanding', the 'removal . . . of causes of [transatlantic friction]', in part through the promotion of 'an atmosphere of mutual confidence and friendship which would admit of free and frank discussion', since differences of interest would, 'for historical reasons', necessarily continue to exist.[21]

How did the conferences pursue these ends? One way was through what might be called a pressure cooker, or distillation effect, of concentrated social intercourse. The meetings were remarkable for the intensity of interaction they promoted.[22] A way these aims were pursued is revealed in the construction of agendas and the priorities these reflect. Their focal points included East-West relations, the Soviet threat, the question of communism in the West as well as the East, the possibilities for European neutralism and anti-Americanism, the question of the 'uncommitted peoples' in the context of the Cold War struggle, decolonisation and Third World development. In addition, other more economic issues such as trade expansion and currency convertibility were often discussed. Also on the agendas were the promotion of an appropriate form of European integration, the structure of NATO, nuclear weapons and the development of nuclear energy, as well as the frequent reviews of topical issues. The nature of these agendas is similar to many of those of the Trilateral Commission.[23]

Only in 1976 when Prince Bernhard (the Chairman) was implicated in the Lockheed bribery scandal, was no meeting held. Thereafter Lord Home, former Conservative Prime Minister of Britain, took the chair. Bilderberg has no permanent membership, although a steering committee has always existed to organise meetings and invite individuals to attend and/or present papers. Previous attendees are, however, kept in touch with ongoing discussions.

Like the Trilateral Commission, Bilderberg has been frequently accused by right-wing and populist-nationalist critics within the United States of being an unseen hand, or super-government of plutocrats, which rules the Western world (extreme variants of this claim even suggest that the conspiracy involves Bolsheviks).[24] For example, in 1971 the right-wing *Manchester Union Leader* charged that Bilderbergers were given advance notice of Nixon's New Economic Policy, making it possible for them to make US$20 billion in quick profits. Other accusations from the right included Bilderbergers' co-ordinated support for Gaston Deferre against de Gaulle in the French presidential election of 1964; the overthrow of the Portuguese dictatorship; and the successful attempt to capture the mineral riches of Angola and Mozambique by the 'Rockefeller cabal' which, it was imputed, orchestrated Bilderberg.[25] In less sensationalist vein, nationalist criticisms are contained in a number of insertions into *Congressional Record*, occasionally accusing American Bilderbergers of treasonable behaviour, that is, of consorting with representatives of foreign governments without authority, thus violating the Logan Act.[26] Another item in *Congressional Record* noted the frequent attendance of United States intelligence chiefs, foundation heads and West European Social Democrats. It then stated that CIA funding of European leftist parties, often through the conduit of the foundations, had been significant in their postwar success.[27]

The corporate liberal perspective was the strongest one in the American section. In the Kennedy administration, 'Bilderberg alumni' (a term used by C. D. Jackson of the CIA and a Bilderberg steering group member) were especially prominent, in the persons of Dean Rusk, George McGhee, George Ball, Walt Whitman Rostow, McGeorge Bundy, Arthur Dean and Paul Nitze. Virtually every American Bilderberger was also a member of the Council on Foreign Relations. Bilderberg was also frequented by individuals representing east coast banking and financial interests. Many key figures from Republican administrations also attended, reflecting, in a simple sense, the fact that Bilderberg meetings are non-partisan. The key factor of inclusion was the degree to which an influential individual was, or could become, sympathetic to the basic purposes of the meetings. Prominent in the American section were the network of Rockefeller interests, in contrast to the importance of the House of Morgan in the Round Tables.[28]

The Bilderberg meetings were of great significance for the United States since they helped to enlarge the membership of the American elite 'which could approach world development with a more internationally-oriented frame of reference'.[29] This fact should be interpreted in the context of the rise of anti-New Deal sentiment in the United States in the early 1950s, and reactionary tendencies in the shape of McCarthyism. The meetings created opportunities for inaugurating transnational networks and groupings. Indeed this process was furthered by often very heated debates, analysis of which make a nonsense of the idea of a conspiracy. The debates meant different things to different people.[30]

Bilderberg, of course, was only one private Atlantic council in which this process occurred. Other private institutions with similar aims were the Atlantic Council of the United States (founded in 1961 by Christian Herter, Will Clayton and other Americans), the Anglo-American Ditchley Foundation (founded in Britain in 1958, first meeting in 1962) and the Atlantic Institute for International Affairs (also founded in 1961). The Atlantic Institute's public relations literature relates that it was originally conceived as 'a sort of public arm of NATO'. At the governmental level the OEEC, formed under the United States Economic Cooperation Act of 2 April 1948, and its successor, the OECD, became official counterparts. These, of course, are only elite bodies in a vast series of international governmental, political, cultural and economic interactions and exchanges which have formed the substance of relations between the Atlantic countries. Nonetheless, Bilderberg is credited in Alden Hatch's biography of Bernhard as the birthplace of the European Community, as well as generally serving to maintain alliance cohesion during the difficult years of the 1950s and 1960s when the Atlantic Alliance was in the process of formation, considerable achievements by any standards.[31]

FORMATION OF THE TRILATERAL COMMISSION

Let us now discuss the factors which led to the creation of the Commission. The catalyst was strong opposition to some of President Nixon's policies of the early 1970s. The wider context was a pervasive view within the Western and Japanese foreign policy establishments that the international system was entering a period of crisis or transition.

In this context, the Nixon–Kissinger world-view was judged to be outmoded and therefore dangerous for the evolving liberal international economic order. A widespread anxiety developed in establishment circles throughout the Trilateral world as the perception grew that America's hegemonic power was entering a phase of substantial relative decline. At a deeper level, elites were worried that there was a growing lack of congruence between what J. D. B. Miller called the 'economic and political worlds', the former becoming characterised by an increasing global integration, the latter persistently fragmented, with political decisions largely made at the level of the nation-state.[32] This emerging view therefore involved not only the perception of a change in the global distribution of power, implying more fluid political possibilities, but also a profound change in the nature of the relationship between world political and economic structures. At the same time, the long postwar boom appeared to be running out of steam and nationalist forces, particularly in the developing nations, seemed to be better organised and more threatening to the West and Japan than at any time since 1945. The questions which liberal elements in the American establishment now confronted were at two levels, theoretical and practical. Were policy-makers really able to grasp the nature of new conditions and understand their implications? Were their theories and concepts of the world and how it worked relevant or outmoded? What were appropriate means for coping with perceived challenges to the interests of the West and Japan, and the postwar capitalist system more generally?

With respect to United States policy, in the early 1970s, two broad strands of interpretation and practice were important. On the one hand was that of the old, but dispirited east coast establishment, Atlanticist in orientation. Its perspective was premised upon the view that peace and prosperity required the integration of economic and political forces in a series of collective frameworks (such as stronger international regimes) to cope with the tensions generated by an age of growing international interdependence. Committed to liberal international economic objectives, it stressed consultation and cooperation with allies so that their views would be weighted in the making of American policy. The other perspective was premised both on a realist and traditional conception of the international system, forged at a time when the United States had been largely self-sufficient. In this view, the United States had only relatively brittle allegiances to other states.

The ubiquity of conflict and rivalry in the interstate system called for careful and, if need be, secret diplomacy. The game of states was one of the never-ending struggle for survival and supremacy. This view, somewhat over-simplified for the purposes of exposition, was exemplified in some of the policies of the Nixon–Kissinger years. Their conservative-nationalist perspective saw 'internationalism' as only desirable when it directly furthered the domestic interests of the United States. Thus Nixon was willing to espouse policies towards allies which were more unilateral and based upon a narrower calculus of American 'national interests'. It interpreted international economic practices in Bismarckian terms, that is, as a product of a more fundamental balance of power. Nixon argued that as the capacity of the United States to act as the key balancing force had eroded, and as the liberal economic order appeared to be working against American material interests, the United States should have no hesitation in repudiating its rules and norms of behaviour or else recasting them on American terms.

Indeed, David Calleo, in *The Imperious Economy*, argues that the Nixon administration symbolised a new phase in United States economic policy, one which contrasted with the Keynesian policies of perpetual boom (exemplified by budget deficits even in years of rapid economic growth) which characterised the Kennedy–Johnson years. In the 1960s, the United States was more globally oriented, and concerned to shape the contours of the international system in an activist, or what has been called a 'social imperialist' fashion. Nixon's policies coincided with a period of more threatening international conditions for the United States and were essentially defensive. They were designed to reconcile the United States to a partial retreat from global leadership. Nixon set the context for the next two presidencies by indicating the willingness of the United States to subordinate (long-term) global concerns to a narrower and sharper assertion of (short-term) national interests. This characterisation of Nixon's foreign (economic) policy was very widely shared in Europe and Japan, as well as in American establishment circles.[33]

Of course, each perspective is represented here as an ideal-type: neither corresponds to exact practices, which mixed the two. Nonetheless, at the heart of each was a quite different conception of foreign policy. Each emphasised, respectively, 'the management of interdependence', and 'the management of the balance of power', as concepts for the organisation of American policy. Both, however, assumed that by the late 1960s American predominance had come to an end and each advocated different strategies to manage American relative decline.

The Nixon–Kissinger doctrine, with its stress on 'regional influentials' (such as Iran) and on 'burden sharing' seemed to represent an American retreat from globalism and a potential new isolationism. The internationalists, by contrast, argued for a reconstructed hegemony, in which more political weight would be given to Japan and West Germany (and the European Community countries more generally). It has become by now a historical commonplace to note that Nixon's policies repudiated this internationalist vision. Indeed, immense strains within the United States primary allian·e developed from the unilateralism of Nixon's New Economic Policy ⸱ ᶜ 15 August 1971. At the time, Federal Reserve Chairman, Arthur Buɪns, warned against the ending of the convertibility of the dollar into gold, adding that 'Pravda would write that this was a sign of the collapse of capitalism.'[34] This policy was a response to a growing United States balance of payments deficit and the pressure put on the dollar, the central international currency in the Bretton Woods system of fixed exchange rates, partly by virtue of the growing international mobility of capital. In addition, the West European and Japanese economies had begun to grow faster than the United States, reflected in the rising strength of other currencies such as the deutschmark and the yen. Discussions had been under way to secure some kind of realignment of currencies but no international agreement had been forthcoming. So the United States decided to act unilaterally in order to secure change on its own terms. The suspension of convertibility was intended to secure an effective devaluation of the dollar relative to other currencies, giving a competitive edge to American exporters. Apart from the 10 per cent import surcharge, political pressure was put on East Asian countries to slow down their import penetration of the United States, and on the European Community and Japan to further open their markets to American exporters. The moves were designed to supplement the monetary measures in giving American producers a unilateral competitive advantage against foreign companies and to help stop American unemployment from rising.

Nixon was rewarded with a very favourable domestic public reaction, although his moves antagonised many liberal internationalists. However, as James Reichley observes, the defection of the Republican high-priests of economic liberalism like Arthur Burns (and to a lesser extent Milton Friedman), as well as the 'desertion of much of the US business community' sapped the will of those faithful to postwar United States international economic orthodoxy. At any rate, transnational liberals such as Phillip Trezise, Assistant Secretary of State for Economic Affairs; Fred Bergsten, Assistant for International Economic

Affairs to Henry Kissinger on the National Security Council (Kissinger was not apparently involved in the making of the economic policies); and Ambassador to the European Community, Robert Schaetzel; resigned their posts. Along with others from outside the administration, such as Richard Gardner and Richard Cooper, they wrote articles roundly condemning the policies.

Indeed Bergsten had warned Kissinger that Secretary of Treasury John Connally was a 'xenophobe', whose stance encouraged a 'disastrous isolationist trend' in United States policy. However, Kissinger's 'reticence' on economic questions meant that he failed to intervene. A severe crisis in American-Allied relations lasted for four months.[35] Cooper, equally blunt, stated that such 'high risk' tactics might generate the first international trade war since the 1930s. Nixon's tactics had been notable both for their secrecy and the absence of international consultation with the main allies of the United States whose interests were badly damaged.[36] The policies were perceived by liberals as taking place against the background of a wider, inchoate trend of economic nationalism, itself an *ad hoc* response to threats stemming from the internationalisation of economic activity. As Bergsten put it:

> By and large, the major political source of the recent resurgence of economic nationalism, particularly in the United States, [has been] relatively immobile domestic groups pressing the government for protection of their share of welfare in the competition with transnational competitors. It is not a situation in which foreign economic policy is used to enhance state power but in which short-term problems of the distribution of economic welfare, particularly for groups whose interests are hurt by increasing international transactions, exert strong pressure on foreign economic policy, *regardless* of the implications for interstate power or even the aggregate welfare of national society.[37]

The dangers in Nixon's policies, from this vantage point, were the way they nurtured 'domestic' forces, and, by undercutting the welfare of key allies, undermined the international consensus which was needed to manage the system effectively. Such economic strains were compounded by allied dissatisfaction with other aspects of United States unilateralism. Allies continued to be alarmed by the war in Vietnam, to a degree because the war effort was partly financed internationally (because of American willingness to print dollars). The unilateral opening of detente with the Soviet Union, other moves such as the secret diplomacy with China and the soybeans embargo on Japan (which was thus deprived of significant supplies of its major source of protein), were variously interpreted as injurious to key allied interests.

Summarising much allied criticism of Nixon's policies, Kissinger's academic rival Zbigniew Brzezinski claimed that American uni-lateralism challenged three assumptions upon which the postwar order had been built. These were, first, that Atlantic co-operation was 'both practical and desirable'; that movement towards West European unity was essential for such co-operation; and that at some point Japan 'would be added to that central framework'. Second, the moves undermined the premise that a liberal international economic system would parallel and reinforce the political system and allow for 'the maintenance of democratic institutions'. Third, the policy of detente weakened the presumption that 'Communist countries and par-ticularly the Soviet Union would remain fundamentally outside of that international system' and have the function of 'objectively unifying' the West.[38] Brzezinski added that by 1974 all of these assumptions were in 'severe jeopardy', partly because of 'contagious unilateralism'. He also noted the pursuit of 'narrow national self-interest' by Japan and certain West European countries during the first oil crisis of 1973–4.[39]

It was in these circumstances that internationalist forces in the United States began to mobilise. The Trilateral Commission was launched from within the Bilderberg meetings by David Rockefeller.[40] Very soon many Bilderbergers joined, despite the fact that many Europeans were resistant to the inclusion of Japanese at the high table. Europeans felt that this would reduce their influence over the Americans. Cooper, Schaetzel, Trezise, Gardner and Brzezinski all became early members, and Brzezinski became the Commission's first director. They envisaged the Commission as a private pressure group which would attempt to influence governments in the direction of more consultation and to reshape American hegemony into a more collective, tripartite format. At the 1974 Bilderberg Conference in Mégève, participants included individuals who became either members of the Trilateral Commission, or directly associated with its activities, such as Giovanni Agnelli, the Fiat tycoon; American political scientist Graham Allison of Harvard; American economist, Miriam Camps; James Chace, the editor of *Foreign Affairs*; Director of the London School of Economics, Ralf Dahrendorf; European Community bureaucrat Etienne Davignon; André Fontaine, the editor of *Le Monde*; and United States General Andrew Goodpaster (later to become Chairman of the Atlantic Council). Also in attendance was Bernhard's former private secretary and later Principal of the European University

Institute, Max Kohnstamm, who became the first European Chairman of the Commission.[41] This selection gives an indication of the type and rank of some of those involved.

The Commission drew upon other networks, in addition to those noted in the first section of this chapter, such as Bilderberg, the Atlantic Institute and Shimoda. In addition, two further networks were important, and provided prototypes for Commission activities. One was organised through *Interplay*, a prototype for the Commission's magazine, *Trialogue*. A second was formed through 'Trilateral' conferences of economists, launched by the Brookings Institution. The method of the meetings became the model for the Commission's own task forces, and the *Triangle Papers*. Gerard Smith and Henry Owen, two of the initial conceptualisers and organisers of the Commission were involved in each of these ventures, and later set up in a Washington law partnership together when they left government at the end of the Carter administration in early 1981.

Smith, a Rockefeller in-law and widely-respected and trusted diplomat (he was American negotiator for the SALT I treaty), launched *Interplay* in 1967. Originally conceived as a magazine of European–American affairs, it soon broadened to cover Japan and East Asia. Apart from Smith, founder members of its international advisory board included many individuals important in setting up the Trilateral Commission.[42] During its short lifetime (the magazine ceased publication in 1971) it contained articles from a wide range of 'Atlanticist' writers. Indeed, the list of contributors is almost an intellectual *Who's Who* of advocates of the Atlantic idea in the 1960s and early 1970s.[43] Many of these writers also attended Bilderberg. What was also significant about this magazine was its capacity to draw upon some of the very best Western minds in the field of international relations (most of whom were also Atlanticists). Its rationale was based on the concept of interdependence which its editor, Anthony Hartley, suggested had come to dominate the thought of the forward looking elements of the Atlanticist elites. The magazine justified itself in terms of the emergence of a 'supranational convergence of problems' caused by the far-reaching historical process of social and economic integration which had taken place in the postwar world, a process which had gone furthest in the North Atlantic economies. Hartley observed:

> A mutual concept of responsibility must unite countries with a high standard of living where competition for power once divided them . . . If the civilisation of the late 20th century fixes itself in rigid patterns of thought, it will break and crumble to dust. But it is the *business of the intellectual to provide a remedy for this mental ossification by*

drawing the attention of his rulers to the existence of new problems and the need for new attitudes of mind in facing them. In 1967 the speed of communication and the increasing cosmopolitanism of the intellectual community allow this task to be carried out on a level above old national oppositions and ideological feuds . . . contrary to Marx's celebrated phrase, to understand the world is also to change it.[44]

The early preoccupations of *Interplay* were with the unity of the Atlantic Alliance, the relationship between European and American civilisation, and the debate over the United States war in Vietnam.[45] Gradually contributions began to focus on Japan. The January 1970 issue of the heretofore mainly Atlanticist journal contained the first such articles by N. Hagihara, Ronald Dore, Kiyoshi Nasu, Anthony Hartley, and W. P. Hunsberger. Long before he became a *cause célèbre* in the West after Francis Ford Coppola's controversial 1984 film of his life, Yukio Mishima was the subject of an essay which argued that the ritual suicide of the ultra-nationalist novelist might produce profound political effects in Japan, since there was widespread sympathy for his opinions in the Japanese Self-Defence Forces. Mishima's self-sacrifice might become a rallying point for Japanese 'fundamentalism'.[46] Other essays on Japan were remarkably prescient, anticipating developments in the 1970s. For example, various authors warned against Congressional opportunism and Japanese myopia, each of which, it was argued, might disrupt relations with America's 'strongest and strangest bedfellow'.[47] Other contributions discussed potential American–Japanese economic frictions and East Asian fears concerning a resurgence of *samurai* militarism and Japanese nationalism (the latter tendency encouraged in the 1980s by Prime Minister Nakasone). However, *Interplay* paid very little attention overall to what has been called the 'weakest link' of Trilateralism: Japanese–West European relations.

The second initiative under discussion did include a Euro-Japanese link. This took place under the auspices of the Brookings Institution, in association with the German Kiel Institute for World Economics (the director of which, Herbert Giersch, was a Bilderberger) and the Japan Economic Research Center in Tokyo. Whereas *Interplay* was a mainly political journal with individual contributors, the Brookings 'Tripartite' studies were intended to be collective efforts of economists. These were to reflect major currents of economic analysis from the European Community, Japan and North America. The main organisers were Henry Owen, Phillip Trezise, Max Kohnstamm, and the well-known Japanese economist, Saburo Okita. They brought together experts to consider economic questions from a shared, 'Trilateral' perspective.

These reports, which began to appear in 1972, were the product of discussions of about fifteen experts. They generally embodied the interdependence perspectives of American economists like Bergsten and Cooper.[48]

Noting, in 1976, that similar efforts to 'reconcile national autonomy in economic decision-making with international economic interdependence' had been made 'regularly over the years by public officials', notably in the Economic Policy Committee of the OECD, Trezise stated that the initiative was 'intended to complement such efforts in the knowledge that a group of private economists can often speak with greater candour than government officials'. The 1976 conference 'was inspired by the realisation that both the inflation of 1973–4 and the recession of 1974–5 were aggravated by the failure of policy-makers in each country to take adequate account of the cumulative effects of developments and policies in other countries'.[49] Important Trilateral Commission members were closely associated with these meetings.

After David Rockefeller's 1972 Bilderberg speech, the Trilateral Commission was constructed. The initial work was done by a small group of Americans. These were David Rockefeller, Brzezinski, Owen, and Professor Robert Bowie. Also important were Gerard Smith, Marshall Hornblower, Governor William Scranton of Pennsylvania and Japan expert Professor Edwin Reischauer of Harvard University. These individuals had advocated ideas compatible with those in Rockefeller's speech. For example, Bowie, as Director of the Harvard Center for International Affairs, had instituted Japanese and European fellowships and exchanges at the Center. Brzezinski, in his book *Between Two Ages*, published in 1970, had called for a 'community of the developed nations' to meet the challenges of the coming 'technetronic era'. Brzezinski had also written a book on Japan in 1971 called *The Fragile Blossom*.

It is worth emphasising here that initiating the Trilateral Commission without David Rockefeller is as unimaginable as *Hamlet* without the Prince. Without Rockefeller's imprimatur, the proposals of Bowie, Trezise and Brzezinski might well have disappeared from the drama in the manner of Rosencrantz and Gildenstern from Elsinore. Rockefeller's unique international influence was mentioned in most of the interviews I conducted with Commissioners, and he was always cited as *the* key figure. Indeed, at least initially, Rockefeller recruited virtually each member personally. The assessment of Rockefeller's influence is substantiated by the careful empirical research of Thomas Dye, who claims that Rockefeller was by far the most powerful man in the United States in the late 1970s.[50] In addition, alumni of the Rockefeller group have often become top foreign affairs personnel for the United States. These have included John Foster Dulles, Dean Rusk, Henry Kissinger and Cyrus Vance. Rockefeller's importance was reflected in the threat (later withdrawn) by the Japanese establishment to pull out of the negotiations to set up the Commission upon learning that Gerry Smith and not Rockefeller was to become the first North American Chairman.[51]

The practical ideas for constructing the Commission were subsequently formalised by a group drawn from the United States, Western Europe and Japan, at a meeting at the Rockefeller estate in the Hudson Valley on 23–4 July 1972. This group included Bergsten; Bowie; Brzezinski; McGeorge Bundy of the Ford Foundation; Karl Carstens representing German interests; Guido Colunna di Paliano representing Italian interests; François Duchêne, the Director of International Institute of Strategic Studies, and Jean Monnet's former private secretary; Rene Foch representing the French; David Rockefeller and his close friend and Harvard roommate George Franklin; Henry Owen; Max Kohnstamm; Bayless Manning, the President of the Council on Foreign Relations; with Kiichi Miyazawa, Saburo Okita, and the so-called 'facilitator', Tadashi Yamamoto of the Japan Center for International Exchange, all representing the Japanese.

Exploratory meetings were then held with the leaders of Western Europe and Japan and approval for the organisation's purposes was obtained. The initiative was viewed as of the first importance in Japan, since there was a growing feeling on the part of some Japanese leaders that they were being wrongfully excluded from key private international forums, such as Bilderberg. For example, in 1973, former Prime Minister Sato candidly expressed the view of the Japanese establishment, observing that the transatlantic institutions of cooperation were inadequate to deal with the rising power of Japan and China. Around the same time, Tomisaburo Hashimoto, Secretary-General of Japan's ruling Liberal Democratic Party (LDP), a confidant of Premier Tanaka and a senior member of the Diet, 'denounced the world's major powers for excluding Japan from important international councils' and for lack of consultation on issues of significant concern to Japan.[52]

Funds to set up the Commission were obtained mainly from David Rockefeller and the Ford Foundation, and after further consultations with the Japanese, an informal advisory council was established. The Commission was created by spring 1973. In June 1973 a group of key executive committee members met in Washington to give further direction to the programme and saw President Nixon. In October 1973, the first full meeting of the executive committee took place in Tokyo, to consider the work in progress of task forces appointed earlier in the summer.[53]

What these initiatives illustrate is first, that a range of informal elite and intellectual networks were in existence prior to the formation of the Trilateral Commission. Second, they show that the Commission sits within much wider networks, which also include meetings for business purposes, other conferences for multinational business (such as the Salzburg seminars), social, civic or educational purposes (for example, the Aspen Institute for Humanistic Studies), meetings of political, media, academic and business leaders at weekend retreats (such as at the all-male Bohemian Grove in the California Redwoods), and gentlemen's clubs. There are also a host of *ad hoc* conferences on a range of issues involving participants from the Atlantic and Pacific regions. There is also a thickening web of bilateral linkages across the Atlantic, and between the United States and Japan. In addition there are numerous multilateral contacts in international organisations, as well as meetings of finance and other ministers, and of government officials at lower echelons. Since 1976 there have also been annual Western Europe–Japanese ('Hakone') conferences inaugurated by Trilateral Commissioners Kohnstamm and Okita. These conferences, held annually in the wake of Commission plenaries, involve about thirty to forty established and up-and-coming figures drawn from the same fields as those in the Commission. The accent in these meetings is on nurturing future leaders. Taken together these forums and other activities suggest that the Commission is a 'network' of 'networks'. It represents a 'point of irradiation' of the kind referred to by Gramsci, in the quotation at the beginning of this chapter.

7 AIMS, ACTIVITIES, ORGANISATION AND MEMBERSHIP OF THE TRILATERAL COMMISSION

Here I outline the aims, activities and institutional form of the Trilateral Commission and discuss the material, political, and intellectual capabilities and institutional forces represented, especially in the United States. The organisational aspects can be grouped into three phases: construction and establishment (1972–4); consolidation and decentralisation (1975–9); and geographical extension (since 1979). As in the seven-power summits, the overall aim of Commission activity is to build a strategic consensus, based upon the highest common factor of Trilateral agreement.

AIMS AND OBJECTIVES OF THE TRILATERAL COMMISSION

The initial stated objectives of the Commission were, first, to involve 'significant groups of leaders' from the three areas in working together 'on matters of common concern' to lessen 'communications breakdowns' and to develop a 'shared understanding' of common problems. Second, the Commission was intended to 'propose policies' which the Trilateral states could follow, particularly in the economic, political and military fields, with respect to each other, the developing nations and communist states. 'In the cases where it is not possible to reach agreement on what ought to be done, it may be possible to agree on certain things which ought not to be done.' Crucially, the Commission would 'suggest approaches to common domestic problems' in order to assist in mutual education, and to 'assure' that domestic policies 'do not raise obstacles to effective cooperation'. Finally, the third objective was 'to foster understanding and support of Commission recommendations both in governmental and private sectors in the three regions'.[1]

Thus the Commission set daunting tasks for itself, namely to oppose a return to the mercantilist policies of the 1930s, to integrate Japan into the core of the American alliance system; and to change the orientations of the foreign and domestic policies of the major capitalist powers so that they might become more congruent with a globally integrated economic structure. It involved, as the Japanese Secretary of the Commission, Tadashi Yamamoto, put it, an effort to 'internationalise' the outlook of the ruling elements of the three regions.[2]

This was perceived as less of a problem for Western Europe, with the partial exceptions of West Germany and France. West Germany was still in a process of political rehabilitation after Nazism. For Germany, the Commission provided a significant opportunity to use its growing political influence in a private, multilateral context, where the sensitivities of other peoples would not be publicly offended. The French were initially suspicious of the Commission, partly because of the mercantilist French bureaucracy and the Gaullist nationalist tradition. These were significant obstacles to the internationalisation of the outlook of French elites. Japanese diplomatic activity had also focused its postwar efforts on political rehabilitation after the inter-war rise of militarism. Beyond this, internationalisation in Japan faced much greater barriers than in Western Europe. This was because of its closed economy, structured to promote export-led growth, its very powerful mercantilist bureaucracy and highly developed sense of Japanese identity and national interest. The potential for a resurgence of Japanese nationalism has been referred to in chapter 6. Yamamoto stressed the fragility of the position of Japanese internationalists, in a country where there seemed to be a pervasive 'fat-headed', 'Japan as number one' materialist form of nationalism emerging. This created problems for the nation's elders, whose leadership was cast in a Japanese Confucian tradition of deference and obedience to authority: their leadership is undermined if perceived as beholden to foreign interests. Internationalist leaders are treated with suspicion, in a way which has parallels with the nativist-populist tradition in America. This explains the initial reticence at joining the Commission by some members of the Japanese establishment. Yamamoto recounted that Japanese leaders eventually concluded, however, that the Trilateral Commission could perform its most useful purpose for Japan if it helped to sustain the internationalism of the United States.[3]

The internationalisation process has substantial obstacles in sections of the American leadership, the outlook of which was often forged in the early postwar years when the American political economy was largely self-sufficient. Moreover, moralistic elements in American political culture generate apparently contradictory policies. On the one hand is a strong isolationist and inward-looking tradition, represented in 'bring the boys home' Mansfieldism. On the other, is a more outward-looking moral universalist tradition, seen in Carter's human rights crusade of the 1970s, which generates policies often insensitive to the interests of other states (for example in sustaining acceptable East–West political relations). A further and major problem in the American case (discussed in chapters 4 and 5) is that of internationalising the realist-mercantilist outlook of the American security complex.

To facilitate the internationalisation process the Commission decided that 'Heads of a number of the major internationally oriented institutes in the three regions will assist the three Chairmen and the Director of the Trilateral Commission in the formulation of the Commission's program' (of policy studies). It was envisaged that some of the proposed reports 'might be prepared in collaboration with one or more of these institutes and at the very least close contact will enable the Commission to benefit from many ideas and to avoid undesirable duplication'.[4] The individuals involved in this process have included the heads of Brookings, the United Nations University in Tokyo, and the International Institute of Strategic Studies in London.

Why were intellectuals seen as so important? The answer to this lies in a view of the primacy of politics in modern international relations. This is why, in the initial statement of objectives, Max Kohnstamm stressed the necessity that intellectuals relate their theory to the actual practice of the ruling establishments of the three regions. The mobilisation of intellectuals was crucial because, as Brzezinski put it:

> It has been often said that this decade is witnessing the surfacing of economic issues as the predominant concern of our time. Yet, paradoxically, the effect is to reiterate the *primacy of politics*. Today, even apparently strictly economic considerations must increasingly be viewed from a political and even philosophical standpoint, for the appearance of more intimate global interactions, not to speak of trilateral interdependence, has the effect of politicising most issues – be it soybeans, or raw materials, or foreign investments. Accordingly, overt political acts and *perhaps even the creation of new political structures* will be needed to cope effectively with what may appear to be now essentially technical or economic problems.[5]

Brzezinski suggested that an inchoate global political process had emerged, a process which required structure and order. An attempt was therefore needed to narrow the gap between the perceptions of politicians (which were nationalistic, narrow, and short-run in nature) and the more long-term, global perspective implicit in the outlook of advocates of the Commission.[6]

The Commission's first plenary meeting took place in Tokyo, at the headquarters of the Keidanren, on 21–3 October 1973. It was addressed by Japan's Prime Minister Tanaka, and members had presentations on the Japanese economic and political situation, discussed proposals for the Commission policy programme, and the monetary task force's interim report. The Commission issued its first public statement of intentions and purposes. This was in three parts.[7] Part I defined the modern condition of interdependence which generated the need for increased Trilateral co-operation to 'counteract economic and political nationalism'. Nationalism generated new problems and frictions in Trilateral relations which 'endanger not only their well-being but affect adversely the other regions'. Further, 'although the risks of nuclear confrontation have diminished, world peace and security are still to be given a lasting basis', whilst simultaneously there were 'serious risks' to the global environment amid shortages in world resources. Shortages 'could breed new rivalries and widening disparities in mankind's economic condition' and were 'a threat to world stability and an affront to social justice'. In this context, Trilateral countries, 'in view of their great weight in the world economy and their massive relations with one another', bore a 'special responsibility for developing effective cooperation, both in their own interests, and in those of the rest of the world'. The statement stressed, 'the aim must be effective cooperation beneficial to all countries, whatever their political systems or stages of development'. Part II outlined procedures and rules to govern political and economic interactions between the Trilateral countries. Trilateral states should 'cooperate more closely, on the basis of equality' and co-ordinate policies where common interests were at stake. They should avoid unilateral actions 'incompatible with their interdependence' and 'detrimental' to others. Finally, the Trilateral countries were urged to 'take advantage of existing international and regional organisations and further enhance their role'. Part III related to the 'creative role' of the Commission. It reiterated the themes of generating common will and mutual responsibility through getting Japanese, North Americans and West Europeans to work effectively together, through a 'sustained process of consultation and mutual education'. These purposes have remained fairly constant throughout the Commission's existence.

ACTIVITIES

To further its objectives, the Commission would organise meetings, at a number of levels, in order to promote elite interaction and disseminate Trilateral Commission ideas and policy proposals through publications, public statements, private briefings and more generally through the influence and good offices of its members.

Meetings have been of seven main types. The first is national, allowing each section to co-ordinate positions, sometimes through consultations with domestic opinion leaders and influential individuals, and occasionally with the establishment press. The second type is regional, where different national groups congregate for the same purposes, again often meeting significant people who are not members (for example, the European group meets the members of the European Commission). Third are plenary meetings, initially held every six to nine months, and later held annually. Here the elites of the three regions interact. Members sit in alphabetical order at formal sessions, rather than in national, political or factional groupings. This is said to promote interaction and avoids the kind of oppositional debate found, for example, in the British House of Commons. At this level, the highest common denominator of agreement on the definition of problems and operative concepts is pursued, partly through myriad social interactions in bars, corridors and at receptions. At informal sessions, spouses are invited, and are entertained in social events and banquets. Commission staff organise a lavish 'Ladies Programme' which operates in parallel with the formal closed sessions. At the 1983 Rome Plenary this involved a Gucci fashion show, visits to several palaces, galleries, and restaurants, and an audience with the Pope at the Vatican for members and spouses. At plenaries, the Commission invariably meets the senior personnel from the host government (these meetings are rotated around the three areas), and holds a press conference to disseminate ideas. In addition, Commission Chairmen and Deputies have met regularly, and the Executive Committee, its main policy-making body, meets as circumstances dictate, and at least twice a year. Finally, there are *ad hoc* and task force meetings called for specific purposes, some of which are combined with social events and dinners.

The most important of the Commission activities is its plenaries, and the interaction between the elites of the three regions they promote. Proponents argue that the meetings develop a sense of collegiality and mutual confidence among the members, building the trust and predictability stressed in public choice theory as being important for the development of international agreements. Despite the collegial flavour of the meetings, discussion is open, frank and often heated, and differences over vital aspects of policy are confronted and explored, even when agreement or consensus seems unlikely or impossible (for example, over energy and nuclear proliferation; this

147

and other debates are discussed in chapter 8). The discussions take place under 'Chatham House rules' of non-attribution and are in private session. A careful scrutiny of debates reveals that where major differences of interest exist (such as over energy security, the continuation of detente), the most the Commission can do is to promote understanding of differences and sources of friction.

This process is analogous to, and operates in tandem with, that of the more intimate seven-power summits, which in fact took the form outlined by Commission task force reports produced during 1973–4.[8] When Carter took office, senior officials put in charge of summit preparations had been members of these task forces. The summit 'sherpas' embodied the idea that consultations should 'strengthen transnational networks', foster 'transnational coalitions' and should seek to resolve substantive policy differences in part through the creation of inter-governmental machinery. Under the supervision of former Commissioners, the summit process became increasingly institutionalised, with an elaborate set of preparations and follow-up mechanisms.[9] The growing summit preparatory groups managed to develop a climate of mutual trust, a certain degree of autonomy and created a kind of 'collective personality to some extent independent of the governments', although the summit 'sherpas' were in all cases very close to their leaders, and thus, to domestic politics.[10] This process mirrors Commission consultations with experts in preparation of task force reports and other initiatives.

Plenaries always consider task force reports and members circulate 'Trilateral memoranda' to contribute to discussions. Also reviewed are future research topics and possible new members. The press is informed of the general drift of discussions and selected establishment journalists are admitted as observers, along with some government officials (a staffer of the United States National Security Council invariably attends), representatives of foundations (notably Ford and Rockefeller) and kindred bodies, such as Bilderberg and the Atlantic Institute. The plenary meetings, like those in Bilderberg, are very intensive and last three to four days.

The preparation of task force reports is of central importance (see the bibliography for a chronological list). These involve extensive and intensive consultations and drafting sessions, often engaging seventy or more consultants. This increases the extensiveness of Commission activities, increases its legitimacy, and incorporates a range of specialists across the range of issues in the study programme. Each report takes up to two years to prepare. Reports are thus the product of a painstaking consensus-building process, and normally endorse the views of the more far-sighted members of the establishment. Reports and *Trialogue* are distributed free to 'opinion leaders' (of whom, by the mid-1980s, there were about 2,000 on the mailing list in the United States, and about 500 in Japan – I have no mailing figures for Europe), and to members. They are available upon subscription to the public.

What kind of task forces were created, and with what objectives? The first were those on 'matters of immediate urgency', which could draw on research already carried out by other organisations, or which contained suitable policy recommendations which the Commission could adopt. The second were longer-term, and would require original, in-depth research. These would attempt to produce policy recommendations 'for adoption by the Commission'. The third type of study would not be necessarily policy-oriented, and might be more 'academic' in character, concerning 'political, economic, or social issues, yielding perhaps policy implications, though not explicitly designed to generate policy recommendations'. Finally, the Commission would consider publishing annual reports (such reports were in fact produced but not published) and internal information bulletins for members.[11]

Examples of the short-term issues (which of course have a longer term dimension) were current frictions in money, trade and investment; arms control and nuclear proliferation; and relations with developing countries. Examples of longer-term study were given as 'the effect of changes in values on the international system', and 'issues presented by the impact on modern society of science and technology'.[12] Thus task forces were viewed as a part of an ongoing process of attempting to incorporate immediate and long-term developments into a common framework of thought and, at least potentially, a common concept of action.

Other possible topics 'suggested but . . . not yet extensively discussed' were attitudes of elites of the three regions towards each other; a joint proposal on the exploitation of the seabed; joint rules for multinational corporations; 'political implications of new means of social control over man's development and behavior'; educational reforms and their transferability; how the three areas cope with 'the social problems posed by youth and by old age'; and a study of the international consequences of demographic growth. Although my research indicates no further discussion of the last four proposals, they indicate that the Commission was concerned with a wide range of questions. Studies would encompass analysis from political sociology, social and behavioural psychology, demography, political economy, educational theory and practice, as well as international relations in its narrower politico-military sense.

Brzezinski stressed that the longer-term, in-depth studies were intended to define, on a Trilateral basis, the 'nature of the problem, and the formulation of policies that enhance both trilateral cooperation and the commonweal'. A typical report would contain a general statement of the problem, a specific discussion of the 'sources of friction, of policy disagreements, and an analysis of the more basic, structural problems', and 'specific policy proposals, both interim and longer-range', with a final section devoted to 'concrete policy proposals designed to reach the general goals'. The studies would start with immediate problems (such as monetary and trade relations and the political setting of Trilateral cooperation), and then move on to wider questions (such as global development: relations between North and South, resource questions, and 'moderating the Global Ideological Conflict').[13]

ORGANISATION AND LEADERSHIP

Constituted as a non-permanent organisation, the Commission has operated since 1973, reviewing its purposes and impact every three years (in Trilateral jargon, each 'triennium'). If members vote convincingly in favour, the Commission continues to operate. It is organised along regional lines (although national sections meet together), with a small administrative staff supporting co-ordinating activities. Each region is led by a Chairman and Deputy Chairman. Day-to-day activities are handled by three regional directors. Overall coherence and direction is provided by a high-powered Executive Committee. Thus the Commission has an inner core of leaders, rather like a political party, who combine experience, connections, knowledge, and mobilisation capacity, as well as the ability to represent and give weight to diverse interests. The New York office originally provided much of the initial impetus. After 1975, however, activities became increasingly decentralised. Apart from this, no major organisational changes have taken place. At the time of writing, the Trilateral Commission had continued to function at least until 1989.

The fact that the Commission renewed itself every third year since 1976 is not surprising, since the Ford Foundation concluded that the benefits of the Commission were primarily restricted to its members (for example, introductions into wider networks, platforms for attempts to gain high office). Following complaints by funding agencies such as the Ford Foundation along these lines (and indeed suggesting that the Commission was in danger of becoming a geronto-cracy) new, younger blood was injected into the American group after 1979, and a further infusion took place in Japan in the mid-1980s.[14] Since 1984 the American section rotated certain membership positions to continue the process of rejuvenation, and widen the networks incorporated.[15] Let us now consider specific aspects of organisation.

The Chairmen

In the organisational plan, it was expected that the Chairmen would devote 'a substantial percentage of their time to the venture . . . in view of the difficulty of the Commission's work'.[16] The role of Chairmen and Deputies is to take responsibility for the development of overall strategy. Chairmen are elected by the regional membership groups. Each Chairman is therefore said to represent, symbolically and politically, the consensus of (elite) opinion of each region.

The North American Chairmen have both been American. Gerard Smith was the first, until he left to become President Carter's Ambassador-at-Large for Non-Proliferation Matters (1977–80). David Rockefeller took over after having refused Carter's offer of the post of Secretary of Treasury. North American Deputy Chairmen have been Canadians. The first was former Canadian Minister of Foreign Affairs (1968–74), Mitchell Sharp. The second was Jake Warren, ex-Chairman of the Bank of Montreal and former Canadian Ambassador to the United States (1975–7). European Chairmen all have had strong connections with the European Movement, since the Commission espouses European unity. These were first, Max Kohnstamm of the Netherlands and second, since 1975, Frenchman Georges Berthoin, the International Chairman of the European Movement (1978–81). Like François Duchêne, Berthoin is a former principal private secretary to Jean Monnet. The Deputies have been the Anglo-French Duchêne, and Egidio Ortona, former Italian Ambassador to the United Nations and the United States (1958–61 and 1967–75, respectively).

The Japanese Chairman from 1973–85 was Takashi Watanabe. He had no deputy until 1979, when Nobuhiko Ushiba was appointed. Both Watanabe and Ushiba were key figures in helping to shape Japan's international economic strategy since 1945. In 1985, Watanabe resigned as Japanese Chairman to become President of the Japan Credit-Rating Agency, set up in the context of Japan's financial liberalisation efforts. He was replaced by Isamu Yamashita, former President of Mitsui Engineering and Shipbuilding and Vice-Chairman of Keidanren (Federation of Economic Organisations). Yoshio

Okawara, Japanese Ambassador to the United States (1980–5), advisor to the Japanese Minister of Foreign Affairs and Executive Advisor to Keidanren, became Japanese Deputy Chairman. Okawara was also Vice-Chairman of Sumitomo Corporation and Chairman of Sumitomo Corporation of America.

The Executive Committee

At the heart of the Commission is the Executive Committee (Excom), which is 'the principal policy organ . . . responsible for policy recommendations'. The Excom uses its considerable influence to recruit new members and obtain funding.[17] It is a microcosm of the wider network of interests and affiliations in the Commission. Given the degree of travel involved and the busy schedules of all concerned, attendance at Excom meetings is very high, usually in the region of 80 per cent.

Interests represented in the Excom are (not unexpectedly) the same as those of the wider membership, that is transnational business, internationally oriented political leaders and bureaucrats (usually with substantial experience at high levels), senior academics, and the occasional moderate labour leader and media representative. However, the nominal affiliation and the particular position of any Excom member at any point in time reflects a part, and often a small part, of that individual's activities, influence, and experience: this is true for the majority of Commission members.

An exemplar is Robert S. McNamara. In his varied and extensive career, he has been a Professor at Harvard and, following service in the United States Air Force, was the President of Ford Motor Company (he was at Ford between 1946 and 1961). As the American Secretary of Defense (1961–8), he built up and diversified the United States nuclear arsenal, as well as presiding over the Pentagon during the Vietnam War. At the Pentagon, as Stanley Hoffman observed, there was 'an exhausting contest between military leaders eager for more bombs and a Secretary of Defense caught between belated lucidity and stolid loyalty to the President'.[18] In the 1980s, along with Gerard Smith, McGeorge Bundy and George Kennan, he proposed the renunciation of a central tenet of NATO strategy, the right of pre-emptive strike. This was the 'no first use' of nuclear weapons proposal.[19] As reformist Chairman of the World Bank (1969–81), McNamara set about reorienting many Bank programmes towards the recognition of basic needs from a more complex socio-economic view of long-term development issues. He has also been a prolific author and his publications include *The McNamara Years at the World Bank* (1981), *The Essence of Security* (1968), *One Hundred Countries – Two Billion People* (1973), and *Blundering into Disaster* (1986), as well as writing task force reports for the Commission. In addition, he has held many trusteeships and company directorships during his career. His experience therefore synthesises theoretical and practical aspects of education, management, warfare, public service and development banking, all crucial to Commission deliberations.

Many of the businessmen involved, like McNamara, hold directorships of a number of companies. Most of the firms concerned have two things in common: they are large and draw a substantial and perhaps growing proportion of their profits from activities and assets overseas.[20] The Excom brings together men (only one woman has ever been a member) of similar outlook and with wide experience and connections. Like the Chairmen, the Excom is intended to reflect the balance of national memberships and interests. Other examples of Excom members are Harold Brown, the former American Secretary of Defense; Henry Kissinger; Giovanni Agnelli, the President of Fiat; John Loudon, Chairman of the Royal Dutch Petroleum; and Otto Graf Lambsdorff, former West German Minister of Economics. Japanese Excom members, like the European, have very strong American connections, either through education, diplomacy or business. Japanese Excom membership has contained more businessmen than its counterparts in America and Europe.

Key Japanese Excom members since the beginnings of the Commission have been Okita, Miyazawa and Ushiba. Okita was the architect of successive governments' economic planning. Miyazawa, widely tipped during the 1980s to become a future Prime Minister, until discredited in the 1988–89 Recruit scandal, represented a neoliberal tendency within the ruling Liberal Democratic Party (JLDP). The late Japanese Deputy Chairman, Ushiba, joined the Excom in 1974 after his three years as Ambassador in Washington, served as the Co-Chairman of the America–Japan 'wisemen's group' in the 1980s until his death on 31 December 1984.[21] The Ushiba family has strong connections with Mitsubishi, Sony, and the Nippon Credit Bank. Nohubiko and one of his two brothers have held important cabinet posts. The matrimonial connections of the three brothers and Nohubiko's four sons include a chamberlain to the late Emperor and also to the Tokugawa family (which ruled Japan for almost three centuries until the Meiji restoration in the 1860s).[22]

Directorate and secretariat

In the first three years the Commission had both a director (Zbigniew Brzezinski) and in 1975–6, a deputy director (Christopher Makins, Fellow of All Souls, Oxford, and a former British diplomat in Washington). This reflected the Anglo-Saxon origins of this form of private diplomacy, as well as the fact that the drive to set up the Commission was American. These posts were intended to give intellectual and political direction to the Trilateral Commission. In 1976, Brzezinski left to become National Security Advisor to President Carter, and Makins took a fellowship at the Carnegie Endowment. It had been initially anticipated that the directorship would be rotated throughout the regions. Instead, a decision was made to decentralise the organisational form.

German political economist Wolfgang Hager of the European University Institute was first European Secretary. Hager has since faded from the Commission scene, perhaps as a result of his subsequent advocacy of a form of Euro-mercantilism. George Franklin was the first North American secretary (leaving an important post as Director of Studies at the Council on Foreign Relations to take the position). The energetic Yamamoto became the first, and to date only, Japanese secretary. When the central directorships were abolished, Franklin became the holder of the new post of co-ordinator (this downgrading reflected opposition within the ranks to Brzezinski's style, and in particular his attempts to publicise and press for Commission positions with governments). The three secretaryships were continued, and Charles Heck, a teaching fellow from Yale (specialising in transnational corporations) was appointed North American Secretary. Former IISS and Sussex University research fellow Dr Hanns Maull (an expert on energy and the Middle East) replaced Hager as European Secretary in 1976. After completing a Commission study on energy strategy, Maull left to take a media post in Germany and later a lectureship at Munich University. He was succeeded by former *Figaro* columnist and holder of a doctorate in political philosophy, Martine Trink, in 1979. Trink departed in 1981, to be replaced by Paul Révay, also French, and a former bureaucrat. The directorships were created in 1982, and upgraded the secretaryships. In 1989, directors were Heck, Yamamoto and Révay. Earlier in the 1980s the post of co-ordinator was abolished, and Franklin joined the Excom. Thus the Japan and North American sections have the most continuity in terms of administrative posts.

In addition there is a small administrative staff of about six to ten persons in each regional office. Until 1985, when it ceased publication, Francois Sauzey, a Frenchman, and a former fellow of the Atlantic Institute, was the editor of the Trilateral Commission's journal, *Trialogue*, which was produced in New York.

REPRESENTATION AND COMPOSITION OF MEMBERSHIP

Commission membership overlaps with what I have called an 'international establishment'. Such an establishment, which has grown in importance since 1945, consists of the intersecting domestic establishments of a range of capitalist countries.[23] This can be said to be the ultimate source of the strength of the Commission, in that the parts interact synergistically to produce a greater whole.[24] This whole has been enlarged since the foundation of the Commission. The membership partly reflects the twin processes, transnationalisation of economy and state, since many members are associated with transnational fractions of capital and corresponding elements of the state that I have discussed in earlier chapters. The concept of the international 'establishment' partly captures a social process which links these 'political' and 'economic' levels.

After the founding and consolidation phases, membership was extended. Since 1979 Spain and Portugal have been allowed entry, and Greek membership is planned. The 1986 membership of around 320 members rose from about 190 in early 1975, and nearly all were men. In contrast to Bilderberg, however, the Commission has a higher proportion of academics and policy intellectuals, and does not include serving members of government. (See Appendix 1, at the end of this book for details.) The higher proportion of intellectuals reflects a recognition that contemporary international relations are seen as more complex than when Bilderberg was created.

As with almost any organisation there are different ranks of membership, formal and informal. At the upper end of the organisational hierarchy is a superior stratum of 'established patriarchs': senior politicians, top bankers and corporate heads, higher ranked academics (policy specialists) and influential lawyers. At the lower end is a tier of 'up and coming' people who may rise to the top in coming decades. These individuals provide a continuing body of people imbued with the 'Trilateral idea', pre-empting any future Trilateral 'leadership crisis'. Within these ranks is a diversity of engagement in Commission activity, since some members are much more active than others. For example, Walter Mondale is generally regarded as not having been very active, whereas individuals such as Richard Cooper, Karl Kaiser, and Otto von Lambsdorff were very active, when not in public office. I will now flesh out the nature of the membership in terms of national representation, and put it into economic, political, and intellectual categories.

National representation

The nations represented are all the European Community countries, except Greece (Europe section); the United States and Canada (North America section); and Japan (Japan section). This excludes a number of important capitalist nations. Thus Australia and New Zealand have been concerned at their exclusion, although there were Australian observers and a speaker at one of the Tokyo meetings. No Third World countries have members, although some of their elites have been consulted in the preparation of reports. Also a large and specialised group of Commission members met the Chinese leadership in Beijing in 1981. At one stage the Commission intended to hold a meeting with the Indian elite, and discussed the possibility of a meeting with Brazilian leaders, but these did not materialise. The Commission had set up a meeting with the Soviet elite, due to take place in 1980, but this was aborted in 1979–80.

Japan has disproportionately high membership numbers (since an aim is to internationalise the outlook of the largest possible number of Japanese). This also explains why, in the late 1970s, West European members refused to allow Bilderberg or the Atlantic Institute to merge with the Commission (which might have appeared rational, given the overlap in activities), and why Japan also resisted this. The Europeans were concerned at the possible dilution of their influence over the Americans in Bilderberg, and the Japanese wished to sustain their privileged position in the Commission. Resistance to a merger also indicated that a fully developed 'Trilateral' consciousness still had a long way to to.

Economic forces represented

One key to unravelling the material interests of the Commission is to ask the question, 'which interests are excluded?' There is no representation given to small-scale capital, capital which is essentially 'national' in character, and the interests of military producers are much less prominent than was the case in Bilderberg where the likes of Dassault and Boeing were strongly represented. Also, organised labour is not given significant representation in the Commission, whereas it had greater, although still minor, representation in Bilderberg.

The economic interests represented are predominantly those of internationally mobile forms of capital. The corporate membership is easily definable, and comprises the heads or deputy heads of giant transnational firms and banks, as well as agribusiness and trading companies. Only a very few union leaders have membership. Firms represented are at the apex of world economic hierarchies and at the vanguard of the transnationalisation process. These companies have privileged access to the massive growth in the Eurocurrency markets, and borrow funds at cheaper rates of interest than weaker competitors. With respect to manufacturing and financial concerns under consideration, the vast majority of their investments during the 1970s and 1980s were geared towards increasing capital-intensity or technology-intensity. Thus their expansion has not tended to generate substantial rises in employment. Most of these firms were also able to escape the worst effects of the recessions of the 1970s and 1980s, where the burden of adjustment was shouldered by less technologically advanced, less productive, and more immobile national capital, and associated labour working in sectors with these characteristics.

Individuals associated with such companies are influential in policy-making circles, although their influence on certain issues may be minimal. Maximum impact is to be anticipated over economic policy, on two levels: in terms of lobbying (the behavioural or direct form of the power of capital, outlined in chapter 5), and in terms of their role in creating a climate of expectations and anticipations which come to reinforce the structural (market) aspects of the power of internationally mobile capital. In the major Trilateral states, notably the United States, Britain, West Germany and in Japan, transnational firms and large banks have significant influence over the climate of exercise of power, whereas the situation in other European countries, notably France and Italy, is more complex, with trades unions and left-wing parties having significant influence. However, in all these states, the need to maintain a suitable 'business climate', one which compares favourably with that elsewhere, is of paramount importance to their governments, often irrespective of their political complexion.

By the mid-1980s, about two-thirds of the world's largest 100 public companies were affiliated through individuals having Commission membership, in fields including banking, financial services, insurance, chemicals and pharmaceuticals, utilities, computing, communications and electronics, automobiles, and trading companies, as well

157

as energy and commodities concerns. Not listed in the top 100 rankings were very large private companies like Cargill and Bechtel, which had Commission members. If publicly quoted, these firms would probably be in the top 100. Most of the industry leaders had Commission members.[25] Japanese corporate membership is centred round the predominance of the resurgent *zaibatsu* combines, Mitsui, Mitsubishi, Somitomo, and the smaller combines which did not reappear in their previous form, but which reemerged and were united in groups centred on large banks, especially Fuji (the successor to the Yasuda *zaibatsu*), Dai-Ichi and Sanwa.[26]

Apart from connections with major financial and industrial corporations and extensive links with government, Commission members have been influential in business associations, media enterprises, important (American) law firms, and civic institutions in their respective countries.[27] The European membership's affiliations are strong in European and other international institutions, as well as civic institutions at the national level.[28]

Political forces represented

Again, it is instructive to observe which political forces are not represented. There are no communists, no left-wing socialists (although significant numbers of moderate socialists and social democrats are members), no ultra-nationalists, no populists, and no extreme right-wing elements. What is also significant by its absence is a large proportion of members of the security apparatus. This suggests that the perspectives of the American security complex as well as their counterparts overseas are not fully in tune with the basic thrust of the Commission's ideas. On the other hand, peace groups, environmentalist and anti-nuclear movements are also absent, although the Director of the World Wildlife Fund (whose major patron has been Prince Bernhard), has been a member.

The key political links between dominant elements in modern capitalism and the state are formed in an internationalised policymaking network. The major political interests sympathetic to the strengthening of such links are reflected in Commission membership. Many important centrist political parties have leaders or senior figures who are members. For example, the JLDP and Japan Socialist Party (JSP), the German Social Democratic Party (SDP), the Free Democrats (FDP), the Christian Democrats (the CDU–CSU alliance), and the American Republican and Democratic Parties all have senior members in the Commission, as do centrists in France. Moderate flanks of the

British Labour and Conservative Parties also have members but it has been difficult to involve high-ranking trades unionists. Also in the Commission is former Foreign Secretary and Social Democrat Leader, David Owen, who has been a particularly active member. In addition, there are significant numbers of former diplomats, finance ministry officials, bureaucrats, and former or current members of important international organisations, notably the International Monetary Fund, the World Bank, the European Community, and the OECD.

Thus the bulk of Trilateral Commission members are either internationally oriented conservatives or liberals. Occasionally there are exceptions, such as George Will, the right-wing American columnist. However, this apparent anomaly can be explained by the fact that, apart from his writings, he was a close friend of Nancy and Ronald Reagan: the Commission would hope to incorporate someone who has some considerable, if perhaps temporary, influence in the White House.

Intellectual networks

It is again worth stressing the types of intellectuals who are not members. These include the *literati* and the scribes of the left-wing intelligentsia, a section of whom the Trilateral Commission *Crisis of Democracy* report scathingly referred to as 'value-oriented' intellectuals (such as Noam Chomsky and Richard Falk). The 'value-oriented' intellectuals of the right, such as neo-conservatives like Irving Kristol and Normal Podhoretz, and free-marketeers such as Martin Anderson of the Hoover Institution, are also notable by their absence. Also excluded are scientists opposed to nuclear power on ethical grounds and those who work within the more scholarly traditions of international relations (which constitutes the bulk of academics, particularly in Europe and notably Japan).

Intellectuals are involved because of their ability to combine theoretical and practical aspects of their activity within the Commission's major discourses, which are liberal and functionalist. They are also chosen because of their place in wider intellectual networks, and because of their vantage-point from within their discipline(s). For example, Samuel Huntington, one of the co-authors of the Commission's contentious report, *The Crisis of Democracy*, became President of the American Political Science Association in 1987. He is of course also involved in a wide range of programmes as Director of the Harvard Center for International Affairs. Thus Commission intellectual networks are based on an international circle of theorists and policy

159

specialists who generally tend to direct the major institutes in which they operate. Many of these theorists are also important practitioners (such as Brzezinski, Kissinger, Okita).

The institutes associated with the Commission networks are bastions of transnational liberalism. These institutes often organise conferences with each other, liaise in a variety of ways, and occasionally co-ordinate and/or collaborate on research projects. Key institutes involved, apart from those already discussed are: the Institute of International Economics; the British Policy Studies Institute; economics departments at Yale, Michigan and Harvard; Centre for the Study of Political Economy, Turin; Centre for European Studies, Sussex University; Centre de Sociologie des Organisations, Paris; the European University Institute; the University of Tokyo; and the Japan Centre for International Exchange. International economic organisations are also linked to this network.

Those institutes which focus more on political questions, foreign policy and security matters are, apart from those mentioned above: Harvard Kennedy School of Government; the Carnegie Endowment; the Atlantic Institute; Chatham House and its equivalents the Italian, French, Dutch, Norwegian, and German International Relations institutes. Also involved on economic and political questions are policy-oriented theorists from prestigious universities such as the London School of Economics (LSE), Oxford, Ecole Polytechnique, Hamburg, Munich, Paris, Bologna, Tokyo, Kyoto and Sophia. Other theorists in Trilateral governments are occasionally associated in preparing Commission reports. Many of these international relations scholars are functionalists, with several European theorists having a neo-federalist and pan-European orientation (such as Karl Kaiser). Others advise policy makers in institutions such as NATO.

American academics are very influential, reflected in the original ideas which served as an impetus for the Commission's creation. Several of America's most gifted international economists and political scientists are members.[29] A reason for the large numbers of such economists was given by Gardner Ackley in an interview, when he pointed out that the key economic problems of the 1970s and 1980s were basically international in nature, namely inflation, recession, exchange rate instability, and energy. Some of these problems, for Ackley, involved 'parallel rather than interacting relationships', yet 'over and above this parallelism the international aspect is inherent and inescapable, except by severely dismantling the postwar internationalisation of the economy, which is of great importance in terms of post-war prosperity'. These theorists consistently emphasise the necessity of international co-ordination of policy, under conditions of concentric circles of participation, with the United States at the core, and other Trilateral and developing countries involved in decision-making according to functional criteria.[30] Many of the American academics have held important government and diplomatic posts. For example, both Ackley and Richard Gardner have been Ambassadors to Italy, and Arthur Burns was Ambassador to West Germany during the early 1980s.

American membership of the Commission

By now it will have become clear that the Trilateral Commission is not the people's party. Its American membership, while involving some union leaders, is almost entirely representative of the elite of society.

Although much smaller than the New York Council on Foreign Relations, the Commission is more representative of the American elite, at least in geographical terms and, of course, in the 1980s, David Rockefeller was Chairman of both. Commission membership includes proportionately more members from the Sunbelt, the West and the Mid-West. On the other hand, Sunbelt military-industrial interests are not fully incorporated into the forum although they are nonetheless represented.

The eastern seaboard predominates in terms of geographical representation. The American group are, of course, generally 'internationalists' whereas the concerns of the American electorate tend to be more domestic in nature. Most members attended Ivy League universities, hold postgraduate degrees, and many had some of their education abroad, especially in Britain, with LSE and Oxford providing alumni. Many American members hold law degrees, and are members of influential gentlemen's clubs in New York, Washington DC and elsewhere. They are members of the 'inner core' of the American elite, identified by Dye as those 6,000 individuals who hold significant positions in major American institutions. Many of these individuals hold positions which are 'interlocked' with others, particularly in banks, which he argues, in accord with van der Pijl, were gaining increasing control over the corporate structure in America in the 1970s and 1980s.[31]

Thus the American group represents a part of the spectrum of the American leadership, although important interests and individuals are notable by their absence. For example, although the Commission's publications consistently argue against protectionism on the grounds

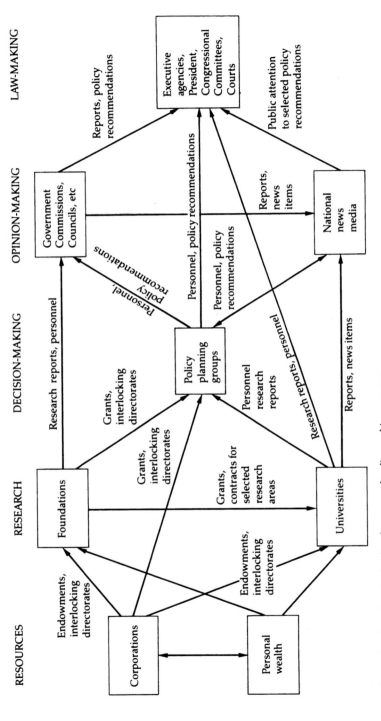

RESOURCES   RESEARCH   DECISION-MAKING   OPINION-MAKING   LAW-MAKING

Corporations

Personal wealth

Foundations

Universities

Policy planning groups

Government Commissions, Councils, etc

National news media

Executive agencies, President, Congressional Committees, Courts

Endowments, interlocking directorates

Endowments, interlocking directorates

Grants, interlocking directorates

Grants, interlocking directorates

Grants, contracts for selected research areas

Research reports, personnel

Personnel, policy recommendations

Personnel, policy recommendations

Personnel, policy recommendations

Personnel research reports

Research reports, personnel

Reports, news items

Reports, news items

Reports, news items

Reports, policy recommendations

Public attention to selected policy recommendations

Figure 7.1 American institutional nexus and policy-making process
Source: T. R. Dye, *Who's Running America?*, p. 212

that it reduces consumer choice and welfare, the most ardent advocate of consumer rights in the United States, Ralph Nader, is not a member. Women are clearly under-represented, as are labour unions. Also, senior members of Congress are few in number, particularly when compared with the large number of academics. Although kept in touch with its activities, Senator Teddy Kennedy is not a member, since by joining he would undermine his base on the left of the Democratic Party. Nor is the Reverend Jesse Jackson a member, perhaps because he is a champion of the American underprivileged. This again reflects the elitist, anti-populist complexion of the Commission.

The institutional basis of the influence of the Trilateral Commission formation within the United States, that is, its place within the relationship between 'political' and 'civil' society, can be summarised by means of Figure 7.1. This, in Gramscian terms, is the framework of a hegemonic, historic bloc within the United States. All stages apart from 'law-making' in this model correspond to the concept of civil society, and indicate its centrality in the making of state policy (especially on economic and social questions) when compared with, say, the Soviet Union. 'Policy planning groups' are central in this oligarchical model of policy-making. The most important of these are the Trilateral Commission, its fraternal organisation the Council on Foreign Relations, the Committee on Economic Development and the Conference Board. Each of these has strong membership interlocks as well as frequent interchanges of personnel with the executive branch and White House staff. The Commission, it will be noted, draws its membership from all stages and institutions in the policy process.

Seen in this way, the Commission is strategically placed at the centre of a diffuse but interconnected elite political process in the United States. Dye concludes that it is 'one of the central co-ordinating points in the entire policy-making process'. Policy planning groups are very important in the United States because of its geographically dispersed and relatively diversified elites. This contrasts with the more centralised power structure of Japan, Britain, and France, where the national leaders congregate in the capital. There is nothing deterministic about this process. What is paramount is that these groups 'endeavour to build consensus among corporate, financial, university, civic, intellectual, and government leaders around major policy directions'. The groups 'are influential in a wide range of key policy areas'.[32] In Dye's oligarchic model, activities of the 'proximate policy-makers' are only the *final phase* of a complex policy-making process largely determined by forces in civil society. The latter structure the options available for the formal law-making institutions. The Commission network is most influential in economic policy, whereas the forces of the political society are more important for security questions. The centrality of the Commission in consensus building within the United States provides a link between the American and the global political economy. This connection is crucial since a number of studies have shown that the American propertied class is tightly connected through networks of kinship and friendship, an efficient system of communication, interlocking directorates, and a unification of basic outlook and political practices.[33] Moreover, as the American political economy has become internationalised there has developed a corresponding link with key elements in the civil societies of the other Trilateral states.

The core of its membership's influence is in the economy. This can be indicated by analysis of the control patterns in American industry. In a recent study of the strategic ownership positions in the *Fortune 500* list of the largest industrial corporations Dye notes that families and individuals held the largest share of strategic positions, surpassing banks and other American and foreign institutional holders of wealth. The diffusion of ownership in the largest American industrial corporations makes possible the acquisition of strategic positions by owning a very small percentage of the voting common stock. For example, in 1981, the largest shareholders in Exxon, the biggest energy corporation and second largest industrial company in the world, were Exxon Trust Plan (2.09 per cent), the Rockefeller family (1.68 per cent) and Chase Manhattan Bank (1.03 per cent), giving an enormous potential for control to members of the Rockefeller family, which also had an effective controlling position in Chase Manhattan.[34]

The largest group of stockholders after family groups (who held 28.55 per cent of total value of stocks as well as 424 associated strategic positions) in big American industrial corporations were banks (21.1 per cent of value of stocks and 486 strategic positions) and other financial holding firms (22.7 per cent of value of stocks and 860 strategic positions). These numbers are from a total of 2,156 identified strategic positions, with an associated total stock valued at $170.2 billion out of overall industrial assets in 1981 of approximately $795 billion.[35] Thus the majority of strategic positions in these corporations (and potential control) lie with family groups and the banking-finance complex in the United States. This shows the degree of integration in the control patterns in American corporate capitalism.

These findings relate the 'inner group hypothesis' of control in American capitalism. The inner group is influential across a range of holdings and uniquely situated to integrate the interests of large numbers of corporations. Thus, in the context of the networks and linkages indicated above, the vanguard elements, represented in organisations such as the Conference Board (which represents blue-chip American corporate capital) and the Trilateral Commission, are able to develop a general class consciousness and cohesion. This process involves rotation of corporate leaders into and out of the American executive branch. What is suggested here is that it is possible to denote a relationship between the transnational class fractions discussed earlier and steering patterns in American capitalism. My analysis indicates a link between these elements and the Trilateral Commission. This link is highlighted by the financing of the Commission.

FINANCING THE TRILATERAL COMMISSION

In the mid-1980s the North American section cost about US$ 2.3m per 'triennium' to run. It received no financial support from the American government. Since it had no endowment or substantial accumulated reserves, the Commission was consistently required to justify activities to sponsors.[36] Here the Commission was successful, at least with respect to corporate contributions, which increased as a proportion of overall funding from 1973. This also would appear to be the case with respect to the other regions.[37] It should be noted that members pay their own travel and subsistence expenses when attending meetings, which prevents a number of people (such as trade unionists) from contemplating active membership. Thus the real costs of the Trilateral Commission are much greater than the budget actually reveals.[38]

In 1973–6, 10 corporations provided about 12 per cent of receipts. In 1976–9, 16 corporations provided about 17 per cent. A big change took place in 1979–82, when 35 corporations provided about 38 per cent. This rose in 1982–5 (as of 30 June 1984) to almost 50 per cent of receipts, from 66 corporations. For the first time corporate contributions exceeded foundation support. This showed a wider corporate appreciation of the Commission's efforts, as well as an expanding membership base. However, in 1983–4 the Commission encountered for the first time 'serious trouble in finding the resources to cover its full range of planned activities'. It decided to discontinue the publication of *Trialogue* on the grounds of expense, and because the ranking of its priorities was meetings, reports and *Trialogue*, 'in that order'. This decision reflected the view that the 'essence' of the Commission was 'thoughtful interaction among a high-level membership'.[39] During the 1983-5 period there was a significant increase in the numbers of meetings, as the North American section mounted a major offensive to change the 'domesticist' orientation of Reagan's economic policy (see chapters 5 and 8).

Funding has proven more difficult to obtain in Europe (as has information on European funding for this study), but similar sources would appear to have contributed support. For example, German sources covered more than half of European costs in the 1973-6 'triennium', but thereafter contributions had to be raised by national delegations on the basis of relative size of GNP. In the British case most of the funds came from transnational companies such as Rio-Tinto Zinc, the four clearing banks, John Swire, Dunlops and Ocean Transport, as well as, after 1977, £1,000 per year from the Foreign Office at the behest of the Foreign Secretary, David Owen. Even so, raising the US$ 33,000 per annum for British contributions (from an estimated total running cost of European operations of US$ 200,000 each year during 1977-9) proved very difficult.[40]

Japanese funding comes from similar sources to those in Britain, although here the Commission draws upon the resources of the important Japan Centre for International Exchange, which is mainly Japanese government funded, and the Keidanren, the very influential employers' organisation. I have, however, been unable to gain precise details of Japanese funding, although the rather large proportion of business interests in the Japanese membership would suggest that Japanese corporations provide substantial support.

COMMISSION MEMBERS IN GOVERNMENT

Whereas many original members had held high office in government, the Commission first received world-wide notoriety when more than twenty of its members filled senior positions in the Carter administration. The individuals concerned included the President, Vice-President Mondale, Secretary of State Vance, Secretary of Defense Brown, National Security Advisor Brzezinski (who had been the Director since the Commission was founded) and Secretary of Treasury Blumenthal. Co-founders Owen and Bowie were appointed respectively as Ambassador-at-large for Economic Summits (and senior White House advisor on international economic relations) and Deputy Director of the CIA. Carter subsequently appointed former Trilateral Commissioner, Paul Volcker, as Chairman of the Board of Governors of the Federal Reserve.

While American members are the most influential,. Commissioners have consistently filled a significant number of high government positions in other member countries. In Japan, three key members, Mssrs Ushiba, Miyazawa, and Okita (all at one time or another foreign ministers) have been leading figures in the shaping of Japanese policy, and the Commission has been enthusiastically endorsed by each Japanese Prime Minister since its inception. Some of the many West European members who have held high office have already been noted. Others include Lord Carrington who became Secretary-General of NATO, and a number of senior figures in the European Commission. In aggregate, Commission members have been directly or indirectly extensively involved in the making and co-ordination of foreign and economic policies in most of the member states since at least the early 1970s.

POLITICAL ACCEPTABILITY OF THE COMMISSION IN THE UNITED STATES

The first thing to be said in this section is, as will be evident from the above, that both major political parties, especially their moderate elements, generally tend to support (or not oppose) the Commission's activities. The main form of opposition to the Commission's basic ideas has, in fact, come from elements of the American security complex. First, however, we will discuss some of the criticisms from other points on the political spectrum.

A problem for the legitimacy of the Commission enterprise stems, naturally, from many of the forces it was set up to oppose, especially right-wing and nationalist-mercantilist forces. Here, criticisms have ranged from the abstruse to the exotic. To date, this challenge has been mainly a political irritation, although some members, when running for political office, have been 'targeted' (that is smeared) by right-wingers keen to eradicate the Commission's moderate and liberal Congressional support. In this vein, Commission members have often been the target of what Congressman Barber Conable called 'ultra-nationalists' in America.[41]

Even within the mainstream parties, however, the Commission's ideas and activities have been contested. Dangers to the Commission at the populist level were, for example, reflected in Ronald Reagan's attack on the Commission to discredit George Bush's candidacy in the 1980 presidential election. Because of this, virtually all American politicians have worried about their Commission membership because of its impact on their political acceptability and popular credibility.

Commission members interviewed usually told anecdotes concerning taxi drivers, hotel managers, constituents and day-to-day acquaintances who had claimed that Trilateral 'fat cats' and 'Washington insiders' were running America. The Commission, at least in the United States, had an image problem. In view of these assaults, the Commission decided to take its case to the people, and Charles Heck and George Franklin conducted over fifty TV and radio interviews during 1979–80, to dispel 'myths'. Public relations activity generated hundreds of newspaper articles (many of which were written by Commission members, their relatives, or friends). This helped refurbish the tarnished image, as did the fact that Reagan appointed former Commissioners in his administration (such as Caspar Weinberger and General Alexander Haig), and had accepted Bush as Vice-Presidential candidate in the 1980 election (albeit under pressure from senior Republicans like Henry Kissinger and Gerald Ford).[42]

The threats to the Commission have come, predictably, from the traditional nationalist right in the United States, represented by Senator Barry Goldwater, who inserted several articles into *Congressional Record* which bombarded the Commission with denunciations similar to those made against Bilderbergers (noted in chapter 6). Goldwater apparently provided much of the material to the sensationalist journalist, Craig Carpel, who ran a widely-read series in *Penthouse* magazine, suggesting that the entry of Commission members into the American government heralded the death of American democracy, with Brzezinski cast as Doctor Strangelove.[43] Even more outlandish was the controversial American Labor Party, led by the former left-winger, Lyndon Larouche, whose critique of the Commission was made on mercantilist grounds, peppered with accusations that Brzezinski and others had plotted to assassinate its leaders. In addition, it attacked the Commission for not giving unconditional support to an arms race with the Russians and for not being wholehearted in its endorsement of the SDI.

Another more obscure line of criticism came from a group associated with the Lehrman Institute in New York. It blamed the Commission for endorsing policies which had led to the demise of the American dollar, effectively demolishing the postwar international financial system.[44] These 'gold bugs' advised people to put their wealth holdings into gold. One reason for this opposition was that the Commission's first task force report advocated a more fully-fledged international currency, which, *à la* Keynes, the authors called bancor.

Also, there was populist current (with some elements in common with the traditional nationalist right). This opposed transnational firms, which were believed to want to create a one-world government and destroy American sovereignty. This claimed that financiers in the Commission were behind the Panama Canal 'sell out' (seen as orchestrated by Commission member Sol Linowitz), so that the Panamanian government could repay its debts to American bankers. This populist strand was linked to American agrarian interests, but not agribusiness (which was strongly represented in the Commission). A notable populist orator, from the small-farmers' American Agriculture Movement, was John L. Lewis. His arguments were influential during the late 1970s and early 1980s in Texas and the Mid-West. Lewis alleged that the Commission was part of a world-wide conspiracy to destroy the American way of life. His claims were expressed on cassette tapes, widely circulated in agricultural areas. According to Lewis, the goal of this conspiracy was world government, which necessitated control of the world's food, energy and monetary system. Lewis claimed that Trilateral 'fat cats', notably the Rockefellers, through their high interest rate policies, were driving American farmers out of business, buying up their land at 'Rock' bottom prices (sic).[45]

Beyond these typically American responses, there was also widespread criticism, not only in the United States, on more familiar political terrain. Much of this originated in hypercritical reaction to the Trilateral Commission's *Crisis of Democracy* report, which sought to identify conditions under which American society could be more 'effectively governed'. This was widely interpreted, in America and overseas, as an attack on liberal democracy. Thus opposition to the Commission embraced not only the right and populists, but also the liberals and the left, including elements in the American intelligentsia. Apart from outrage that the Commission could produce a report which suggested that a period of self-sacrifice and democratic retrenchment was necessary for the United States to cope with global crises, many on the centre and left objected to the idea that the cause of many of these problems was the American people, rather than the Ivy League establishment elite which had led the United States into the devastating affray of Vietnam. This line of argument was represented in Holly Sklar's edited collection, *Trilateralism: Elite Planning for World Management*, which sold over 20,000 copies.

What is most significant from the point of view of the Commission is the liberal–mercantilist cleavage. Michael Klare was one of the first to identify this when he wrote a short paper arguing that the Commission's 'Traders' (reflecting the international capitalist interests) were opposed by the 'Prussians' (nationalist, protectionist, hard-line groups, particularly in the security complex).[46] This latter group was much less cohesive than the former in terms of its economic base and was united as much by its opposition to internationalist finance and the old Atlanticist establishment as by any other factor. Whilst Klare's general point is compelling, it should be pointed out that several defence and aerospace companies were, however, clearly visible in the membership of the Commission (such as Boeing and Hewlett-Packard). Nonetheless, declining smokestack industries are scarcely represented. What seems crucial is the opposition from the forces of the American military-industrial complex, represented, for example by the American Security Council. These forces were successfully mobilised between 1978 and 1986, with resulting enormous increases in military expenditures. It was to this part of the 'Prussian' grouping that the Reagan administration was swiftest to respond.

In retrospect, popular mistrust of the Commission really developed after the election of President Carter, who had run on an anti-Washington, moralist and populist platform. Antipathy to the old establishment in Carter's inner circle was reflected in his chief of staff, Hamilton Jordan's widely-quoted remark, 'I should say we've failed' (if the old guard of the likes of Vance and Brzezinski took key positions in the administration). The reconstruction of the Commission's legitimacy therefore took some time.

How important was this opposition, or should we say notoriety, for Commissioners in their own countries outside of the United States? I have already referred to the ambivalence of Japanese popular reactions, and the widespread mistrust of internationalists there. However, most of the mainstream Japanese press, as well as leading elements in both major parties, the JLDP and JSP, were supportive of the Commission, with criticisms coming from neo-nationalists, and opposition from within the bureaucracy. Nonetheless, here, the Commission became an object of deference, awe and curiosity after Carter's election. Slowly, Japanese public opinion has become increasingly supportive.

What was the reaction in Europe? In general, a similar situation has emerged to that in Japan, although criticism was left-wing, as well as from nationalist forces which have been suspicious of the Commission (the Japan Communist Party has also been suspicious of the Commission, but organised labour has shown little direct opposition).

In Britain, there has been virtually no mention of the Commission in the press, and it has never surfaced as a political issue. This was less so elsewhere. Excom member Paul Delouvrier, reflecting on this from a French perspective, argued that the 'too great success' of Carter's victory was a major weakness for the Commission: Carter's election and appointment of Commission members created political disrepute elsewhere. The French press took to likening the Commission to a *pouvoir occulte*, or *synarchie*, a mysterious organisation possessing joint sovereignty with governments. Since Raymond Barre was Prime Minister of France at the time of Carter's election, the Commission was perceived, particularly by the French left, as a kind of capitalist springboard for elevation to political power (this viewpoint was also to be found in Italy). Thus its very success posed problems for the French group, undermining its attempts to recruit trade unionists.[47] This was in contrast to the situation in West Germany (where it has not really been at issue, and where strong initial support was given to finance Commission activities). Several prominent West German trades unionists have been members, including the leader of the Federation of German Trades Unions, Heinz-Oskar Vetter. German trades unionists have also acted as rapporteurs for Commission task forces.

Like all mainstream political leaders, Commissioners have worried about terrorism from extremist groups (especially when in Germany in 1977). However, apart from the assassination attempt on the life of President Reagan in 1981, on the day that he was due to meet the Commission's Chairmen, Commission meetings have passed without violent incident.

Delouvrier reported that at the 11–13 June 1978 plenary of the Commission, Carter indicated that, although happy to receive the members at the White House, and pleased with Commission efforts, he was still attacked for his earlier membership of a 'too capitalist, too establishment' organisation. Carter added that this posed political problems for his administration. Carter's problems were, of course, to be much greater in the near future than any created by his association with the Commission. Soon to follow was the Iranian hostage crisis, the 1979 recession and the collapse in domestic and allied confidence in the credibility of White House leadership. The Commission had therefore suffered a (temporary) and widespread decline in legitimacy because of the strong link between Carter and its point of view. This set the scene for the Republican victory in the election of 1980, with the new President intent on bringing a right-wing 'Reagan revolution' to American politics.

However, an examination of the personnel changes in the Reagan administration suggests that, ultimately, the Reagan revolution, the military build up, and the Reaganite tide of populism were contained by the establishment. Although there were initially far fewer former Commissioners in senior posts than in its predecessor, those sympathetic to the broad thrust of the Commission's positions gradually came to the fore. By 1988, these included George Shultz at the State Department, Frank Carlucci at the Pentagon, James Baker at Treasury, and Howard Baker and David Abshire in the White House. Other members of the administration more in tune with the Reaganite right had either left the administration or were discredited, to the vociferous complaints of their supporters.

8 THEORETICAL AND PRACTICAL ASPECTS OF THE TRILATERAL COMMISSION

This chapter focuses on agendas and the topics discussed at Commission meetings since 1973. This allows insight into the difficult and often elusive process of the forging of Trilateral consensus and also into some aspects of the consciousness-raising role of the Commission.

Given the importance of the United States in the international relations of the major non-communist states, a key question here is: under what conditions did a gulf emerge between American government perspectives and Commission perspectives? A related issue (discussed in chapter 9) is how far the Commission helped to promote internationalisation of outlook in American and Japanese leaders, and what practical consequences this may have had. The content of debates is reflected in Commission publications (listed in Appendix 4, along with a list of members interviewed). My exposition seeks to highlight major disagreements in the debates. However, interviews with members and officials suggest a consensus often emerges, which appears to be at its greatest on economic questions. There has been virtually unwavering support for measures which would serve to move the world economy in a more liberal direction, under managed conditions. The exceptions to this have been Japanese recalcitrance and 'Trilateral' economic relations with communist states.

The stages in the Commission agenda were marked by first, a stress on the theme of global interdependence and the necessity of international policy co-ordination (1973–9); second, wider consideration of security issues which broadened the agenda (this occurs after 1977, and preoccupies the Commission during 1979–81); and third, a return to centrality of economic questions, as dissatisfaction with Reagan policies surfaced in the early and mid-1980s. This was accompanied by an emphasis on the need for arms control. Thus stages have overlapped. Questions addressed have often been long term in nature, which gave continuity to the agendas.

There was a fairly high degree of correspondence between the agendas of the Commission, the seven-power summits and the United States, in the economic sphere (with the exception of the early Reagan years). On security questions, American domestic forces tended to shape the Commission's agenda. The Commission intended to pursue more co-operative relations with the Soviet bloc, and, as its initial plans revealed, to 'moderate the Global Ideological Conflict'. However, the resurgence of Cold War sentiment meant that the Commission sought a united stance against the Soviet Union, especially after the failure of the SALT II ratification, and the Soviet invasion of Afghanistan, but the Trilateralists were unsuccessful in this. This failure reflected a deep rift between the West Europeans and the United States and, to a lesser extent, Japan.

Let us now examine the evolution of the debates. These will be grouped, for purposes of exposition, into interdependence issues, security issues, and international economic questions of the 1980s.

INTERDEPENDENCE ISSUES

The issues here are both economic and political, global and 'Trilateral'. The early agenda aimed to consolidate the concept of complex interdependence in the pattern of thought of members, and indirectly to that of a wider audience. On the economic side, predominantly Trilateral issues such as the monetary order (1973–5, 1978–9, 1984–6); and macroeconomic co-ordination (1976–7, 1984–6), were consistently being discussed. More global issues on the agenda have been energy and nuclear proliferation (1974–9); North-South questions, including trade, food supplies and debt (1973–8, 1981–3, 1987); the management of global commons, notably the oceans (1974–6), space (1983), science and technology, including ecological questions (1987); the conduct of international business (1976); and the overall nature of the international order (1976–7, 1982–4). On the political side, discussions focused on the reform of international institutions and consultative procedures (1974–6); the governability of democracy (1975–9); and the cultural and social contrasts between Japan and the West which create barriers to the imperatives of interdependence (since 1975, at every plenary held in Japan). Let us deal selectively with these debates in chronological sequence, until the late 1970s, in order to indicate their evolution. Some of the interdependence issues of the 1980s are discussed in our third section.

The first meeting was in Tokyo, 21–3 October 1973. The location symbolised the commitment to treating Japan as an equal, a gesture considered as of historic import in Japan. The meeting considered monetary reform and the state of Trilateral political relations. The second major meeting was in Brussels, 23–5 June 1974, a location intended to signify the Commission's commitment to the European Community. Discussion involved relations with developing countries and the energy crisis. The Commission produced a public statement. This recommended joint action to increase aid to developing nations, increased international monetary co-operation in order to help recycle OPEC surpluses accruing from the oil price rises, promoting the unity of the Trilateral countries in the context of a co-operative and non-confrontational approach towards OPEC; and reform of the international trading system in a more market-oriented direction. Implicit in these debates was severe criticism of Nixon's policies.

The first major North American meeting was held by the Excom in Washington DC, 8–10 December 1974. The same issues were discussed as in Brussels, with the addition of 'inflation and politics'. The Commission publicly advocated the creation of a Bank for Fund Recycling, a proposal which was, however, not taken up by OPEC, which was expected to foot almost all of the bill. However, the Commission's proposals appeared to persuade Henry Kissinger to change the State Department's negotiating tactics, which until 1975 had been based on uncompromising opposition to OPEC. George Ball, the prime articulator of the Commission position, had heavily criticised Kissinger for tactics which were bound to antagonise OPEC, and divide the Trilateral countries.

The second Japanese meeting, in Tokyo and Kyoto, 23–7 May 1975, involved extensive seminars on cultural, psychological, political and economic aspects of Japanese society, and a review of the global redistribution of power. Americans and Europeans were the object of this 'educational' exercise. This was followed by heated discussion of the study on governability of democracies. This study implied that domestic democratic processes needed to be constrained, so as to increase state autonomy to 'manage interdependence'. In effect, the report suggested a move towards a neo-liberal state. In this sense it was a political counterpart to the McCracken Report discussed in chapter 5. The premise of the report was challenged by many Commission members, and by guest speaker Ralf Dahrendorf. He argued that the 'problem' was that there was *insufficient* democracy, particularly at the enterprise level. This prompted the Commission to later embark on a study of industrial democracy. In 1979, Kiichi Miyazawa was able to state that the worst period of the 'crisis of governability' has passed, with a 'new realism' replacing the activism on the early 1970s.

Observations by other members revealed less confidence in such conclusions for Europe.

Other agenda items were commodities and the oceans. Here Brzezinski warned that the Trilateral North–South policies ran the risk of forcing a denial of co-operation by developing nations. His speech reflected worries at the rise of 'resource power'. The Commission decided to place global issues at the heart of its agenda so as to defuse North–South conflicts. Discussion of commodity and energy problems preoccupied members at the 29 November–2 December 1975 Excom meeting in Paris, and resulted in a joint statement reiterating the case for a co-operative approach. Also discussed were nuclear proliferation and the spread of civil nuclear technology, industrial democracy, and East–West relations.

In 1976 the plenary was held in Ottawa, to emphasise the importance of Canada, a nation which took on added significance, given its vast natural resources. International business ethics were discussed (in the shadow of the Lockheed scandal) in light of revelations of corrupt practices by numbers of American corporations in their attempts to secure foreign business. The Commission recommended international surveillance of such practices, and the enactment of mutually reinforcing codes of conduct by the Trilateral powers (this only occurred in the United States, where legislation was quickly repealed because it had not been reciprocated in Japan or Europe: American firms therefore lost business). The Commission stated that bribery undermined arguments in favour of the market system and damaged the legitimacy of transnational enterprise. Again on the agenda was increased macroeconomic co-ordination with stress on strengthening the role of the OECD, the World Bank, and the IMF. The Commission advocated extensive consultations amongst the Trilateral powers 'at all levels' to help create a wider framework of co-ordination. To advance this goal, a special meeting was arranged with senior members of the Ford administration and Congress, in Washington DC, on 12 May 1976.

The first plenary of 1977 was held in Tokyo (9–11 January) following Carter's election as President. This was a source of elation amongst many members. Here the main focus was on macroeconomic co-ordination and trade frictions, in the context of the 'locomotive' and 'convoy' debates. At this point, the membership appeared to endorse an international Keynesian approach, stressing co-ordination of policies as a prerequisite to a successful strategy. There were widespread fears of the political repercussions of a failure to reverse the stagflationary conditions which had prevailed for much of the 1970s.

Reflecting the last vestiges of American–European consensus on detente, the Commission also discussed the means by which Trilateral–East European relations could be made more co-operative.

On 26 May 1977, a special meeting was held with the President of the European Commission, Roy Jenkins, and other key European Community officials. The Trilateral Commission consistently endorsed European integration both as a means of levelling disparities between different parts of the European Community (which, if uncorrected, would tend to promote protectionist policies in weaker economies) and in order to promote more coherent European political positions, particularly in trade where the European Commission had jurisdiction. This contrasted with contradictory positions taken by recent American Republican administrations, which appeared to encourage a strong European Community (as a bulwark against the Soviet Union) while simultaneously desiring weak economic competitors in Western Europe.

The 22–5 October 1977 Bonn meeting pursued similar arguments and discussions, with the focus on energy and nuclear weapons proliferation, food production in developing countries, and East–West relations. The food study was instigated by the Japanese section and administered from the Tokyo office. The study was an attempt by the Japanese to deflect criticism of the pattern of its aid giving (many Commission members saw this as being primarily motivated by concerns of market access in Asia) and to increase the legitimacy of Japanese involvement in Asia, where memories of Japanese imperialism were strong. Since 1977, Japan gradually moved to increase its aid contributions substantially, some of this being, indirectly, for security purposes (for example, to Turkey and Pakistan).

At Bonn, significant differences emerged between the United States and its allies on nuclear energy and proliferation. This debate indicated the limits of agreement among the Commission countries when there are rival interests based on different degrees of national vulnerability. Whereas the United States defined energy-security questions in global terms, Japanese and Europeans stressed national interests (with apparently all participants, some of whom were leaders of nuclear agencies, subscribing to the view that nuclear power was necessary). The debate took place against the backdrop of limited progress in shaping a common energy strategy since the 1973–4 oil crisis, largely because of the confrontational tactics pursued by the (much less vulnerable) United States, and a *sauve qui peut* mentality amongst its allies. Here Kinya Niizeki (Japan Atomic Energy Commissioner) pointed out that Japan was 'the extreme example' of an industrially advanced country with 'no indigenous energy sources'. Japan was entirely dependent on imports. A shift from oil to coal (entailed in the Carter energy programme) would mean 'heavy reliance' on imports from the United States and Western Europe. Thus Japan 'ascribed very much to the use of nuclear energy', and even here, since Japan had no uranium, it had to rely on imports. Considering the risk of proliferation, Niizeki added: 'There is no international consensus on the best way to develop nuclear energy while preventing such dissemination [of plutonium] . . . it is our basic position that our energy concerns should not be overlooked in the name of non-proliferation.'[1]

The seminar debated the costs and benefits of the fast breeder reactor – a benefit being that it was, as a German participant stressed, 'the only option to avoid being submitted to a possible cartel of uranium suppliers'. (This is because fast breeders use fifty times less fuel.) Another German, reflecting a common judgement, said the Trilateral countries faced an antagonistic breakdown of the 'old consensus on nuclear non-proliferation as it emerged in the sixties'. The impression was that 'international agreements [had been] replaced by unilateral policies' (by the United States) which 'amounted to a denial of nuclear energy'. Indeed, some European participants sensed that American proposals (such as the setting up of a 'nuclear bank', controlled by the United States) were intended to lead to an 'unacceptable monopoly situation'. Count Lambsdorff referred to American policies as 'nuclear imperialism'. Such comments reflected severe friction between the West German and American governments over this question. These difficulties were exacerbated by the well-known personal contempt Chancellor Schmidt had for Carter.[2]

Energy conflicts heralded a turbulent period for intra-Trilateral relations, which were badly undermined by the divided response to the oil crisis of 1973–4. This was despite large numbers of ex-Commissioners in the United States administration. Energy controversies continued at the 11–13 June 1978 Washington plenary, overshadowing debates on industrial relations. Attendance at this meeting was large (200 out of 280 members), but observers relate that the atmosphere was very tense. Members debated the new energy report (No. 17, see Appendix 4 for details), which 'aimed at outlining a co-ordinated strategy for the trilateral governments to secure an orderly transition to a new generation of energy technology as reserves of hydrocarbons are increasingly unable to meet energy needs'.[3] The idea of a concerted strategy was endorsed, with some

178

stressing the need for rapid development of nuclear power. Once again, however, non-proliferation issues were very divisive.[4] Overall, a lack of confidence was expressed in the prospect of a viable consensus which could underpin an improved non-proliferation regime.

The session turned to the Middle East (a region constantly disputed before and since). It was argued that the key threat posed to the Trilateral countries was the possibility that a new embargo might reopen the type of divisions which had emerged in 1973–4. Several participants expressed renewed criticism of American energy policy, which was based on the 'misleading assumption of an early energy shortage'. It thus lacked credibility. Other discussion touched on strengthening the role of the IMF; intensifying the 'special relationship' between the United States and Saudi Arabia (but not forcing the Saudis to increase output massively since this would erode their position as 'swing producer' and undermine Saudi influence in OPEC); and a discussion of policies towards China and the Soviet Union in the energy field.

The state of Trilateral relations was reviewed in a special edition of *Trialogue* (Winter 1980). Central to considerations again was energy, which can be considered, during the 1970s, as a conclusive failure of Trilateral co-operation. Crucial here was the United States, where domestic interests, lack of a coherent energy policy, and the conduct of American foreign policy, had the effect of undermining the interests of its allies. In the 1980s market forces, in the shape of a decline in demand due to recession and closures of smokestack industries, and new sources of energy supply, eventually undermined OPEC power.

SECURITY ISSUES

The security debates were in three phases, initially focusing on Europe and the Middle East, then widening to encompass the Pacific and the Americas. The first and second phases concentrated on East–West questions. The first discussions were held by the Excom in 1975, but the first plenary discussions really began in 1977. Early dialogues were framed by the desire to continue detente with the Soviet Union and to normalise relations with the People's Republic of China. Two task forces were created in 1976 and 1977, the first favouring wider economic and functional co-operation with the Soviet Union, and concerted attempts at arms control. The second was more confrontational, reflecting anti-Soviet feelings on the rise within the United States. Of these, the first was, and still is, probably closer to the mainstream American position in the Commission. This twin track approach was similar to the CIA 'Team A' versus 'Team B' assessments of Soviet power in the 1970s, made by different task forces. Each was, respectively, optimistic about the US position relative to that of the Soviet Union (Team 'A'), or extremely pessimistic, calling for a rearmed America to meet the Soviet challenge (Team 'B'). These studies were commissioned by George Bush whilst he was the Director of the CIA. Whilst Team 'A' stressed that peaceful co-existence and some limited co-operation was possible between the United States and the Soviet Union, Team 'B' saw the relationship through a more traditional Cold War lens, with little prospect that the two superpowers could live and work peacefully together: conflict was endemic between two fundamentally opposed nations and social systems. In the latter view, the major guarantee of peace was a substantial strategic and military advantage in favour of the United States: a major military build up was therefore imperative to reverse the gains made by the Soviet military during the previous decade.

A second phase of discussion of security concerns emerged in 1977–8, with the first such debates at full plenary level. These were initially catalysed by growing concern over Carter's human rights policies, considered as unilateralist moralism by many members. Debates intensified following the Soviet invasion of Afghanistan. Japanese leaders generally endorsed the American definition of the consequences of the invasion, that is, as having global repercussions which demanded Trilateral solidarity. The prevailing European interpretation, premised on the desire to continue detente, was that Afghanistan was a regional issue which did not concern them directly. With respect to energy, security and East–West questions, debates at the 1977 Bonn meeting had also reflected enormous divisions in policies. American policies were generally identified as the primary source of friction. The next cycle in East–West security questions concerned relations with China, and East–West relations after Brezhnev, including East–West economics.

The third phase, from the early 1980s, saw a widened security agenda, encompassing questions concerning the Americas (where United States policies had been criticised by many Europeans) and East Asia (which was delicate for Japan). In 1985–6 a study of East Asian security was mainly conducted from the Tokyo office.

Over the life of the Commission, there was considerable evolution in Japanese outlook, with its leaders gradually perceiving their security role in more global terms after initial resistance. In its nascent strategy, it was intended that the Commission would discuss security questions. In the initial phase, the Japanese resisted open discussion of security matters, for a number of reasons. First, Japan did not want to be seen to be a part of a Cold War International. A second was the sensitivity of Japan's East Asian neighbours, who had ugly memories of Japanese aggression in the 1930s and 1940s. Third, the American-imposed 'peace' constitution severely limited the potential military role of Japan. Fourth, the vast majority of public opinion was against an increase in Japan's military power, partly reflecting and reinforcing a taboo on discussing security matters in postwar Japan. A final, practical reason was that Japan did not have sufficient specialists to interpret security questions with enough sophistication, and discussions in this sphere would have to have the construction of an intellectual apparatus.

Let us take 1977 as our starting point for detailed discussion of the debates, since, at the time, the leaders of all major Trilateral countries (Schmidt, Giscard d'Estaing, Callaghan, Fukuda, Trudeau, Andreotti and Carter) had pronounced themselves devotees of the Trilateral idea and in favour of increasing co-operation and avoiding unilateral or mutually damaging actions. This is in contrast to the more sceptical approach of President Reagan (at least during most of his first administration) and Mrs Thatcher in Britain after 1979. These debates had their ground prepared by a special edition of *Trialogue* in Summer 1977 which included essays from Yevgeniy Rusakov, New York correspondent of *Pravda*, and Fuji Kamiya, Professor of International Relations at Keio University (the first Japanese to write on security questions for the Commission). Kamiya stated that the Commission's approach to East–West relations (in report No. 13) took a piecemeal, issue-by-issue approach, an approach which might yield very specific forms of co-operation. However, 'certain fundamental barriers' were impossible to overcome using this method. One was the foreign policy stance of the United States, that is, its unilateral human rights policy, which implied interference in the domestic affairs of the Soviet Union. This unilateral tendency persisted despite the seven-power summits in Rambouillet and San Juan.[5] Criticism of the Carter policy (which was defended on two occasions by National Security Advisor Brzezinski as reflecting the 'historical inevitability of our times') was repeated consistently in Commission debates.

Rusakov stated bluntly that Trilateralism 'may just come to a formula, "NATO plus Japan"'. Reflecting the deteriorating climate of American–Soviet relations, Rusakov alleged that the United States was 'more concerned with the whims of its hawkish politicians [for example, Jackson and Stevenson Amendments, COCOM] than in trade with the socialist states'. Rusakov agreed with Kamiya's view of the human rights campaign, suggesting it 'reflected an isolationist trend', and 'disregard' for the 'interests and opinions of other countries, including its allies.' This view was partly shared by Henry Kissinger. He feared that such a campaign might undermine a number of 'friendly regimes' (presumably in Argentina, Chile and Iran) and create a confrontational climate towards the Soviet Union. This might cause a crackdown on dissidents in the East and retard Jewish emigration. The latter part of Kissinger's position was shared by most Commissioners.[6] Indeed, even former Commissioners in the administration were disturbed by Carter's evangelical approach to foreign policy, pointing out the contradictions in a President prepared to condemn 'merchants of death' supplying arms to authoritarian and repressive regimes, whilst simultaneously authorising the largest arms export drive in American military history.[7]

With 'high politics' now on the agenda, at the 1977 Bonn plenary, disagreements quickly arose over the nature of communism in the West and the East. Richard Löwenthal, Professor Emeritus of International Relations at the Free University of Berlin, argued that Eurocommunist movements threatened the 'very cohesion of the west'. At the same time, it was impossible to prevent communists entering government if elected. Others stated that communist participation in government might 'critically weaken' the American commitment to Europe. Others favoured a 'constructive policy of [economic] recovery' as 'our best chance' to encourage a 'positive evolution' of political forces away from the left. More generally, the Commission agreed that Europe's deepest problem lay in its cohesion, in the face of 'rising protectionist tendencies and growing disparities in economic growth.' This theme of 'Europessimism' recurred in subsequent debates.

By contrast, 'Nippo-Communism' was seen as less threatening in the Far East, where the key issue was the role of China and the Soviet Union. Speakers emphasised that Japan was not interested in any peace arrangement with the Soviet Union which did not involve China. Discussion encompassed the Korean peninsula (with criticism of Carter's intention to withdraw American ground forces), the specific vulnerabilities of the Soviet Union, especially in technology and food; the vulnerabilities of the West, exacerbated by national industrial competition; their energy vulnerability when compared with the energy-rich Soviet Union; and an emphasis on the 'crucial importance' of the European Community as a 'pole of solidarity' (sic). The Community was praised for helping to 'equalise disparities' which exacerbated national rivalries.[8]

Notwithstanding these anxieties, a confident Brzezinski outlined the priorities of the new administration. Criticising Kissinger's approach, he stressed that the United States objective was to 'assimilate East–West relations into a broader framework of cooperation, rather than to concentrate on East–West relations as the decisive and dominant concern of our time'.[9] He added that in contrast to the flexibility and inherent dynamism of the West (despite the current crisis period), the East manifested a condition of 'meta-stability', namely a condition of rigidity which fractures when challenged by dynamic processes. Eurocommunism had two sides, one being its undesirable impact on the West since it helped legitimise communism, the other on the East, where it legitimised pluralism and variety, and as such might be a source of change. It might help to promote a stage of de-Stalinisation and/or a stage of de-Leninisation, since internal regimes varied from one party to another. Brzezinski stated American opposition to communist parties participating in West European governments. However, if such parties became 'minor partners in government' and were 'insulated from the general leverage of power' they 'might not behave in a fashion' which was 'disruptive or dangerous'.[10] Brzezinski then linked the expansion of East–West economic linkages to developments in other areas, notably progress on SALT and related security matters, although the administration did not have very much control in the area of trade, where Congress was much more significant. He then reemphasised the importance of the human rights policy.[11]

The next plenary was Tokyo, on 22–4 April 1979. For the first time there was an extensive interchange on 'China and the International Community'. This discussion prepared the ground for an unprecedented Commission meeting with Chinese leaders in 1981. By now, exchanges on security issues, anathema to Japan at an earlier stage, became a norm. The Commission published a special edition of *Trialogue*, as the SALT II Treaty reached the floor of the Senate. Here, Karl Kaiser, a close associate of Chancellor Schmidt and one of the Commission's key European intellectuals, highlighted the West European stake in the passage of SALT II, and European anxieties at the fact that significant forces in the United States were attempting to repudiate a serious process of arms control. Kaiser crisply outlined four implications of a Senate rejection of SALT II for Europe: it would undermine alliance cohesion; calculability in international relations; United States leadership of the West; and conciliatory elements in the Soviet leadership.[12] Kaiser stated that disagreement between the United States and Europe was becoming increasingly visible, on 'both the necessity and the content of detente policy'. The American concept of detente was global, competitive and dominated by the conflict with the Soviet Union. It was focused on security. By contrast the European view was Eurocentric, covered a larger spectrum of issues, and assigned a greater role to smaller East European powers. These differences were 'most noticable' between West Germany and the United States, but reflected a common European viewpoint. Kaiser stated, 'Such a common view became visible, for example, in their critical perception of the Carter administration's handling of the human rights issue.'[13]

The 1980 plenary was in London, on 23–5 March, and was dominated by repercussions of the Soviet invasion of Afghanistan, and the Senate rejection of SALT II. Attendance at this meeting was 30 per cent greater than at the previous European plenary. Some Commissioners described 1980 as a year of 'disarray' and 'turbulence'.[14] Japan Secretary Yamamoto became increasingly disturbed by the emergence of 'single-issue Trilateralism', that is, a preoccupation with Soviet conduct.[15] Nonetheless, most Commission members argued that it was self-defeating to lump all security developments into a 'global balance'. The evolution of regional balances, in the Middle East, Europe, and East Asia, was crucial. Security was a broad concept, involving access to raw materials and energy. Many security questions escaped 'purely military remedies'. Most speakers called for a nuanced response to security questions. The tendency was to state that allies would have to be more directly *involved* in resolving security problems, rather than simply be *consulted* by the United States.[16]

However, discussions took a major step forward at this meeting. A new willingness emerged, on the part of Japanese leaders, to move towards American positions. As was noted earlier, up to this point the Commission had intended to meet the Soviet elite, but decided finally to shelve this after the Polish crisis.[17] This appeared to confirm a shift within the Commission towards some adoption of, or tolerance towards, new Cold War positions adopted by the United States. A crucial presentation was made by Kiichi Miyazawa, 'To Meet the Challenge'. This was interpreted by key Commissioners as signalling the willingness of Japan to more comprehensively forge a 'Trilateral alliance'. Miyazawa began by stating that at the outset, the Commission was not intended to become 'an actor in the ideological struggle with the Soviet Union'. However, in the aftermath of the invasion of Afghanistan: 'We feel today that the need is greater for us to close ranks in our endeavour to strengthen . . . an alliance of common values in order to defend freedom and democracy against the challenges arising out of the most recent world developments.'[18] Such words could have been uttered by John Foster Dulles. Nonetheless, divisions emerged over interpretations of, and responses to, the Afghan crisis. The Europeans generally viewed the invasion in terms of Soviet weakness. The United States interpreted the move in terms of Soviet expansionism and as an aspect of East–West conflicts.

The 1981 plenary was held in Washington DC, on 29–31 March 1981, and coincided with the assassination attempt on President Reagan. The East–West question again dominated discussions, and the clash between the three regions continued, a fact only emphasised by presentations made by key members of the Reagan administration. Since American political and public opinion had moved clearly in an anti-Soviet direction, Commission members concluded that the United States would rearm, and try to cement its growing military links with China. The consensus expressed was the Western Alliance was now 'at its lowest ebb in its existence', with major differences in perception and strategy separating the United States and Europe.[19] The Commission decided to re-examine concepts of security by launching a new task force, *Trilateral Security*, an initiative meant to parallel that of the Council on Foreign Relations and its counterparts in West Germany, Britain and France.[20] Noteworthy here, given the Miyazawa speech cited above, was a contribution from Hiroshi Kimura of the Slavic Research Centre, Hokkaido University. Kimura stated that the broad consensus of Japan's political scientists was that the best guarantees of Japan's security would come, not through military measures, but through commerce, technological cooperation, cultural exchange, etc.[21]

The Commission finally met the Chinese leadership in Beijing, on 20–3 May 1981. The symposium, whilst in some ways appearing to be a dialogue of the deaf, in others reflected the steady change in Chinese politics which had taken place since the Cultural Revolution. Many members of the Chinese delegation were policy academics. The Trilateral group had members with expert knowledge of China. Discussions featured: Chinese modernisation, domestic trends in the Trilateral countries, global issues, and policies towards the Soviet Union. The Commission's 'special delegation' met Deng Xiao Ping for two hours. During the sessions, the Chinese made their usual attacks on Soviet 'hegemonism', whilst simultaneously emphasising the fact that they would not allow Trilateral countries to use them against the Soviet Union. By riposte, there was a speech (some might call it a lecture) from David Rockefeller, criticising certain aspects of China's economic policies, stressing China's need to adopt a more accommodating attitude towards foreign investment if it wanted to be considered a viable economic partner by Trilateral states.

Changes in the East–West climate also caused the Commission to embark on a second 'overview' study. This task force study, discussed in Tokyo (4–6 April 1982) was, *Sharing International Responsibilities*. Seen as at the heart of the Commission's work, the report 'dominated much of the three days of the plenary'.[22] (This report is sufficiently central that it is more fully discussed in a separate section below.) The objective of the meeting and task force was to help shape a consensus on a new division of labour within the alliance. The question of how to share responsibilities was at the centre of a heated debate at Tokyo on economic warfare. This initially hinged on evaluation of American sanctions against Iran and the Soviet Union. It then widened to include broad questions of strategy. Many Europeans challenged the view that sanctions were efficacious or wise in a political sense, reflecting a distinct Euro-American division, with Europeans tending to argue that immense political benefits were gained from increased trade. From the American side, the argument was that sanctions had more effect than met the eye (despite costs imposed on American agricultural exporters). An economic task force report (No. 24) was criticised because it suggested that sanctions – which fell far short of economic warfare against the Soviet Union – had little effect. A compromise emerged, combining strong support for reviewing and perhaps strengthening COCOM, with market principles: non-restricted trade and other economic relations were to be allowed to develop on a market basis. This compromise reflected attempts to synthesise economic liberalism with a 'hard-line' realist position. The aim was an 'overall political strategy for economic relations [since the real problem was to] exercise leverage on Soviet decisions on the allocation of capital and investment'.[23] In this view, there were four main economic burdens on the Soviet Union, that is: those stemming from its credit rescue of Eastern Europe, from its arms build up, from the development of Soviet agriculture, and from the development of Siberia. One Commissioner observed:

> Helping the Soviets in the credit rescue of Eastern Europe and supplying agricultural commodities allows them to devote more resources to armaments . . . The Trilateral aim should be to influence Soviet decisions on allocation of GDP. If we have this point in focus, everything can be deduced from it with regard to a meaningful strategy – and we need a strategy, not just denial actions.[24]

Backing this argument was a widespread view that the Soviet economy was in crisis, giving the Trilateral countries substantial leverage if a common policy could be found. To advance formulation of political questions involved, the Commission published a special edition of *Trialogue* in 1983, *The Heart of Europe*, focusing on East–West European relations, and prospects for change in the Soviet Union. Amongst others, this featured contributions from Milovan Djilas and Leslek Kolakowski, mainly aimed at educating American members in complexities of *Mittel Europa*. At the 17–19 May 1986 plenary in Madrid, members debated the report on the *Next Phase in Trilateral–Soviet Negotiations*. David Rockefeller, having recently returned from a meeting in Baku between American and Soviet businessmen, announced that the Soviet Union was now prepared to discuss joint ventures and was becoming more flexible in outlook.

The examination of East–West questions was taken further with a long topical session, 'After Rekjavik', led by Henry Kissinger, at the 1987 plenary in San Francisco, the first to be held on America's west coast (21–3 March). The United States National Security Advisor, Frank Carlucci (successor to the discredited Admiral Poindexter) also addressed the Commission. Security questions were also encompassed in discussions of a task force report on 'Science and Technology in Trilateral Relations', although here the main focus was on the development of a Trilateral regime for managing the diffusion of high technology and scientific knowledge, with the stress on moving away from military definitions of the question, and towards Trilateral co-operation and collaboration.

Earlier, at the 1984 plenary in Washington, there had been discussions on Latin America. European and American differences again came to the fore, following publication of a special edition of *Trialogue* in March 1984, *Sovereignty and Intervention*, in the wake of the invasion of Grenada. The question of intervention, as the editor of the journal observed, 'tests our very conceptions of political order and international life'. Commissioner Richard Gardner stated that the invasion had resulted in the 'unprecedented isolation of the United States from its allies', noting that Trilateral countries failed to support the United States and the United Nations because they 'disbelieved the US version of events [which was] a commentary on the state of trust and confidence between countries that are supposed to be allies and close friends'.[25] Mario Vargas Llosa, the Peruvian novelist, stated that apart from the invasion of Grenada being an obvious violation of international law, it held ominous political consequences for Washington as well as for the cause of democracy throughout Latin America.[26] The Commission debated the Kissinger Commission report on Central America, with Europeans stressing it could not erase decades of 'erratic' American policy in the region. An Italian member noted that American reaction during the Falklands crisis (vacillating between support for Argentina and Britain) 'Will have long-standing effects and has created an enormous amount of ill-will toward American partisanship towards the British case'. He then itemised persistent American support for 'the most odious dictatorships in the name of security policy'.[27] Latin American issues were also discussed at the 1987 plenary in San Francisco, with Vargas Llosa, Enrique Iglesias (Uruguayan Foreign Minister) and Marcilio Marques Moreira (Brazilian Ambassador to the United States) giving presentations. A task force report, *Restoring Growth in a Debt-Laden Third World*, also emphasised Latin America, although here the issue was treated mainly from the point of view of Trilateral economists and bankers.

THE INTERNATIONAL ECONOMY IN THE LATE 1970S AND 1980S

Economic issues addressed in debates since 1979 concerned international financial instability, gyrations in exchange rates and capital flows, recession and unemployment trends, trade, North–South relations and the debt crisis. Particularly at issue were the global costs and benefits of Reagan's economic policies. Also of concern was the question of uneven economic development and its long-term implications for the Trilateral alliance. In this context, the relationship between economics, security, science and technology, in 1987, had substantial significance.

It is clear that Commission members prefer expansionary economic conditions, and fear the consequences of protracted recession for political stability, in Trilateral and especially in indebted developing nations whose governments were forced to cut living standards to pay foreign debts. Wider fears, at the level of the world economy are also seen in continual allusions in Commission literature to the potential for a return to conditions akin to those of the 1930s. Anxiety was also evinced at the long-term political consequences of continued European economic stagnation.

These concerns were also reflected in the Commission's consistent stress on the need for an internationalised political process so that market interactions were more orderly and stable. This theme was evident throughout its debates, although American conservatives favoured the market-oriented approach rather more strongly than European social democrats. Nonetheless, there was a convergence in orientations towards economic strategy among the Trilateral countries in the mid-1980s, after the initial domesticist, *laissez-faire* approach of the first Reagan administration (see the Volcker speech cited in chapter 5). American policies became closer to those favoured by the Commission. Japan continued to liberalise its domestic economic structure in ways congruent with prevailing Commission ideas.

Indeed, the Commission took a lead on a number of economic questions in the 1980s, advocating the changes in IMF and World Bank funding later made by Reagan, and pushing heavily for realignment of exchange rates. Thus, whilst the American security complex apparently determined many of the questions on the Commission's security agenda, in the economic sphere the Commission was at the heart of a range of forces which led the way in reversing the tide of the Reagan revolution. Where Commissioners had less impact was on the massive American budget deficits, which productive sectors of capital, most allied governments and the Third World leaders had all criticised.

Let us now review the evolution of the economic debates. Discussions at Tokyo, 22–4 April 1979, centred on payments imbalances and international financial stability, against the backdrop of rising oil prices and a growing crisis of confidence in American economic policy. Fierce criticism of American economic policies here may have had some effect on the American decision to change course, although the market's lack of confidence was the crucial factor. The shift in policy involved the use of monetary aggregates, allowing interest rates to fluctuate freely. These measures were widely acknowledged to represent a revolution in American economic policy. As Calleo notes, the onset of the decade of the 1980s was accompanied by turmoil in the markets, and a threat of a 'catastrophic liquidation of the dollar's role as a reserve currency'.[28]

The other key change was in the oil market, where between December 1978 and April 1979, dollar prices of oil rose by 120 per cent, the first significant increase in real price since 1974. This helped to fuel inflation and increased the length of a recession which Federal Reserve Chairman Volcker had apparently intended to be a short, sharp, purgative shock to defeat inflation in the United States. As a result, a Commission report, written in early 1979, was rendered rapidly obsolete and never published. This illustrates the power of the market to defy the analysis and anticipations of even the most informed economists.[29] Noteworthy here, however, was that the Commission welcomed Japan's reaction to the recession. Japan moved to liberalise its exchange markets, rather than through the export-oriented strategy of the first oil shock, when it effectively shifted the burden of adjustment onto other countries (see chapter 9 for more detail).

Commissioners were alerted to the dangers of Reagan economic strategy *vis-à-vis* the Third World at the 1981 Cancun summit. In 1981 the Commission published a special issue of *Trialogue* on these issues, and launched a task force study (No. 27). This report was seen as building on the work of the Brandt Commission. Overall, the Commission endorsed the view that renewed growth and liberalisation of Trilateral markets was crucial to the possibilities of long-term development. However, it stressed that a market oriented approach could not, in itself, solve the problems of the poorer countries. This was a direct criticism of the Reagan policies of the time.

On 4–6 April 1982, the plenary was in Tokyo, with over 200 members and guests in attendance. The shadow of world recession and rising unemployment was cast over the conference, and debate raged on the implications of the rising American budget deficits, which were roundly criticised. However, inflation in the OECD area was falling, and in late 1982 there was an easing in American monetary policy, so that 1982–3 was a period of transition from severe recession to slow expansion. At the plenary, members were warned of the possibility of an intensification of the debt crisis by Adam Malik, the Vice-President of Indonesia. The recession was interpreted as contributing to political problems between the allies. Brzezinski stated that there was a risk of 'fracture' in the well-established forms of political and economic cooperation. He stressed that problems of some newly-industrial countries and oil producers be moved to the centre of the political agenda. The current oil glut was dangerous, since it was provoking serious political and social instabilities. There was a mounting 'liquidity crunch' in several 'key countries' 'with all sorts of unpredictable consequences'.[30] Retrospectively, a Commission report stated that the:

> Reagan Administration was forced by the Mexican crisis of August 1982 to abandon its 'benign neglect' of the Third World Debt problem, and of the IMF. It subsequently maintained a basically cooperative mode *on those issues*, but this cooperation did not spill over into the macro/monetary field until a crisis loomed *in that area* in 1985.[31]

The Rome plenary was held during 17–19 April 1983. The most important economic event of 1983 was the mild recovery (many professional economists had been predicting such an upturn since 1980). The expansion was partly linked to changes in economic policy. In many OECD countries (notably the United States and Japan), restrictive monetary policies were eased, and this, combined with the United States expansive military Keynesianism, helped fuel an OECD growth rate of 2 per cent. In the United States, unemployment fell from its late 1982 peak of 11 per cent to 8.2 per cent, but rose in Europe to almost 11 per cent, and in Japan from 2.4 to 2.7 per cent. The European Community concluded an agreement with Japan to protect its crisis-hit industries. Real interest rates were at unprecedentedly high levels for this stage in a recovery, whilst profits rose dramatically. The American dollar continued to appreciate, and the American trade deficit reached US$ 70 billion.[32] The high interest rates were interpreted by many Europeans as undermining the possibilities of a Euro-recovery. This prompted a session at the next plenary on 'Living with the United States'.

The Commission endorsed the IMF's case-by-case approach to the debt crisis (it called this the '1983 strategy') which involved a wide network of banking interests led by the Fund. Banks provided new lending as a *quid pro quo* for stringent performance requirements, that is, under Fund conditionality. The assumption was that a combination of austerity and improving world economic conditions would improve the creditworthiness of debtors, and allow voluntary lending to be resumed by private banks. This process involved a reversal of the traditional relationship between the Fund and the banks: whereas previously the IMF had given its imprimatur to induce banks to co-operate, the new agreements 'stipulated that the provision of its facility was contingent on satisfactory bank participation'. In addition, the *Williamsburg [Summit] Declaration on Economic Recovery*, issued on 30 May 1983, emphasised the need for co-ordinated domestic and international economic policies, and 'provided a strong endorsement of the new classical economics', stressing that the way to promote recovery (and thus help to solve the debt crisis) was through reduction in structural budget deficits.[33] The vehicle of the Group of Five (G5) capitalist nations (the United States, Japan, West Germany, Britain and France, plus the managing director of the IMF) became an important means of moving towards convergent economic patterns. This indicated the growing importance of the IMF and of finance ministries in what the Commission calls a 'vital core' of key states, that is for setting the agenda for international economic strategy. This can be interpreted as a part of the wider process of the transnationalisation of the state.

In Rome, apart from a speech by Paul Volcker (soon reappointed Chairman of the Federal Reserve), the Commission had reports on progress of the GATT. Edmund Wellenstein argued that the GATT Ministerial Meeting of 29 November 1982 'contributed to pushing national policies in the right direction, away from short-term, shortsighted, beggar-thy-neighbour actions'. This was all the more remarkable since world trade was in its second year of contraction, falling in 1982 by over US$ 100 billion.[34] The Commission also discussed their development task force report (No. 27) which criticised the United States for failing to reinforce the World Bank and other development agencies and for using aid and trade policies almost entirely for strategic and political objectives.

The 1983–5 period saw both economic growth in North America and Japan. There was an intensification of Commission activity, with more frequent meetings urgently focused on the management of the world economy. When the Commission convened once again on 1–3 April 1984, in Washington DC, it registered its highest ever attendance. There was the usual reception at the White House with the President, Vice-President and their spouses, but on this occasion news coverage was prohibited, so as not to inflame the Reaganite right. Special sessions were held on the American economic and political scene in the election year. Here the discussion suggested that Walter Mondale was out of tune with what Daniel Yankelovitch called the new *zeitgeist* of forward-looking possessive individualism. Reagan and the other Democratic front runner, Senator Gary Hart of Colorado, were more in harmony with it. A Reagan electoral victory was predicted.[35] Other speakers noted the shift in the political consensus on economic policy in the United States towards a more 'new classical' or monetarist stance. Further criticism of the budget deficits was made. It was widely held that the dollar was too high, was fuelling the American trade deficit, consolidating protectionist tendencies in the American labour movement and in Congress. The session on 'Living with the United States' revealed continuing differences over American economic policy, and worries on the part of the Europeans over the implications of the SDI. This was followed by a seminar on the international financial situation led by Jacques de Larosière (Managing Director of the IMF) and Jesus Silva-Herzog (Mexican Minister of Finance).

The main topic in 1984 was, however, the long-term implications of changes in the economic relationship between the Trilateral countries. This followed a survey of the Trilateral countries in the international economy of the 1980s (No. 23). In the Owen *et al.* report, *Democracy Must Work*, there was a recommendation that Japan, in view of its massive surpluses, should make new multi-billion dollar commitments to security expenditures and to economic aid, and recommend that Japan should provide all the US$ 3 billion then needed to replenish the World Bank's aid programme (the shortfall was because the United States had limited its contributions by the same amount). These recommendations built on earlier calls for a unilateral Japanese initiative in *Sharing International Responsibilities*. *Democracy Must Work* painted a grim picture of economic and political disarray among Trilateral countries, and urged Japan to export more capital, particularly to Europe to help regenerate its sagging economy. Implied at the meetings was that, if Japan failed to respond, it would undoubtedly face an increase in protectionist measures. The boldest demand was that Japan should take over part of the United States's global defence burden. This was significant because the influential Saburo Okita was one of the three co-authors of the report, so widespread consultations with Japanese leaders had undoubtedly been made prior to publication. Proposals were made for a 'six point package deal' which should be adopted at the 1984 London Summit. Summit partners were asked to agree to co-ordinate foreign exchange parities and create a 'flexible' system; Europe should increase its conventional defences; each should try to find an agreed approach to developing nation debts.[36] At this time, the United States's Cabinet level Trade Policy Committee, chaired by (former Commissioner) Special Trade Representative Bill Brock, was scheduled to meet and consider retaliatory steps if Japan refused to liberalise import quotas on American agricultural products.

The Commission held a special seminar in New York in late May 1984, on 'Europe's Future', which discussed the most problematic part of the *Democracy Must Work* report, that of 'Europessimism', namely the relative decline in West European economic and technological performance. Speakers included former Secretary of State Alexander Haig; Horst Schulman, Chancellor Schmidt's representative at the seven-power summits; Michael Howard, Regius Professor of Modern History, Oxford University; and Etienne Davignon, Vice-President of the European Commission. Davignon stated that there was a 'new consensus' maturing in Europe, along the lines of 'decreased state involvement and a return to more flexibility'.[37] It was pointed out that the theme of Europe's decline was not new, and its political stability amid very high levels of unemployment was remarkable. This suggested that Europe's long-term prospects were, in fact, hopeful. Indeed, a theme of 'Euro-optimism' was emphasised in the 1987 task force study on Science and Technology, where it was argued that European potential was considerable, especially in fundamental research. Also, its initiatives in more applied areas would begin to bear considerable fruit, especially after 1992, when the unification of the European Community's internal market would be completed.

In February 1985, in New York, the North America section of the Commission met to discuss the 'huge and growing trade imbalance' between Japan and the United States, and associated economic issues. Remarks were made by Yusuke Kashiwagi, Chairman of Bank of Tokyo. He stated that in 1984 Japan had taken steps to liberalise capital markets, to moderate its external surplus by promoting increased capital outflows and to allow the yen to be used more freely as an international currency. These measures fell considerably short of American demands, although they bore the hallmark of gradual progress in terms of the internationalisation of the Japanese economy. Moreover, the changes were underpinned by a broad domestic political consensus, including the Japan Socialist Party.[38] Japanese measures were part of a growing Trilateral consensus on the need for more co-ordination in the exchange and capital markets, for a more growth-oriented strategy, to reverse stagnation in Europe and deal with the debt crisis. This consensus was reflected in the September 1985 Plaza Agreement. It had emerged at the Commission's 21–3 April 1985 Tokyo plenary.

After a reception at the Prime Minister's official residence, Nakasone held a private meeting with the Commission Chairmen. They discussed trade frictions, the world economy and the SDI. In addition, Commissioners considered two new task force reports on *Agricultural Policy and Trade* (No. 29), and *East Asian Security* (No. 30). The Commission heard a speech by Martin Feldstein (Chairman, Council of Economic Advisors 1982–4, and Reagan's chief economic advisor), on 'American Economic Policy and the World Economy', held a special session on the 'Soviet Challenge', and debated the theme of 'East Asia in Transition'. Reflecting the new consensus in Japan, Kiichi Miyazawa spoke on the need to expand the Japanese economy and moderate Japan's export surplus. Commissioners heard from Haruo Maekawa (outgoing Governor of the Bank of Japan) on Japan's financial liberalisation. The Commission Chairmen publicly recommended a series of measures for the world economy, including the need for the Trilateral governments to:

> Engage in more intensive discussion of international monetary imbalances, notably misalignments and excessive fluctuations of exchange rates. Meetings at an appropriate level can lead the way to a thorough reassessment of the principles underlying the international monetary system.[39]

The Commission held a follow up dinner, in June 1985, in New York, focused on international economic issues, and heard an address by former French President Giscard d'Estaing. In July 1985, the

Japanese held a consultative meeting on the same questions, led by Isamu Miyazaki, and discussed the new Commission study, *Conditions for Partnership in International Economic Management*. On 25–7 October 1985, in Paris, the European members convened to discuss Davignon's contribution to the report. This was followed by another special North American meeting, held on 13–14 November 1985, in Washington DC, discussing economic and security strategy, with presentations from Senator Sam Nunn (co-sponsor of the Nunn–Roth Amendment on Conventional Forces in NATO) on 'Security Strategy', and Paul A. Volcker on economic questions (see chapter 5). Nunn's speech was delivered against the backdrop of European and Japanese misgivings about the wisdom of SDI, and anxiety at the lack of progress on arms control.

The 1986 plenary was held on 17–19 May in Madrid, to pay tribute to the emergence of liberal democracy in Spain, and the entry of Spain into the European Community and NATO. The members met King Juan Carlos and Prime Minister Filipe Gonzalez. A Japanese business delegation to Spain preceded the plenary. They discussed the politically charged issue of agricultural trade, the future of economic relations with the Soviet Union and held extensive deliberations on international economic management. The members heard speeches by Arthur Dunkell, Director-General of GATT, on agricultural and other trade subsidies, and by Thomas Enders, United States Ambassador to Spain, attacking the European Community for undermining the interests of American grain producers. Also discussed was African development. A particular focus of the Madrid debates was the progress of economic liberalisation in Japan. Commissioners discussed the 1986 Maekawa Report, said to make a 'historic shift' in Japanese policies towards ever-greater economic openness.

In 1987, in San Francisco, reflecting renewed emphasis on growth-oriented economic policies, the Commission heard from Michel Camdessus, Managing Director of the IMF, and returned to the issue of unemployment/employment trends and their implications. Commissioners heard speeches by Heinz Klunckner (ex-President of West Germany's second largest union, the Public Services and Transport Workers'), Lester Thurow (Professor of Management at MIT) and Ginko Sato (Director-General of the Women and Minors Bureau, Japan Ministry of Labour). Viravan Amnuay (Chairman of Bangkok Bank) outlined prospects for the Asia/Pacific economy. The Commission also discussed Third World indebtedness, in the form of a detailed debate around a high-powered task force study co-authored by Martin Feldstein (by then Professor of Economics at Harvard)

Hervé de Carmoy (Director and Chief Executive, Midland Bank International), Koei Narusawa (economic advisor to the President of the Bank of Japan) and Paul Krugman (Professor of International Economics at MIT). This was called *Restoring Growth in a Debt-Laden Third World*. The preparation of this report involved consultations with almost a hundred Trilateral experts from government, academia, business and the financial media. Consultations involved over thirty top international bankers. The emphasis in the report was again on growth-oriented policies, so as to provide the long-term conditions for resolving the debt problem.

The final issue, one of the first importance for the long term, discussed in 1987, was international aspects of science and technology. I have no information about the debates, so here I summarise the content of the draft task force report, presented by a team led from the Tokyo office and including Harold Brown, the former American Secretary of Defense. Here it was pointed out that scientific endeavour was inherently a universal activity, with progress and innovation the result of complex interactive and reiterative processes across national boundaries and scientific disciplines. However, regulations were made from a national perspective. This inhibited scientific advance and retarded growth in global welfare, created trade and other frictions, and skewed scientific research in a military direction.[40] Political and economic factors had led to a neglect of ecological and environmental concerns, most of which could only be resolved through international co-operation.[41]

The report argued that there were two main dangers to be avoided: narrowly nationalistic and sector-specific industrial policies.[42] It proposed that each Trilateral country should contribute to a pool of fundamental research, the fruits of which should be openly exchanged. Second, it stated that trade in proprietary technical knowledge should be governed by market principles (except where there were clearly defined national security considerations or when significant 'economic disruption' was likely). Third, it advocated establishment of an 'effective international legal regime', with basic standards and procedures to be incorporated into the GATT Uruguay Round. Fourth, it suggested Trilateral governments should reduce barriers to 'transnational business relationships' (for example, joint ventures, partnerships, wholly-owned subsidiaries). Fifth, governments should not discriminate against firms on grounds of 'nationality of ownership'. Sixth, national regulatory systems should be transparent and 'fully disclosed'. Seventh, national systems should be harmonised to allow for potential economies of scale. Recognising the clash between intensifying international competition and national security considerations, the report argued that freer flows of knowledge and technology between Trilateral countries would both increase economic growth and enhance security. Too wide-ranging an application of COCOM restrictions was divisive. Only those dual-use technologies which could be shown to be militarily essential to the Soviet Union and its allies should be restricted. The transfer of sophisticated military technology, or that with military potential (such as nuclear reactors) was a matter of 'international concern' and needed 'appropriate' safeguards. To co-ordinate security and economic considerations in these fields, the report advocated widening the remit of the OECD and NATO, involving Trilateral countries excluded from each on these issues.[43] It also suggested an evaluation of the potential of 'an international institute for science and technology policy'.[44]

THE TRILATERAL THEME 'PAR EXCELLENCE'

Let us now return to *Sharing International Responsibilities*, written in 1981–3, which the Commission described as the Trilateral theme *par excéllence*. There were three main purposes for the report: to set an agenda for the 1980s; to advance the process of the internationalisation of Japan, by involving Japan in a comprehensive political framework; and to moderate Reagan's unilateralist policies.

The report was by Nobuhiko Ushiba, Graham Allison and Thiérry de Montbrial, respectively, a diplomat, a political scientist and an economist. The authors were assisted by six special consultants, and thirty-four others, seven of whom were members of the Harvard programme on American–Japanese relations. Very few West Europeans were involved. By contrast, for *Trilateral Security*, and *East Asian Security*, which concentrated more heavily on military matters, most theorists consulted were either American or West European, although the latter report was the only one written by a single author, who was Japanese (an experiment not repeated since it was felt that it 'exposed' the author in undesirable ways).

One of Reagan's policy goals in the early 1980s was to force a sizeable and swift increase in Japanese defence expenditures. One of the purposes of report No. 25 was to contain this pressure and allow for a reconsideration of Japan's global role under more politically acceptable conditions. Interviews with Commissioners indicate that this report was very successful in helping Japanese consensus to emerge. Thus many Japanese were involved. Only by building a strong body of domestic opinion could Japanese leaders contemplate

197

anything other than a rhetorical extension of their restricted politico-military role. Prior to this report, the Commission and other groups were working to nurture a corps of specialists equipped to theorise the practical consequences of such a change in Japan's role.[45] In the early 1970s, Japan lacked such theorists, something which continues to be a problem, especially with respect to articulating Japanese positions persuasively abroad. This has been referred to as the 'Okita Syndrome', namely that Saburo Okita is usually the only Japanese expert most foreign audiences have heard of. As a result he is beseiged with invitations to speak overseas, whereas the few others who could carry out such duties are much less in demand.

The report stated that forces outside the Trilateral regions threatened the international order of the 1980s more severely than at any time since 1945, with potentially catastrophic global consequences. The Trilateral countries – because their stakes were so high and their capacities so great – had a special responsibility to preserve the *status quo*. Underpinning the study were normative commitments to the liberty of the individual, representative government, the market economy, 'an international order that encourages efficiency and equity through specialization and trade', and 'an international political order based on national self-determination and evolution'. These words are very similar to those used in the Commission's first-ever public statement of purposes in Tokyo, 1973 (see chapter 7).

Four threats to international order were identified: neutralism and alliance cohesion; Soviet military power; the plight of the poorer nations and East–West confrontations in the Third World and the Middle East; and threats to the Trilateral countries' domestic ability to govern. The authors outlined concepts from public choice theory to clarify the issues connected with sharing responsibilities: 'the positive-sum game' of international trade; the Ricardian notion of comparative advantage; the concept of public goods; and the 'free rider' problem. The dominant message was the necessity for leadership groups in the Trilateral regions to agree on basic concepts, mobilise collective resources under agreed criteria, counter threats and achieve their normative commitments.

The authors analysed different attitudes and political trends in the Trilateral countries. Japan came out worst: it was most susceptible to accusations of 'free riding' in security and development areas, and to the charge that it had not accepted global responsibilities concomitant with its massive economic power. The Japanese worried more about economic than military threats. They were scapegoats for the economic decline of Europe. They were anxious about protectionist trends in the United States. They were concerned about possibly reckless American policy in the Middle East.

The authors identified American paternalism towards allies and the disproportionate burden it carried to maintain international order after 1945. It was clear that the United States now refused to 'pick up the tab' in the same way. Its attitude was becoming more narrowly self-interested as a result of changes in American domestic politics and increased consciousness of the outside world, partly linked to a novel 'experience of failure' in foreign policy. The net result was a sense of American decline. While Japan became moderately more globalist, the United States retreated towards nationalism and unilateralism. Many American theorists were beginning to view the world through strategic lenses, as they had in the 1950s and early 1960s. Detente had become a 'foreign' word and arms control ceased to be a centre-piece of America's strategy. Two distinct views had emerged: that of the Reagan administration which perceived threats primarily in terms of their Soviet dimensions; and the alternative (and dominant Trilateral Commission) view of threats as 'variegated challenges' in which the Soviet Union played an important but 'rarely decisive' role.

Looking at Europe the authors contrasted the promise of European union and laborious progress towards that end. National rivalry was played down in the account of causes for this delay, which were seen as primarily economic – the crisis of the 1970s and 1980s being held chiefly responsible. Europe's economic ills allowed less room for manoeuvre and increased its vulnerability to world economic conditions: a vulnerability far greater than that of the United States or Japan. The authors noted a 'lack of political leadership or coordination' at precisely the moment when the web of interdependence had become more tightly woven. This was the central contradiction in European politics. The report implied the need for more political discipline in order to meet Europe's external challenges – the theme of the 1975 report, *The Crisis of Democracy*. The enlargement of the European Community paradoxically made it more difficult to progress towards a politically unified Europe.

The authors emphasised different views of the Soviet threat which had emerged after Afghanistan. Western Europe relied more heavily on East–West trade, more so in a period of economic crisis. This resulted in a tendency to placate the Soviets. The United States, with much smaller risks in such trade, was more likely to be confrontationist and unilaterally to impose its positions on Western Europe, as in the Siberian pipeline sanctions. Europeans inclined to argue that the Soviet system was in difficulties while Americans stressed the increasing Soviet military threat. The two positions were very far apart. Europeans were alarmed at Reagan's tendency to see a Soviet hand behind crises and instabilities throughout the Third World. The report stated that differences might lead to a danger of 'decoupling' Europe and the United States, a perennial theme in the literature on Atlantic relations for the last twenty years.[46]

European views on Japan were similar to those held in the United States except that they were founded, according to the authors, on a more fundamental ignorance. Japan's economic penetration of Europe was feared and there was concern that strengthening American–Japanese ties might be at the expense of Europe. Japan was not generally seen as a 'natural ally'. However, no concern was expressed at a possible resurgence of Japanese militarism. More worrying, it seems, to France and Britain in particular, was that the growth of the arms industry in Japan (though it might enhance Trilateral security overall) could mean a loss of their arms markets (as inevitably the Japanese would compete successfully). The Euro-Japanese flank of Trilateralism contained little sense of mutual solidarity except among a select few.

The picture painted of the state of Trilateral relations in the early 1980s is thus close to that which emerges from scrutiny of Commission debates and meetings: one of strain, stress and diverging perceptions of interest and threat. Turning to the future, the report did not attempt to prescribe formulas but sought to point out key threats to the Trilateral countries and give guidelines for an allied division of labour in the areas of: international economic management; the Soviet threat; and North–South relations. With respect to the first set of issues, the authors argued vigorously for the defence of the liberal trading system, strengthening the GATT, including services, investments and intra-firm trading, and declared that the GATT and OECD should be more active in monitoring trade. They repeated consistent calls for more frequent consultation and coordination of macroeconomic policy. Further, they demanded a 'major Japanese initiative'. Japan should take 'unilateral steps to open its market' to head off protectionist pressures in Congress and the European Community.

Their consideration of the 'conceptual basis' for diagnosis of East–West relations led to a prescription for world strategic summits (based on intensive staff-level consultations). These would hammer out differences, build a common conceptual framework and optimise the alliance's military stance. Military policy itself should continue to 'couple' Europe and the United States in 'the strategic, political and psychological sense', increase NATO's conventional capacities, complicate Soviet calculations through the enhancement of individual nations' self-defence forces and develop co-ordinated approaches to political and security issues in the Middle East.

To cope with potential challenges from the South, the report argued that demands for a New International Economic Order should be taken seriously and steps should be taken to integrate newly industrialising nations into the international order, by engaging Third World nations more actively in international economic institutions. The Trilateral countries should open their markets to Third World imports and substantially increase the flow of aid – Britain, Japan and United States were singled out for criticism on this last issue. On the political front the model of the Contact Group on Namibia was cited as justifying more involvement from 'indigenous groups' to produce solutions to Third World political conflicts where Trilateral countries had vital interests. The proliferation of nuclear weapons should be avoided, although the report argued for the 'peaceful diffusion' of nuclear technologies to the Third World, an issue which caused major divisions amongst the Trilateral countries in the 1970s. This last point reflected a victory, at least in the Commission, for the positions of Japan and Western Europe.

A HIGHER GOAL: GLOBAL COMMUNITY OR THE WITHERING AWAY OF COMMUNISM?

The aim of fostering a practical Trilateral consensus is a very difficult, sometimes impossible, objective. However, international conferences such as the Commission, the Pugwash Conferences (which includes scientists and the Soviet elite), and Bilderberg are bound up with the emergence of a wider international establishment. The significance of this is often underrated or completely ignored in the international relations literature. The Commission appears to serve as a gyroscopic force in allied relations and, perhaps, a moderating influence on the unilateralism of the United States. It is also a consciousness-raising institution. As we will see in chapter 9, it has been important in influencing the outlook of Japanese and other leaders in a more 'internationalist' direction and for encouraging economic liberalisation in Japan. In this regard, the Commission's influence appears have been greatest on economic, rather than security questions, although there were signs, in the 1980s, of a major change in strategic thinking in Japan, as well as a move away from Cold War policies of all-out military build up in the United States. Both of these shifts have been endorsed in the Commission (as well as, of course, by many others in various forums).

Moreover, it is crucial to acknowledge that the Commission has focused the attention of its members on longer-term questions, not always from a narrowly materialist and self-interested perspective. This is reflected in recent development reports, as well as work on global science and technology. This contains international proposals for monitoring ecological threats, sharing scientific data (involving better access for developing nations) and a shift away from emphasis on military research and development, especially in the United States.

In conclusion it is important not to overstate the divisions within the ranks of the Commission. Whereas there are considerable differences manifested in the approach to a range of specific problems, there is a bedrock of shared assumptions which give coherence to the Commission enterprise, reflected, for example, in the science and technology proposals. These were consistent with others in the fields of trade and capital flows, calling for general measures with a high degree of transparency, geared towards the salience of transnational forces, with an emphasis on benefits to be reaped from economies of scale in a globally integrated high-technology marketplace. These assumptions to a large extent reflect the interests and world-view of dynamic, internationally mobile forms of capital, as well as internationalist elements within the establishments and state bureaucracies of the major capitalist states. The fact that there are often frictions within these ranks is to be expected: contemporary international relations are configured by a dialectic between conflict and co-operation.

The issue of interests provokes the deeper question: how does the Commission see the long-term goal of its efforts? The Commission is committed to a stable structure of world order which would promote, amongst other goals, the internationalisation and expansion of capitalism. It has advocated certain universalist values, such as the integrity of scientific research, commitment to global economic welfare and the preservation of the ecosystem (though not global equality). What are the ends of such lofty principles? Certainly they are not the ones desired by Engels or Lenin. In a phrase which echoed Hartley's metaphorical inversion of Marx (see chapter 6), the authors of *Democracy Must Work* state that their study was part of a wider goal to 'devise a global system where the communist philosophy withers and has no new converts'.[47]

9 HEGEMONY, KNOWLEDGE AND THE LIMITS OF INTERNATIONALISM

There are four sets of questions which need to be answered in this conclusion. The first three relate to the levels of analysis outlined in chapter 1. The fourth relates to the role of ideas, ideologies and knowledge in the study of political economy. What are these questions?

First, has American hegemony relatively declined, and does hegemonic decline have the implications for international economic order suggested in the neo-realist/liberal theory of hegemonic stability? Second, to what extent is America affected by transformations in the political economy, especially the process of transnationalisation? That is, what is the relationship between American and transnational hegemony? Third, what have been the American (and Japanese) responses to these changes, and how do these relate to the agendas and debates in the Trilateral Commission? Fourth, what does the role of the Commission tell us about the importance of ideological apparatuses in the constitution of international relations? In the final section I relate the substance of this study to criteria for the evaluation of different approaches in political economy which are noted in chapter 1: scope, consistency and reflexivity.

CHANGES IN AMERICAN HEGEMONY

There have been substantial changes in the international distribution of material power since 1945. These changes, if understood in inter-state terms, have led to a shift away from a bipolar towards a more multipolar world. There has been a diffusion of economic and military capacities, in relative terms away from the United States and in favour of its key allies in Western Europe and Japan (particularly in the economic sphere) and the Soviet Union (particularly in the military sphere). Thus, American hegemony, defined in terms of the power of one state relative to others, may have declined, although my argument emphasises that the United States has managed to sustain much of its relative power and structural dominance in an impressive way. However, most arguments concerning the consequences of such changes have misinterpreted their implications for the contemporary international economic order.

Realist and world systems theorists discussed in chapters 2, 3 and 4 have argued that, by opting for a movement towards a liberal postwar international economy and rebuilding its allies through the export of capital, the United States was, like the aged King Lear, creating the conditions for the breakup of its empire (and for the re-emergence of mercantilist economic blocs). Whereas Lear lost the appetite for power and rule, clearly this is not true for American leaders. The realist analogy to the tragedy is perhaps correct in one respect: of the King's daughters, Japan tended to behave like the ungrateful daughters Goneril and Regan, taking advantage of American generosity: the Japanese mercantilist state banished the King's corporations from their lands. While the Western European states can hardly be compared to the chaste and good Cordelia (who despite being wronged by her father, continued to show him compassion), they largely welcomed the King's corporations. The argument even holds for France, despite its Gaullist challenges to American hegemony. Moreover, Japan became more willing to share the burdens of empire with the United States and moved gradually to liberalise its economy. This has remained true even for the European Community. Although the United States has frequently been unhappy about the Common Agricultural Policy, this appears to be the exception rather than the rule. Recent American anxieties concerning the form that the consolidation of the European internal market might take after 1992 have resulted in a series of moves to preempt any strong Euro-protectionist tendencies which would work against major American interests: the US–Canada Free Trade Agreement and the strengthening of the powers of the President in foreign economic policy in the 1988 Trade Act are examples of this.

The military change concerns the loss of American primacy relative to its key rival, the Soviet Union. More broadly, there has been a global diffusion of military power, such that the use of military intervention to achieve economic and political ends by the major powers is more problematic. In the 1980s, it proved more difficult for the United States to justify foreign intervention, because of the so-called 'Vietnam syndrome'. This continues to be the case despite Grenada and the bombing of Tripoli. On the other hand, it may transpire, that Afghanistan has similar effects on Soviet attitudes to those resulting from

Vietnam for Americans. It is also worth emphasising that Soviet interventionism (and general military capability) has never been as 'global' as that of the United States. The United States has in place the Rapid Deployment Force should it need to mount a significant intervention in the Middle East or elsewhere. The Soviet Union is, of course, still very strong in Europe, but is totally overshadowed by the United States in the Americas and to a lesser, though still significant extent, in the Pacific.

It is easy to overestimate the relative decline in United States military power, especially if alliances are taken into consideration. The collective capacities of NATO plus Japan are much greater than those of the Warsaw Pact. The fact of China's long-standing antagonism towards the Soviet Union, and its desire to act as an independent military force in Asia seriously undermines the Soviet military posture (and explains President Gorbachev's attempts at Sino-Soviet *rapprochement*). Moreover, the United States and its allies probably have better weapons than the Soviet Union (see chapter 4). In addition, between 1978–86 the United States showed a formidable capacity to rearm and develop exotic new generations of weapons. This put the Soviet Union on the defensive, raising Soviet fears of a widening of the American–Soviet technology gap (also a worry for many of the NATO allies in Europe). Now there is a much closer strategic relationship between the United States and Japan. If Japan becomes militarily stronger during the 1990s this will be largely at the expense of the Soviet Union, in favour of the United States. On the other hand, the Reagan rearmament was accompanied by massive budget deficits with much of the increased expenditures indirectly paid for by foreign purchasers of American government bonds (especially by Japanese). The limits to the sustained growth of such expenditures appeared to be reached by 1986.

By the same token, the Soviet Union's economic performance was lacklustre and perhaps even more significant constraints may apply to the future development of Soviet military power, than to that of the United States. Indeed, it may be argued that the Soviet Union and its Warsaw Pact allies have begun to experience a substantial structural crisis of their planned economic systems. This crisis is much more fundamental than that experienced by the major capitalist states of the West. This is because of the constraints and limits imposed by the social structure of accumulation of existing socialism.[1] In the 1980s, this crisis was placing significant constraints on the capacity of the Warsaw Pact to mobilise increases in resources for military purposes.

In aggregate economic terms, moreover, the United States vastly overshadows its Soviet rival, enabling it, because of its massive GNP base, to undertake significant research and development programmes and develop its military-industrial structure in a dynamic way. The combined GNP and technological capacities of the United States and its allies massively outweigh those of the Warsaw Pact, Vietnam and Cuba. Nor, indeed, do any of its major allies appear to wish to relinquish American military leadership. The sheer size of American GNP also allows the United States to have much more influence in the Third World than does the Soviet Union through aid programmes. The Soviet Union, particularly after the Polish crisis, did not have a great deal of surplus for foreign aid, and it is difficult to imagine that it could afford another Cuba. A crucial weakness for the Soviet Union here is not only its own structural economic crisis (which the reforms proposed by Gorbachev are designed to redress), but also a related secular decline in the appeal of the Soviet model of development in the Third World. This is partly because it has virtually given up on aid provision, except for favoured client states (the Soviet Union also lost considerable Third World support after it invaded Afghanistan). The United States, whilst providing the bulk of its aid to Egypt and Israel for strategic purposes, is still able to give, in absolute terms, much more freely and thereby consolidate its international position.

On a wider plane, the global spread of consumer culture, allied to international pressure on Third World states (and indeed some of the communist states of Eastern Europe) to liberalise their economies assists the spread of transnational business and helps develop new markets (see chapter 5). Here the role of the giant American communications industry is of global significance in terms of the transmission of values which underpin and might serve to develop American and capitalist hegemony. A recent study indicates that 75 per cent of the world communications market is controlled by 80 transnationals. The bulk of such transnationals are American, followed by British and French corporations. In the Third World these firms introduce value patterns native to the metropolitan capitalist states, especially American ones. Such values are embedded in the interpretation and representation of news, in soap operas, crime series, and mass advertising. Of the fifty largest advertising agencies in 1977, thirty-six were American owned, accounting for 81.5 per cent of the revenues of the top fifty. Whereas Western TV has about 5 per cent of air time taken by advertising, advertisers on Third World broadcasting have 12 per cent of air time. The messages carried are of two types, informative and persuasive. These latter contribute to the definition of basic needs and orient cultures towards the American model. Cees Hamelink, of the Institute of Social Studies in the Hague, has argued that because of this, a process of cultural synchronisation is taking place in much of the Third World, around the axiomatic values of possessive individualism and consumerism.[2] The 1990s are likely to witness the growing dominance of international broadcasting by transnational firms given the vast costs of new technologies and systems (such as satellites). This will increasingly involve transnational co-operative ventures between formerly separate national firms, as well as new conglomerates. Satellite technology is likely to enhance the international impact of transnational media companies, in the short run in the 'core' nations, and in the longer-term, world wide. These developments are likely to further undermine any comprehensive attempts to sustain the heretofore dominant pattern of national control of broadcasting, notably in the major capitalist nations.

In terms of its ideological and political struggle with the Soviet Union, the appeal of the United States is generally strengthened if such values and perhaps ideas favouring liberalism become more influential in other countries. However, in this regard the American position is clearly contradictory with respect to the link between capitalist values and human rights. In the 1970s and 1980s, some American conservatives, such as Kissinger and Jeanne Kirkpatrick, worried that human rights campaigns (which can be equated with attempts to universalise American liberal values) would undermine the position of the United States 'friends' in authoritarian countries and, by implication, American security and economic interests. Similar objections to American human rights policies towards the Soviet bloc were also voiced, since this might threaten superpower and transatlantic political relations.

Nonetheless, the spread of American cultural imperialism is facilitated by English (or 'American') as the main international language. Apart from corporate influence, it is cultivated by American schools and universities in other countries, by sponsorship of important foreign university programmes and think-tanks by the American government and the ubiquitous American private foundations. These initiatives promote study and research which tends to be congruent with the American vision of a 'liberal' world order. An example is the backing of social scientific research at the London School of Economics by American foundations since the 1930s. The intellectual networks within the Commission can be interpreted as part of this process, and can be linked to the promotion of a process of the synchronisation of concepts and values at the elite level (see chapter 7).[3]

What is more important for American international power is its relationships with its wealthiest allies. In this regard there may be a certain congruence between American cultural imperialism and bilateral relationships between the United States and allies. The development of capitalist liberal democracy in Japan and Western Europe since 1945, as well as the growing interpenetration of capital and production between them and the United States, has made them more 'organic' than 'tactical' American allies (see chapter 4). This liberal democratisation of Western Europe continued into the 1980s (although here the role of the United States was again ambiguous, for example in Greece and Spain). Nevertheless, each of the major West European countries, as well as Japan, defines its foreign policy positions, even on the question of an integrated Europe, primarily in terms of their effects on relations with the United States. Indeed, it can be said that the foreign relations of European states are stronger with the United States than with any of their European Community 'partners'. This is reflected in the way positions were defined in Trilateral Commission debates and was evident in responses of participants at the European–Japanese Hakone meeting in Munich in 1983, which did not include Americans (see chapter 8). Bilateral links may be cumulative, so that dominant ideas, institutions and material forces gradually become more congruent with those prevailing in the United States.

They may interact in a synergistic way, enlarging America's international power, and its capacity to bring about favourable international 'outcomes'. In some instances this can cut both ways for the United States, for example, the powerful Jewish lobby and Israel itself can be seen as major constraints on American policy in the Middle East. While other nations have attempted cultural imperialism (such as France and the Soviet Union), the United States is uniquely placed to expand on a global basis. One reason for this is America's capacity to attract and absorb people from overseas whilst sustaining a remarkable conformity on the basic principles of its way of life. This gives the United States tremendous power to communicate with other nations, whilst having little to fear from other cultures. This contrasts strongly with Japan and the Soviet Union.

What these observations concerning cultural imperialism underline is American centrality in the world economy. It also has controlling positions in key international economic organisations (notably the World Bank and IMF). Also, American corporations are generally the leading players on the world economic stage: in 1985, IBM (with a market value of about US$ 88 billion) was bigger than the Soviet foreign trade bank Vneshtorgbank (estimated at US$ 70 billion) and

Exxon (valued at US$ 44 billion) was more than half its size.[4] American companies still lead international business, although British, Japanese, West German and French transnationals have eroded American primacy. However, this is less than postwar changes in relative shares of world GNP of each of these nations might suggest.[5]

GLOBAL RESTRUCTURING AND THE STABILITY OF WORLD CAPITALISM

On the basis of evidence presented in chapters 5 and 7, we can suggest that cumulative global economic integration has produced, in terms of the international economic order, a quite different *dénouement* to that of Shakespeare's great tragedy. Whilst furies racked Lear's kingdom and fratricidal conflict tore it apart, the process of liberalisation launched by the United States has not been a self-destructive one. Instead of a collapse of a *liberal international economic order*, we are witnessing a transition towards a *transnational liberal economic order*. The political basis for this order lies in the way that economic integration has cumulatively tied together the economic and political interests of the major capitalist states and those of many developing nations, under American leadership (see chapters 5, 6 and 7). None of this suggests that such an alliance of interests and identities is without frictions and contradictions, some of which are American in origin.

At this point it is worth emphasising that some sceptics have suggested that there has been very little global restructuring since the 1960s, and that the capitalist world of the 1980s is undergoing stagnation rather than structural transformation. As David Gordon puts it, 'We are still witnessing the decay of the older order and not yet the inauguration of the new.'[6] By this he means a decline in the social structure or regime of accumulation which prevailed in the West in the 1950s and 1960s. In part, therefore, his argument accords with my position concerning the crisis of hegemony discussed in chapter 5. Where we differ is that I would argue that a significant structural transformation is now underway, one which might result in a necessarily incomplete, but nonetheless significant movement towards a transnational hegemony during coming decades. This is why the study of international organisations such as the Trilateral Commission is vital, since they provide insights into the way such a transition is theorised and debated by individuals who are associated with large scale transnational capital, and by liberal internationalist intellectuals and political leaders.

Gordon's position calls to mind Gramsci's famous comment, 'The old is dying, the new is struggling to be born – and in the state of interregnum there arise many morbid symptoms.' Such symptoms might include not only images of industrial decay, starvation, war and terrorism, but also what might be termed a near-revolution in the intellectual world, involving a shift away from (though not an abandonment of) the conviction of the older Enlightenment vocabularies with their optimism concerning progress and their certainty (and those of some of the established political parties) about what is wrong with the world. The 1980s has brought a ferment of intellectual deconstruction, doubt, and a level of exploration and contestability notably absent from the debates of the 1960s: in other words, the 1980s has a different tenor and intellectual complexion. This may lead to a phase of intellectual reconstruction in coming decades. To point out such changes is to suggest that there are limits to the economism which persists in much left-wing writing and to reemphasise the importance of a dialectical method for analysing social change. Gordon's approach to the question of global restructuring is typical of the Anglo-Saxon empiricist tendency in much New Left analysis, a tendency which often conflates qualitative and quantitative aspects of social change.

For example, Gordon's essay, published after the research for this book had been completed, argues that the level of the internationalisation of capital in the 1980s was roughly the same as that which prevailed before 1914. He then points out a pronounced tendency in the literature to exaggerate the degree to which there has emerged a globalisation of production and a new international division of labour. As such, the material evidence which is needed to argue that there has been global restructuring is, in his view, notable by its absence. However, whilst Gordon is correct in stating that such globalisation has not gone as far as is sometimes claimed (it has been mainly restricted to the OECD countries and a small number of newly industrialising countries) I would suggest that he provides a misleading interpretation of the trajectory of transnational social forces in the long term. For example, if one accepts that the political, military and economic integration of the OECD countries has developed in a relatively deep-seated and organic way, and if it can be demonstrated that transnational social and political forces are sufficiently entrenched in the wealthiest nations, then it can be claimed that these forces will configure the long-term political and economic pressures exerted on the developing countries, as well as on some communist states. An empirical task of this study has been to point out such tendencies.

My argument does not suggest that nationalist and 'planned socialist' social structures or regimes of accumulation are unimportant, or might be speedily overcome by transnational forces. Quite the contrary. These forces, as in the Japanese and American cases reconsidered in this conclusion, are bound up with an emerging global dialectic, whereby nationalist forces and associated historic blocs are engaged in a struggle with transnational forces and an emerging transnational historic bloc. One of the material elements linking transnational forces is a concentrated, but nonetheless crucial, pattern of cross-cutting investments, in an international economy which is much more institutionalised, integrated and massive than was the case in the early part of this century. This is supplemented by an emerging transnationalisation of the pattern of broadcasting and publishing. This struggle is, of course, taking place in the context of slower levels of economic growth than for much of the post-1945 period, and where, increasingly, concerns are being expressed over the degradation of the environment, levels of unemployment and the costs of global militarisation and fears concerning the likelihood of nuclear war.

What I am suggesting is that the issue of global restructuring needs to be interpreted in normative as well as material terms, and must address the crucial question of the relative political stability of the two phases or periods in question. At the heart of this is the question of quantitative versus qualitative aspects of explanation. Whilst, according to aggregative data, the capitalism of the early twentieth century might appear to have represented a high point of internationalism, it was nonetheless characterised by different social structures of accumulation which emerged in the international context of a world divided into imperial spheres of influence. Moreover, in the phase in question, the forms of consciousness which prevailed among the masses were significantly different to those which pertain today. This earlier phase of capitalist development was both domestically and internationally fragile (with two world wars and the intervening period of extreme instability as evidence of this).

In the 1980s, in the context of a world economy many times bigger in terms of its absolute size, no one would seriously argue that the system is completely stable or without contradictions (some of which I refer to below). However, it is based upon changing, but nonetheless relatively organic, sets of transnational social forces across and within the major capitalist states, whose international relations are now ordered and organised in comprehensive alliance structures. This has created a more complex intermeshing of interests, identities, and ideas, in part along the nationalist-internationalist dimensions. This is why developments in the media, education and in the intellectual world are of the first importance for our argument.

An implication is that any major setback to global capitalism in the 1990s or the early twenty-first century is unlikely to have the kind of repercussions witnessed between 1914 and 1939. My argument therefore suggests the likelihood of further moves towards globalisation in the coming decades, and that the 1980s may prove to be, in retrospect, a decisive decade in such a transition. Some aspects of this transition are discussed below.

TRANSNATIONALISATION AND INTERNATIONAL CO-OPERATION

The transnationalisation of production and exchange is a cumulative process, one which has gone through two major stages since 1945, and seems to be entering a third. The first 'European' stage followed postwar reconstruction and embraced the establishment of the European Community (1950s and 1960s). Here the major flows of overseas foreign investment were from the United States to Western Europe. This was followed by an 'American' stage, during the 1970s and accelerating in the 1980s. West European and Japanese capital invested more heavily in the United States. During this period, Japan generally resisted the liberalisation of its own economy and considerable barriers still exist for foreign capital trying to invest in the Japanese economy. However, gradual liberalisation began to occur after the mid-1970s. We may thus be about to witness a third, 'Japanese stage', as foreign investment rises in Japan.

Within these patterns American transnational corporations continued to expand. These firms came closer to maintaining their share in world markets, than the American economy to maintaining its share in world GNP. Nonetheless, non-American transnationals have grown in size, strength and numbers, relative to American firms. This latter fact has not significantly altered the ability of the United States government to achieve certain of its desired outcomes (such as liberal economic policies, including an open door to foreign direct investment). The United States (and the Trilateral Commission) pressed, in the late 1980s, for further liberalisation of telecommunications and financial services. The prospect of American success in these moves is enhanced if one allows that the growth of transnationals makes for an increased congruence between internationalist interests in Trilateral countries. These trends are linked to the increasing importance of foreign direct investment within the United States, as foreign based corporations come to see access to the American market as increasingly crucial. By the late 1980s this was particularly the case for Japan, which needed a vent for its surplus savings. The transnationalisation process can be interpreted as having the effect of strengthening an emerging transnational historic bloc.

In view of the Japanese leadership's consensus expressed in the 1986 Maekawa Report, and given the massive revaluation of the yen since 1985, two things may well happen.[7] A rapid and unprecedented increase in Japanese foreign direct investment, especially in the United States and Latin America, is to be anticipated in the 1990s, whilst a liberalisation of domestic conditions may serve to increase the transnationalisation of the Japanese domestic economy. Second, since all major currencies appreciated by up to 50 per cent against the dollar since 1985, the surge in foreign direct investment from other nations into America should probably continue, particularly since the price of labour in the United States has become much more competitive in international terms. As was indicated in chapter 5, real wages for most workers in the United States have not risen for about twenty years. This perhaps explained why foreign investors continued to put their money into the American economy. The dollar's fall since 1985 failed to cause a wage-price spiral in the United States, partly because the American labour movement was in almost total disarray and American producers were subjected to stronger international competition.

The massive American budget deficits of the 1980s, coupled with the strong dollar, had the effect of delaying the transnationalisation of the Japanese economic structure: whilst the yen (and the deutschmark) were weak against the dollar, Japanese (and West German) corporations could still concentrate on export-led growth. Since the yen the deutschmark have appreciated in value it gave added meaning to the concept of economic interdependence as Japanese (and German) producers were impelled to become more transnational (this was also the case for sterling and British investments in America). In this context, the process of the internationalisation of the outlook of Japanese leaders in the Trilateral Commission took on extra and continuing significance.

It was also pointed out in chapter 5 that during 1979–82 the increase in the power of internationally mobile capital was accelerated. However, it was by no means clear that the key individual in what David Calleo called the 'revolution' in American economic policies, Paul Volcker, had anticipated these effects. This indicated the degree to which even the best-informed economic theoreticians and policy-

213

makers were working with imperfect knowledge of the 'brave new world' of global capitalism. The Reagan administration, which many suggested would be antipathetic to perspectives expressed in the Commission (that is a long-term view of transnational capital on economic questions) gradually moved its economic policies closer to those preferred by the bulk of Commission membership. The first sign of this was a shift in its stance on Third World debts after the Mexican crisis in 1982–3, followed by the Baker Initiatives of 1985.

The transnationalisation of production and exchange was associated with a huge increase in size and volatility of international capital movements. This explained why the part of the Baker Initiatives on exchange rate parities was undertaken. It also reflected the realisation that the mobility of capital has constrained and influenced the economic policies of governments. This meant that many governments were often forced to maintain high interest rates and, more generally, to offer incentives to induce capital investment (sometimes by imposition and/or threat of trade barriers). In this vein, attempts to reduce inflation in the 1970s and 1980s can be interpreted as a means of offering a more stable, and thus a more favourable investment climate for (foreign) capital. The *communiqué* issued after the G5 and G6 (G5 plus Italy) meetings in Paris on 24 February 1987, illustrated this, in so far as the restoration of higher employment was not mentioned on the list of priorities.

One major conclusion here is that a steering mechanism, within the confines of the wider process of the transnationalisation of the state, is necessary for containing some of the contradictions generated by the liberalisation of markets. Thus an internationalisation of the American economic policy-making process is a necessary condition for the emergence of a more politically developed transnational hegemony. The material basis for this is the rising power of transnational capital (discussed in chapter 5). This power led to certain undesirable consequences, such as the emergence of the debt crisis in the early 1980s. Thus a growing consensus of transnational capital emerged in the 1980s that market forces must be steered by an internationalised policy process, involving dominant elements of the civil societies of the major capitalist states. This implied more of the co-operation and collective management that developed in institutions like the IMF (acting as an 'ideal collective [transnational] capitalist') the seven-power summits and the G5. Moreover, such co-operation would need to encompass political aspects of international order, such as the question of East–West relations. In addition there would have to be a deepening of the world-wide appeal of market values amongst politically and economically significant groups across a range of countries. This would mean that nationalist-mercantilist institutional structures (particularly those opposed to foreign capital) and ideas would need to be undermined on a more comprehensive basis. It would also imply that organised labour would need to be further weakened or perhaps more comprehensively incorporated. Such changes are necessarily long term in nature.

These processes relate to the conditions for an emerging hegemony of large-scale internationally mobile capital. It was argued in chapter 5, and also in chapter 8, that the power of such capital had a cumulative character, transcending changes in the policies of different American administrations. This process was linked to the theme of a crisis of hegemony, in that the overall coherence of the international capitalist system, and the postwar hegemonic settlement between capital and labour have come under significant pressure since the 1970s, with the result that a reordering of political and economic relationships on a world scale was under way by the 1980s. This process is far from complete and is still countervailed by nationalist and mercantilist forces across a range of states (for example in their security complexes), as well as by a range of socialist and populist (such as agrarian) forces. Nonetheless, it appeared to be leading towards what I have called a *transnational liberal economic order*, although the time this might take is a matter for conjecture. As has been noted, these processes have even begun to affect the Soviet Union under Gorbachev. In this light the modernisation of Deng's China also has a wider international significance.

The processes of market liberalisation, however, are now widely perceived to contain contradictions which the transnationalisation of the state is designed to help overcome. As Susan Strange has argued, the sheer size and volatility of international capital and exchange flows can be profoundly destabilising, implying the need for political control. In the Trilateral Commission's general view, international markets need to be collectively managed by an internationalised political process, led by the United States and the major capitalist nations. The provision and maintenance of such an international steering mechanism requires continued international awareness and sensitivity on the part of the United States, as well as specific measures to reduce its budget deficit. The United States ability to reduce its deficit has been strongly circumscribed by a range of domestic political interests, notably its military-industrial complex, which points to a potential contradiction between the United States economic and security interests (and a clash between the realist concepts embodied in the military-industrial complex and transnational liberal concepts). Moreover, this line of argument indicates that economic co-operation between the Trilateral countries is not so much necessitated by a relative decline in American hegemony and the rise of Japan and Western Europe (although this is clearly important), as by a growth of transnationalisation and capital mobility.

A major conclusion to be drawn is that co-operation is potentially at its greatest where 'internationalist' coalitions of interest predominate in the civil societies of key capitalist states, and where there are congruent orientations on the part of the leaders of major state and international institutions. The early 'domesticist' orientation of the Reagan administration would thus be an example of a barrier to such co-operation. The Gramscian metaphor of the organic intellectual helps to capture the theoretical-practical activity which is central to the reconciliation of these sometimes contradictory processes of American and transnational hegemony. For the Trilateral Commission, this is inherently a political issue. For example, a recent Commission task force report on the debt crisis considered the possibility of a new, small agency to catalyse action, supplementing ('adding value' to) the World Bank and IMF, with sufficient resources to provide for the long-term solvency of debtor nations. This agency would comprise 'key, "action-oriented" officials, culled from both the public and private sectors . . . be temporary, with an automatic "self destruct" mechanism . . . constituted very carefully', so as to provide:

> Firstly . . . political momentum. The debt problem is a political issue and requires a political, as well as a technical response. Secondly, it should provide access to the highest echelons of government in the creditor countries, so that it could provide quick, decisive action. Thirdly, it should be fully representative of the present power sharing in the global economy so that Japan and Europe in particular would be given more weight. Fourthly, it should provide a wide socio-political embrace in the debtor countries. Fifthly, it should be given a mandate of total flexibility, governed only by the dictates of efficiency and pragmatism. Sixthly, it should provide an 'image' of a fresh start, unencumbered with the debris of the past. Perceptions, as noted earlier, are crucial in making a process work . . . Nevertheless, it may be that whatever the advantages that could be conferred by a new agency, political objections will in the end prove overwhelming. A feasible compromise would be to adapt and enhance the World Bank to meet these additional objectives.[8]

INTERNATIONAL CONCEPTS AND TRILATERALISM

The activity of organic intellectuals takes place in what Gramsci called ideological apparatuses, of which the Commission is a key example. The wider framework for this is a process of transnational class formation, within which particular forms of class consciousness emerge (discussed in chapters 5, 6, 7 and 8). Such consciousness involves perceptions and interpretation of changes in the global political economy, and the American place within it, as they affect the American, European and Japanese foreign policy establishments and political leadership.

This process of transnational class formation was relatively well developed in the Atlantic circuit of capital before the creation of the Trilateral Commission, exemplified in the membership network of Bilderberg. The leading elements in this class formation were American and the subordinate elements were West German, British, and to a lesser extent, French and Italian modernising elites. The creation of the Commission reflected a need for a wider basis for this formation, involving Japan. This was despite the problems of integration for a culturally unique oriental country into what had been a Euro-American formation.

In this sense, the basic role of the Commission has been in internationalising the outlook of its members. In this process, apart from underlying material forces, intellectuals play a leading role. This process is important not only for Japanese and American leadership, but also for countries such as Spain (which experienced a substantial influx of foreign investment in the 1980s) and Portugal, both emerging from a period of right-wing dictatorship. Thus Bilderberg's function was partly to increase the international sensitivity of the postwar American leadership, a function crucial for the Commission. This explains why the American section of the Commission chose to rotate a proportion of its membership and to hold consistent meetings with members of Congress and potential future leaders (as well as involving some of these individuals as members). This process has had its greatest impact at the level of American economic policy. In the security sphere, the interests and outlook of the American military-industrial complex have tended to predominate, shaping Commission agendas.

By contrast, given the distinctiveness and separateness of Japanese mentality and its long tradition of mercantilism, this process is currently at a very embryonic stage. The Commission is a key forum where what I called the 'incubation effect' operates. This practice is important for Japan since the internationalisation of the outlook of many of its leaders is still in an early stage of gestation. In this light, let us consider the evolution of international concepts in the outlook and practice of postwar Japan. Here an important question for this study is: to what extent has the Commission as a forum been important in promoting such internationalisation for Japanese leaders? This issue is central to the meaning of the Commission since such a development would be a prerequisite for a fully fledged Trilateral alliance. Clearly, the Commission has been one of a number of factors which have served to change what was a predominantly inward-looking and reactive foreign policy viewpoint on the part of the Japanese elite.

Japan: a hesitant internationalism

There have been three stages in the development of Japanese postwar concepts in foreign policy. The first, following defeat in World War II and after signing the San Francisco Peace Treaty of 8 September 1951, was characterised by an inner-oriented perspective. From the early 1950s until the late 1960s, Japan's priorities were reconstruction, economic growth and political rehabilitation. Foreign policy was primarily geared to solving bilateral problems. This generated a low profile in international relations itself based upon dependence on the United States for security, and for maintaining the international economic order crucial for Japan's export-led growth.

The second stage emerged in the 1970s, when Japanese elite perceptions began to change gradually, but profoundly. On the one hand, Japan began to settle some of its bilateral problems, such as the normalisation of relations with China. This helped free Japan from some of its inward-looking mentality. On the other hand, Japanese leaders began to perceive a relative decline in American power, at the same time as Japan felt more vulnerable to disruptions in raw materials, food and energy supplies. Japan became painfully aware of the meaning of economic interdependence, and practised careful 'resource diplomacy' to minimise threats to supplies.

A third phase began in the late 1970s. This involved not only economic questions, but also politico-military ones. Japan's foreign policy became gradually more globalist in outlook. In 1979, the Japanese government moved away from its traditional caution and pragmatism in foreign policy when it came down strongly against both Iran (a major source of Japan's oil supplies) and the Soviet Union. At this point Japan began to identify more forcefully with the concept of a Trilateral alliance. The Japanese government gradually began to increase its military expenditures during the 1980s and moved to consolidate the American–Japanese security links.

It is interesting to compare Japanese responses to the two oil shocks of the 1970s to identify some practical implications of changes in outlook. Japan reacted to the first shock by reasserting its postwar policy of export-led growth. This partly shifted the burden of balance of payments adjustment onto other countries. In the second shock, amid conditions of world wide recession, Japan reacted through an economic liberalisation programme in order to finance its balance of payments. It abolished a 1949 law which forbade foreign exchange transactions *in principle*. On 1 December 1980, a new law reversed the previous principle, allowing all foreign exchange transactions unless expressly prohibited. Whilst this law did not signal complete abolition of controls, as had British legislation in 1979, it was a significant step forward for such a highly mercantilist state. The legislation was the culmination of a long process of domestic consensus building, which had been preceded by the gradual decontrol of domestic capital markets (1977–9). It was also important because Japanese corporations needed to establish foreign financial bases in order to support Japanese trade and overseas investment. These changes, although primarily market-driven, however, were not politically inevitable. It is clear that during the 1970s, Japanese leaders made a fundamental *political* decision to carefully move Japan towards greater economic openness.[9]

At the same time there was also a rise in Japanese neo-nationalism. This phenomenon has been related to the end of the so-called *Age of the Moratorium Man*.[10] What this refers to is that under American domination and tutelage, aspects of the Japanese national character were, so to speak, put into suspended animation. With the perceived decline in American power and a shift away from dependence on the United States, many Japanese sought to redefine their identity in Asian, Confucian terms, repudiating Western Enlightenment universalism. These cultural forces were linked to the rise of neo-nationalism, which differed from the militarist variety of the 1930s, but still saw Japan as not receiving the necessary esteem from foreign countries (it was, for example, outvoted by Bangladesh for a seat on the United Nations Security Council in the early 1980s). Political forces on the right (and some on the left) argued that Japan should pursue a neo-Gaullist foreign policy, once more independent from the United States. Some aspects of this new nationalism (such as worship at Shinto shrines) were, in fact, encouraged by Prime Minister Nakasone. However, partly because of the emergence of a less strident mercantilism within the powerful bureaucracy, nationalist forces appeared to lose some ground to the internationalists in the late 1970s and 1980s. Nonetheless, as Ezra Vogel, Director of the Harvard programme on American–Japanese relations noted, 'At least until now, in battles within Japan between nationalists and internationalists, power has tended to gravitate to the former.' Vogel added that Japan's mercantilist policies still kept savings high, the cost of capital low, and trade barriers in line with national strategy.[11]

Thus, whilst there was a considerable metamorphosis in the outlook of many Japanese leaders, a change partly promoted by their engagement in the Commission, the basic cleavage which emerged was similar to that in the United States: between domesticists (nationalists) and internationalists. This struggle seemed likely to intensify in Japan since transnationalisation of the Japanese economy may lead to similar results for Japanese corporate workers (who experienced significant increases in living standards since the 1960s) to those experienced by many American workers since the late 1960s (see chapter 5). There might be, therefore, a growth in Japanese unemployment and a fall in real wages. In contrast to the United States, there was virtually no social welfare system to cushion these potential consequences. However, an aspect of the proposals of the Maekawa Report was that Japan should focus on building both the social and educational infrastructure to allow painful adjustments to be made and allow Japan to expand its domestic economy in accord with its international agreements.

The United States: the interplay between isolationism, liberalism and geo-politics

In the period prior to World War II the American outlook was predominantly isolationist, despite the emergence of a 'multinational bloc' of internationally-oriented interests discussed in chapter 6. This inward-looking aspect of elite and popular consciousness changed dramatically after Pearl Harbor in 1941, although there remained a strong element of isolationism which continued throughout the postwar period. This was bound up with the fact that the United States was virtually self-sufficient in the period up until the 1960s. During the war, the Council on Foreign Relations and the State Department came to reflect a new outlook and these institutions did much to help shape American postwar plans.

The concept of internationalism advanced by the Council's studies of this period was three-fold. First, the studies advanced the idea of the 'Grand Area', defined as the 'maximum living space' for the

American economy. In effect this meant enlarging the territory for American exporters and investors to expand into. Second, the creation of a Grand Area necessarily entailed a break up of the old colonial economic empires. Thus American theorists advanced the notion of national self-determination, and the need to dismantle colonial spheres-of-influence. Third, and central to the achievement of American aims, was a dual concept of political and economic reconstruction, aimed at bolstering Western Europe and Japan against the spread of communism and ensuring that the old imperialist leaderships did not re-emerge in defeated and allied states, endangering the possibility of world economic integration.

As a consequence, American leaders came to oppose the idea of imposing a Carthaginian peace on the defeated Axis powers. The concepts of the time were still based upon a traditional world view, which combined New Dealism and Wilsonian universalism with geopolitical concepts drawn from the realist tradition. The latter were reinforced by the establishment of the military-industrial complex, the onset of the Cold War and the militarisation of the Atlantic relationship after the creation of NATO in 1949. At this stage, the concept of interdependence held by the American leadership was focused mainly on politico-military alliance and trade. Although America successfully pressed for the open door to foreign direct investment (except in Japan), the pace of such investment was relatively slow. American policies were bound to create frictions with those powers whose leaders saw their sovereignty being eroded by American globalism, as well as their colonial interests being unravelled. Thus much of the agenda in the early years at the Bilderberg conferences was concerned with the resolution of inter-allied tensions, as well as attempting to create a common front against international communism.

By the late 1960s, a more complex view of interdependence began to emerge within the American leadership, at the same time as there was a major American capital export offensive. This flow of investment preceded reciprocal flows of investment from Western Europe to America in the 1970s and 1980s. The creation of the Trilateral Commission was related to advancing this process on a wider geographical basis. It can also be concluded that the onset of the Commission coincided with a clash between earlier international concepts, which shaped the outlook of a previous generation of American leaders and new, more sophisticated and comprehensive conceptions of complex interdependence (see chapter 6). This was epitomised in the clash between the Nixon–Kissinger pentagonal design, with its *realpolitik*, and the more international and multilateral sensitivity of elements which came together to create the Commission. The Nixon shocks of August 1971 were a clear example of a nationalist-mercantilist move on the part of the Republican administration. Since they were in large part aimed at Japan, this gave an added reason for the internationalist wing to remobilise its forces. Its representatives, such as David Rockefeller, Fred Bergsten and Edwin Reischauer, argued that Japan would become more important in the system of interdependence, a system which was likely, in turn, to increase in importance for the American economy.

THE TRILATERAL COMMISSION, INTERNATIONAL CONCEPTS AND AMERICAN FOREIGN POLICY

The emergence and evolution of the Trilateral Commission can thus be interpreted in terms of the interplay of different international concepts in the outlook of the American foreign policy elite. In this respect, its development can be reviewed by comparing the relationship between the Commission concepts and its agendas (as outlined in chapter 8) with the orientations of successive American administrations. In this sense, the Commission can be analysed on two levels: the economic and politico-military. When economics topped the Commission and American government's agenda (1974–7; 1982–6), liberal perspectives associated with American transnational capital would seem to have predominated. When security issues were at the forefront of the agenda (1978–82), the geostrategic, realist perspectives of the American security complex appear to have prevailed, at least until 1986. This tentative conclusion, of course, oversimplifies the complexity of the social forces in question.

The Commission's key concept of complex interdependence was rapidly absorbed into the administration's outlook after the fall of Nixon. Gerald Ford became President, and Nelson Rockefeller Vice-President. Ford was the first American head of state to visit Japan. At this juncture Henry Kissinger largely adopted the Commission posture after his ill-fated 'Year of Europe' and attempts to dragoon allies behind the United States confrontational policy toward OPEC in 1973–4. This was a significant shift for a thinker whose main ideas were drawn from his extensive knowledge of nineteenth-century German diplomacy. The Ford administration thus reflected the key aim of the Commission in its first phase: gaining acceptability for the 'interdependence paradigm' in an era of superpower detente (despite Ford's refusal to allow the word detente to be used in his re-election platform). With so many former Commission members in its ranks, it was no surprise that the Carter administration emphasised allied solidarity in a more complex world, where the management of interdependence was of the first importance. By the middle of the Carter presidency, Trilateralism had become the new orthodoxy in American foreign policy. This was despite significant frictions between the United States and its allies over many aspects of American policy, notably human rights, nuclear proliferation, and macroeconomic co-ordination.

From the mid-1970s, geopolitical definitions of foreign policy were strongly reasserted, partly in consequence of a rising sentiment that the United States needed to reverse its perceived relative military decline since Vietnam. Carter became increasingly wary of the domestic political costs of pursuing increased interdependence with the Soviet Union. The forces of the American military-industrial complex had begun to politically remobilise and pushed for an increase in military capacity. At this stage Japanese and West European elements in the Commission were still keen to sustain detente with the Soviet Union. Nonetheless, the power of the American security complex was such as to cause a shift in Carter policies and, in consequence, in the Commission agenda.

In effect there were, and continue to be, two basic positions in the Trilateral Commission on relations towards the Soviet Union. On the one hand are the 'traders', who seek to incorporate the Soviet Union through increased economic interdependence and functional forms of co-operation, thus hoping to decrease East–West tensions and create the climate for progress on arms control. This was the dominant perspective within the Commission during the 1973–9 phase, reflected in Commission plans to send a delegation to Moscow, as they did in 1981 to Beijing. The Soviet invasion of Afghanistan and the Polish crisis meant that the meeting with the Soviet elite was cancelled. However, this position staged a partial comeback in American policy in the mid-1980s.

The rival, 'Prussian', position, which came to dominate the United States after 1978, maintained that the Soviet Union would only make concessions on arms if it met solid opposition, and if the allies had rebuilt their military strength. From 1979 to 1983, this perspective became dominant in the Commission. As noted above, there was a surprising shift in Japanese views which indicated that Japan was prepared to become a more militarily committed part of an anti-communist alliance. The European, and notably West German, elements in the Commission continued to oppose a confrontationist posture, wishing to preserve *ostpolitik* and the wider East–West detente. On the other hand, Britain shifted towards the American position after the 1979 election, and after Mitterand was elected, the former pro-detente Schmidt–Giscard axis ended. The new French Socialist government moved closer to American positions on the East–West question. Thus from 1974–7 the American position was similar to the mainstream view of the Commission, whereas in 1978–83 the positions taken by the American government reshaped the Commission agenda. This caused a split in its ranks, and divisions over basic concepts used to guide Western responses to the Soviet Union.

After 1982 the Commission began to re-examine the question and produced a report on East–West trade, which appeared to return to the former 'trader' concept, and as such was criticised by 'Prussians' as signalling that the Commission was trying to sell 'capitalist rope' to the Marxist–Leninists. Nonetheless, the Commission continued to review prospects for East–West relations after the Brezhnev era and appeared to conclude that the future Soviet leadership would be more outward-looking, less conservative, more cosmopolitan and more aware of the benefits of global economic interdependence.[12] In this light it was significant that David Rockefeller led a business delegation to the Soviet Union in 1986 and thereafter the Soviet Union announced that it was to permit 49 per cent foreign ownership in Soviet enterprises and joint ventures. With the rise of Gorbachev, the Soviet Union seemed to be returning to policies akin to those of the New Economic Policy of 1924–8, encouraging an influx of foreign capital, and a reinvigoration of the Soviet cultural, political and economic climate. These develop-ments led one astute observer of the Soviet scene to suggest certain policies of the new leadership of the Soviet Union, when compared with those of their predecessors, appeared to harmonise with a number of characteristic Trilateral Commission preferences.[13] For example, the Soviet Union wanted to observe the discussion at the GATT (Uruguay) round as a possible preliminary to joining.

Reagan's massive military build up had the consequence of produc-ing enormous budget deficits, which had significant international repercussions. This aspect of Reagan policies was opposed by most members of the Commission. The Commission consistently backed the imperative of progress on arms control. However, the Commis-sion was, at least during 1980–5, unable to exert a great deal of influence in the security sphere. Indeed, some of its former members (notably Reagan's first Secretary of Defense, Caspar Weinberger) were advocates of massive American rearmament. Elements within the Commission had equivocal feelings over the administration's broader

East–West stance and its attempts to impose extra-territorial application of American law as a means of controlling trade and investment flows for security reasons.

By contrast, Reagan's economic policy (with the perhaps important exception of budget deficits), gradually moved away from its domesticist focus towards a more internationalist stance, one closer than ever to mainstream Commission positions. The early harsh 'market place magic' approach gave way to direct support for a long-term solution to the debt issue. After changes in senior administration personnel of 1985–7, Reagan's policies moved even more towards the Commission's mainstream perspective, as the two Bakers (James at the Treasury, Howard at the White House), Secretary of State George Shultz and the new Defense Secretary, Frank Carlucci, were much more attuned to the international repercussions of American economic policies. A second important arms control agreement (after INF) may be concluded in the late 1980s or early 1990s and it seemed likely that the American arms build up would further decelerate. Characteristic Commission ideas seemed once again to become the prevailing orthodoxy, with the new President, George Bush, exemplifying the return of the establishment perspective.

Although no simple cause-and-effect relationship can be adduced between American policy and Commission positions, what is significant is that the Commission represents the views of the more forward-looking and internationally oriented aspects of the establishments of the three areas. Nevertheless, there was still a significant clash between the outlook of the bulk of the American security complex and that of the transnational interests represented in the Commission. This was reflected in Pentagon attempts to prevent Japan, armed with its 1986 current account surplus of $84 billion, from buying American companies in areas affecting sensitive military production. (The same applied to many European investors.) Thus, whilst the United States appeared to need foreign investment for purposes of economic revitalisation, the Pentagon and nationalist-mercantilist forces in Congress continued to oppose foreign take-overs of significant sectors of American capital (such as semiconductors produced in California's Silicon Valley).[14] The 1988 Trade Act contained a provision allowing the President to block foreign take-overs on grounds of national security (the Bryant Amendment). Although much of the mood in Congress was hostile towards Japanese assets in America, one recent estimate indicated the much bigger stake held by European, especially British, investors. In 1987, this stood at a total of US$ 745 billion, compared to Japan's total of US$ 187 billion.[15]

A possible long-term solution to this problem (from a Trilateral perspective) might be to integrate parts of the American military-industrial complex with those of Japan and certain European countries, along the lines of the Hornet 2000 deal offered in 1988 (see chapters 4 and 5). This solution, if implemented, would be of major significance in that it would serve to not only constrain nationalists in the United States Congress, but also the possibility of Japanese nationalists and elements in Japan's Self-Defence Forces pressing for a neo-Gaullist foreign policy. It would also retard the flowering of a European defence identity and capability. A greater internationalisation of the outlook of both the American and the Japan military-industrial complexes would therefore appear to be crucial for maintaining momentum towards a more organic Trilateral alliance.

A development along these lines would help to reconcile the gap between the emerging global civil society and what Gramsci called the political society. Of course, there is no clear counterpart to the concept of the political society at the international level. At most there is the tendency towards the transnationalisation of the state, that is a reconfiguration of ideological and institutional forces within the state apparatuses of a range of capitalist governments and international organisations. This tendency at least suggests that a sharp distinction between domestic and international political levels is no longer tenable.

INTERESTS, IDENTITY, IDEOLOGY AND KNOWLEDGE

There is an obvious political danger for a closed, private, self-selecting forum such as the Trilateral Commission. Apart from charges of international Freemasonry, the elite nature of the Commission means that it risks the fate of becoming decadent and detached from other elements in the political and civil society. This is apart from its other political problem, in that it is attacked by right-wing parties and groups as a conspiracy, and from the left for its capitalism and authoritarian tendencies. It is also criticised by other states for being exclusive and marginalising their interests from debates which affect them. The epithet 'rich man's club' does describe one aspect of the Commission, although the intensive programmes in the meetings would indicate that there is scant time for a midday 'glass of the warm south' or an afternoon siesta on a comfortable leather couch.

On the other hand, for the Commission to maximise its influence in the economic realm, its members need to have a developed sense of collective identity, reasonably compatible sets of interests and shared frameworks of thought. This compatibility stems from a shared sense of exclusiveness, or *cachet*, a collegial atmosphere and careful selection of members so that there is a basic congruence of outlook on key values promoted by the Commission. This relates to Jorge Larrain's 'positive' concept of ideology, mentioned in chapter 1, that is, the representation of the world view of a class or class fraction.

As my examination of the Commission reveals, the largest measure of agreement, or highest degree of consensus appears to be reflected in the economic realm, where debates are built from axiomatic principles of economic liberalism (with exceptions such as East–West trade, and the conflicts over freedom to export nuclear technology). Divisions have been more obvious at the politico-security level, where considerable divergence between American perspectives and West European perspectives on East–West relations has emerged. On the other hand, Japanese members seemed increasingly willing to endorse American security positions. Despite divisions, at the heart of the enterprise is the long-term management of a changing division of political labour amongst Trilateral allies in order to sustain a world order conducive to internationally mobile capital, constraining the long-term growth of communism. This means that the question of order is simultaneously seen in political and economic, short and long terms. On this basic issue there is wide agreement.

Substantial problems for this enterprise also exist at the practical level, involving the means to achieve these ends. As was shown in the example of the Volcker shift in 1979–82, the knowledge system of the Trilateralists is imperfect, as is any form of social knowledge. Under some conditions this can restrict the outlook of the Commission itself. This relates to the 'negative' conception of ideology. Indeed it is clear that the majority of Commission members were not in favour of a protracted recession as a means to resolve the 'governability' problem relative to domestic forces and developing countries, in part because they feared the political consequences of a prolonged slump for their leadership. This may have reflected, in the outlook of many Commission members, the continued hegemony of a 'political Keynesian' model of order and stability in modern capitalism. Nonetheless, *The Crisis of Democracy* report had earlier suggested that the counter-hegemonic political and cultural movements would probably not outlive a prolonged period of recession.

The recession of 1979–82, in conjunction with Reagan policies had the unintended effect of significantly increasing the structural power of internationally mobile capital. To use Gramscian metaphors, this can be described as an unintended onset of a short-term 'war of movement', in the context of a longer term 'war of position' aimed at establishing a hegemony of transnational capital. This unintended effect is akin to that noted by Leslek Kolakowski, with respect to Lenin's expectation that a European revolution would occur, thus leading him to decide on an armed insurrection in October 1917. Lenin's fortunate errors, 'enabled him to exploit the possibilities of revolution to the full, and were thus the cause of his success'.[16] This raises the question, 'fortunate for whom?' In the Volcker shift these errors were fortunate for elements of internationally mobile capital, notably certain banks. In the latter case, they were fortunate for the cause of Bolshevism.

The tendency in Commission debates is towards an instrumental discourse rather than an analytical one. Moreover, there is an element of contingency in the approaches adopted. Thus what may seem appropriate for analysis and policy at any one period may be pragmatically discarded later. Although many Commission members were economists of Keynesian persuasion, they updated their ideas in an era when a monetarist approach seemed more useful. This underlines the importance of seeing the Commission as part of an ongoing *process* of class consciousness, particularly for members of an exclusive, inner elite group. Indeed, the form of consciousness within this group corresponds to the higher, 'hegemonic level' identified by Gramsci (see chapter 3). Nevertheless, the dominance of establishment perspectives may mean that the forum lacks exposure to new ideas and influences. This prospect caused funding agencies such as the Ford Foundation to press the Commission to introduce 'new blood'. This suggests that the knowledge process is beset with a basic epistemological contradiction, and as such the functionality of its knowledge system can be queried, even in its own liberal terms.

The above argument is reinforced by a review of the Commission's ideological process. The establishment perspective can be linked to a general aspect of the construction of ideologies and ideological apparatuses, namely what Goran Therborn calls 'authorisation'.[17] This involves restrictions on who is permitted to speak, what can be said, for how long, and when. This restriction can be made through the use of only one author (for example, Marx, Buddha), or one type of author (such as Islamic Fundamentalists in post-revolutionary Iran). A second procedure is consistent repetition of a given discourse. Whilst Commission processes of analysis and discussion are more open than these principles suggest, it can be concluded that the nature of the discourses used by its carefully selected intellectuals (partly chosen because they are regarded as experts in a technocratic sense) and consistent use of liberal perspectives entails a process akin to authorisation. This is reinforced by a very elitist sense of identity.

Since the Commission values itself as promoting an educational process, the question which arises, therefore, is what kind of educational process is involved? Commissioners claim that intellectuals gain 'relevance' by constantly checking their ideas and concepts with those in power, or with influence over those in power. Thus on one level, the powerful are educated, as are their educators, the intellectuals. The key intellectuals claim that part of the objectives of the Commission is to correct the 'cognitive processes' of those leaders whose outlook is based in the outmoded ways of seeing and interpreting the political economy. This seems crucial to its function and meaning.[18]

It has already been noted, however, that many of the most influential advocates of realist, geopolitical views (who might be influenced to change their views) are notable by their absence. Their omission means that primary impact is likely to be felt mainly by those already converted, as it might be for members of a political party. However, if the knowledge structures of realist and liberal constellations of social forces continue to diverge or clash, they will prevent attempts to resolve the basic contradiction which the Commission is attempting to resolve: the lack of congruence between aspects of the economic and political worlds. This does not imply, of course, a world government. The rising power of transnational capital is generally assisted by the division of the globe into formally sovereign states (see chapter 5). What is at issue is the degree to which states are hospitable to foreign capital, and the construction of an internationalised policy-process which can help to sustain stability for economic forces.

Writing in the 1950s, C. Wright Mills argued that in the United States there was a 'triumvirate of power', involving 'military chieftains', corporate and political leaders. This 'power elite' was cemented by a congruence of social background, interests and outlook.[19] Wright Mills' thesis was specific to an earlier phase in the history of American capitalism when a broad consensus between the three leadership ranks was possible. In today's conditions, a congruence in the outlook of American leaders is more problematic. Whereas the economic world is ever more integrated and increasingly dominated by giant companies, politics is still largely conducted at the level of the nation-state, notwithstanding a growing process of the transnationalisation of the state. As has been noted, a continuing problem for the Commission and its interests is how to incorporate and modify the outlook of some elements of the security structures and 'internationalise' their outlook, and help to make the Trilateral alliance more 'organic'. This entails a resolution of an overlapping problem: to increase the very weak sense of mutual solidarity between a range of Western European interests and those of Japan, in what has been described as the 'weakest link' of Trilateralism.[20]

THEORY AND HEGEMONY

If it is possible to identify an intellectual pattern in the developments in dominant American international concepts, we should relate this to the study of international relations. In American academic circles there have been two prevailing concepts of hegemony. The first related to the era of American self-sufficiency and Cold War, where the dominant concept in study was a realist one. This was followed by a concept of hegemonic decline, which fused realism with the ideal-typical concept of complex interdependence, generated by the transnational liberal perspective. This more complex concept pervaded American academic work in the field for much of the 1970s. After 1977 earlier realist concepts were reasserted and a clash between this and the interdependence strand emerged. However, to explain this evolution we need a third, and more complex Gramscian concept of hegemony.

With respect to substantive arguments, Shakespeare's tragedies were written in the Elizabethan age when it was perhaps more plausible to analyse international relations in terms of the interaction between discrete rival states, where one state's gain was another's loss. In the more complex modern system, transnational social forces are, however, crucial for our understanding of international power. Thus interpretations of the rise and decline of American hegemony based upon historical analogy and a cyclical view of historical process may be of much more limited value in the contemporary context (see chapters 2 to 4). This argument can be related to the criteria which were introduced to assess the theoretical value of alternative perspectives in political economy: scope, consistency and reflexivity (see chapter 1). These criteria reinforce the justification for our historical materialist approach, relative to other schools discussed in chapters 2 and 3.

The Gramscian approach can be said to be more comprehensive since it allows for a more consistent theorisation and explanation of changes in the contemporary global political economy. This is because it synthesises the interaction of material, institutional and ideological forces, including culture, and gives them, where appropriate, a class dimension. It therefore enables a more complex answer to the question, 'Hegemony for whom?', understood not just in terms of the vocabulary of national or group interests, but also in terms of social classes. By its stress on dialectical social change, using concepts which combine both agency and structure, it is able to avoid the pitfalls of essentialist explanations of the historical process. Our approach also serves to critique the tendency to explain change in terms of an abstracted structuralism of the Waltzian or Althusserian varieties, as well as a contrasting empiricist tendency which prevails in much of Anglo-Saxon social science.[21] The historical materialist approach can be further justified because of its greater reflexivity: the explanation of change in the world political economy systematically incorporates the origins, development and changing role of rival theories and ideologies as part of the historical process. Ideas and ideologies are of fundamental importance for our understanding of political identity and the constitution of interests in both domestic and international politics. In the Gramscian approach, rival theories and intellectual-material networks, such as those represented in the Trilateral Commission, are *part of* the object of our analysis, that is the changing global political economy.

APPENDICES

APPENDIX 1 *Regional and national membership of the Trilateral Commission, 1973–85*

Country	Aggregate members 1973–85		Total in 1973	1979	1985	No. of continuous members[a]	
North America	193		67	94	99	25	
United States		160	59	80	85	25	(35)
Canada		33	8	14	14	0	
W. Europe	227		60	129	140	23	(36)
Belgium		15	5	7	11	3	(3)
Denmark		8	1	3	5	0	(1)
France		34	8	20	23	3	(3)
Ireland		14	6	9	10	2	(3)
Italy		24	10	15	17	4	(8)
Luxemburg		2	1	0	1	0	(0)
Netherlands		13	3	8	4	1	(1)
Norway		7	3	3	5	0	(1)
Portugal		5	n.a.	n.a.	5	n.a.	
Spain		20	n.a.	13	13	n.a.	
United Kingdom		45	9	30	25	4	(5)
W. Germany		40	14	21	21	5	(5)
Japan	131		63	76	80	33[a]	(50)
Total	561	(403)	190	299	319	81	

Note: [a]Japanese total in 1983. In 1985, nine older members left the Commission. Figures in brackets are for 1979. Spanish members joined in 1979, Portuguese in 1980.
Source: Trilateral Commission Membership Lists, 1973–85.

APPENDIX 2 *Breakdown of Trilateral Commission membership by occupational category (expressed as percentage of total members 1973–85)*

	United States	Canada	W. Europe	Japan	Total
Business	21	34	30	46	30
Politics	21	21	40	9	25
Banking	10	13	12	12	19
Academia	20	13	12	19	14
Unions	5	4	6	3	5
Media	5	4	6	3	5
Law	9	8	1	0	3
International organisations	10	0	1	1	4

Note: Given the way members change their primary occupations, for example, into and out of government, this table should be treated as only generally reflecting occupational patterns.
Source: Trilateral Commission membership lists, 1973–85.

APPENDIX 3 *Trilateral Commissioners and staff members interviewed*

METHODOLOGICAL NOTE

The data base for the chapters of this study relating to the Commission is drawn mainly from primary sources. These sources are Commission publications and documents, and interviews with its members, carried out in North America (the United States and Canada) and Western Europe (in Britain, France, West Germany and Italy). Funds were not available for me to visit Japan. The interviews, carried out between 1978 and 1986, lasted between 30 minutes and 2 hours 30 minutes, with over 75 per cent of them lasting at least an hour.

Virtually all interviews were open-ended, concentrating on the way problems were perceived and prioritised. Some were used to obtain specific information. Interviews and consultations were conducted with other experts, including some critical of the Commission perspectives. Access was difficult in the case of Japanese members, partly because of their unwillingness to co-operate, partly because of language problems, but mainly because funds were not available for me to travel to Japan: a major condition for personal access.

In order to sustain access I had to build the confidence of members and staff, and ascertain who were the most important individuals to speak to. This was a difficult, and painstaking process, requiring considerable preparation, in order to consistently justify taking the time up of very busy individuals. I consulted *Who's Who* and other sources in order to know something of the background and area of expertise of members. This was useful for selecting questions and issues for discussion. This method also allowed me to gain access to Commission documents, and to other source items such as unpublished speeches, memoranda, etc., which were often given to me by members or their staff. This process of confidence-building did not, however, gain me observer status at any Commission meetings, although I was granted such status at the 1983 Hakone (Europe–Japan) meeting in Munich. However, my research would suggest that the process is similar in each case. Hakone meetings, of course, are smaller, more intimate, and involve more junior figures than in the Trilateral Commission.

The affiliations of the individuals given below are those current at the time of interview. Where more than one interview took place, the individual's affiliation at the time of the last interview is shown. The place where the (final) interview took place is at the end of each entry.

ABSHIRE, David M. Director, Centre for Strategic and International Studies, Georgetown University: Washington DC.
ACKLEY, Gardner. Professor, Department of Economics, University of Michigan: Ann Arbor, Michigan.
ANDERSEN, Nyboe P. Chief General Manager, Andelsbanken Danebank, Denmark: London.
BENSON, Lucy Wilson. President, Benson and Associates Inc: Arlington, Virginia.

BERGSTEN, C. Fred. Director, Institute of International Economics: Washington DC.

BERTHOIN, Georges. Trilateral Commission European Chairman: London (two interviews).

BOWIE, Robert R. Professor, The Brookings Institution: Washington DC.

BRADEMAS, John. Democratic Party Majority Whip, House of Representatives: Washington DC.

BRIMMER, Andrew Felton. President, Brimmer and Co: Washington DC (two interviews).

BROCK III, William E. Chairman, Republican National Committee: Washington DC.

BRZEZINSKI, Zbigniew K. Professor, Georgetown University Centre for Advanced Strategic and International Studies: Washington DC.

BUNDY, William P. Senior Fellow, Council on Foreign Relations: New York (telephone interview).

CALKINS, Hugh. Senior Partner, Jones, Day, Reavis and Pogue: Cleveland, Ohio.

de CARMOY, Hervé. Chairman, Midland Bank (France): London.

CHAIKIN, Sol C. Secretary, International Ladies Garment Workers Union: New York City.

COLEMAN, Jr, William T. Senior Partner, O'Melveny and Myers: Washington DC (two interviews).

CONABLE Jr, Barber B. Ranking Republican on House Ways and Means Committee, House of Representatives: Washington DC.

COOPER, Richard N. Professor of Economics, Harvard University: Cambridge, Massachusetts (two interviews).

COWLES Jr, John. Chairman, *Minneapolis Star and Tribune* Co: Minneapolis, Minnesota.

DELOUVRIER, Paul. Chairman, Electricité de France: London.

DOBELL, Peter. Director, Parliamentary Centre for Foreign Affairs and Foreign Trade: Ottawa.

DUCHÊNE, François. Professor, Centre for Contemporary European Studies, The University of Sussex: Brighton.

FRANKLIN, George. Coordinator of the Trilateral Commission: New York City (three interviews).

GARDNER, Richard N. Professor of Law and International Organization, Columbia University: New York City.

GARRIGUES, Walker Antonio. General Secretary, Liberal Party of Spain: London.

GAUDET, Michel. President, French Federation of Insurance Associations: London.

GEDDES, Sir Reay. Chairman, Dunlop Holdings: London.

GRIERSON, Ronald. Director, General Electric and Orion Bank: London.

HAYHOE, Barney. MP (Conservative), House of Commons: London.

HECK, Charles. North American Director of the Commission: New York, Rome, London (seven meetings and interviews).

HELLER, Walter W. Professor of Economics, University of Minnesota: Washington DC.

HOFFMAN, Diether. Chairman, Neue Heimat, Hamburg: London.

HOGE, James. Executive Vice-President and Editor in Chief (later publisher), *Chicago Sun-Times*: Chicago, Illinois.

HOLBROOK, Richard. Under Secretary of State, East Asian and Pacific Affairs, State Department: Washington DC.

HOUTHHAKKER, Hendrik. Professor of Economics, Harvard University: Cambridge, Massachusetts.

HUNTINGTON, Samuel P. Director, Centre for International Affairs, Harvard University: Cambridge, Massachusetts.

INGERSOLL, Robert S. Chairman, United States–Japan Economic Relations Group: New York City.

IWADA, Hiroshi. Personal assistant to the Japanese Prime Minister: London.

JOHNSON, Gale D. Professor of Economics, University of Chicago: Chicago, Illinois.

KAJI, Motoo. Professor of Economics, Tokyo University: Munich.

KAMURA, Hiroshi Peter. Japan Foundation: New York City.

KILEEN, Michael. Managing Director, Industrial Development Authority of the Irish Republic: London.

KRAFT, Joseph. Syndicated Columnist: Washington DC.

LITTMAN, Mark, QC. Deputy Chairman, British Steel: London.

LORD, Winston. President, Council on Foreign Relations: New York City (two interviews).

MACFARQUHAR, Roderick. MP (Labour): London.

MACLAURY, Bruce. President and Chief Executive Officer, Brookings Institution: Washington DC.

MAKINS, Christopher. Fellow, Carnegie Endowment for International Peace: Washington DC (two interviews).

MAUDLING, Reginald. MP (Conservative): London.

MAULL, Hanns. Assistant Professor of Politics, Munich University, and former Trilateral Commission European Secretary: Rome (three interviews).

NADEN, Kenneth D. President, National Council of Farmer Cooperatives: Washington DC.

NISHIHARA, Miyasashi. Professor of International Relations, Japan Defense Academy: Munich.

NYE, Joseph S. Professor, Centre for Science and International Affairs, Harvard University: Cambridge, Massachusetts.

ORTONA, Egidio. Commission European Deputy Chairman: London.

PEARCE, William R. Vice-President, Cargill: Minneapolis.

PILCHER, Sir John. Former UK Ambassador to Japan: London.

REISCHAUER, Edwin W. Professor of Japanese Studies, Harvard University: Belmont, Massachusetts.

RICHARDSON, Eliot. United States Ambassador-at-large to the Law of the Sea Conference: Washington DC.

RIDSDALE, Julian. MP (Conservative), and Chairman, Anglo-Japanese Parliamentary Group: London.

ROBERTS, Sir Frank K. International Advisor, Unilever: London.

ROCKEFELLER, David. Chairman, Chase Manhattan Bank, and Chairman of Trilateral Commission North America: New York City (two interviews).

ROLL, Eric. Lord of Ipsden, Chairman, S. G. Warburg and Co: London.

ROPER, John. MP (Labour): London.

ROTH, William Matson. Chairman, Roth Properties: San Francisco, California.

SAUZEY, François. Editor, *Trialogue*: Rome (two interviews).

SHACKLETON, Lord. Deputy Chairman, Rio Tinto Zinc: London.

SCHAETZEL, J. Robert. Former United States Ambassador: Washington DC (two interviews, one by conference phone).

SHARP, Mitchell. North America Deputy Chairman of the Trilateral Commission: Ottawa.

SHONFIELD, Sir Andrew. Professor of Economics, European University Institute: London.

SISCO, Jr, Joseph. Former Undersecretary of State for Security Affairs: Washington DC.

SMITH, Gerard C. Former Trilateral Commission North America, Chairman, and Ambassador-at-large for Non-Proliferation Affairs, State Department: Washington DC (three interviews).

SONNENFELDT, Helmut. Visiting Scholar, Brookings Institution: Washington DC.

SWIRE, John. Chairman, Swire Group: London.

TAFT, Jr, Robert. Senior Partner, Taft, Stettinius and Hollister: Washington DC.

TAYLOR, Arthur R. President, The American Assembly: New York City.

TRAIN, Russell E. President, World Wildlife Fund: Washington DC (telephone interview).

TREZISE, Philip H. Senior Fellow, Brookings Institution: Washington DC (two interviews).

VOLCKER, Paul A. Chairman of Federal Reserve Bank of New York: New York City.

WARNER, Sir Frederick. Former UK Ambassador to Japan, and Deputy Chairman, Guinness Peat International: London.

WARNKE, Paul. Partner, Clifford and Warnke: Washington DC (two interviews).

WATANABE, Takashi. Chairman of the Japan Trilateral Commission: London.

WATTS, Glen E. President, Communications Workers of America: Washington DC (two interviews).

WEINBERGER, Caspar. Vice President, Bechtel Corp: San Francisco.

YAMAMOTO, Tadashi. Secretary and later Director of the Japan Trilateral Commission: Munich (three interviews).

de ZULUETA, Sir Philip. Chairman, Antony Gibbs Holdings Ltd: London (two interviews).

APPENDIX 4 *List of Trilateral Commission publications (chronological sequence)*

TRIANGLE PAPERS 1973–87

All these task force reports are New York, Trilateral Commission publications, except where stated otherwise.

1 *Towards a Renovated World Monetary System* (1973). Authors: Richard N. Cooper, Motoo Kaji, Claudio Segré.

2 *The Crisis of International Cooperation* (1974), François Duchêne, Kinhide Mushakoji, Henry D. Owen.

3 *A Turning Point in North–South Economic Relations* (1974). Richard N. Gardner, Suburo Okita, B. J. Udink.

4 *Directions for World Trade in the Nineteen-Seventies* (1974). Guido Colonna di Paliano, Philip H. Trezise, Nobuhiko Ushiba.

5 *Energy: The Imperative for a Trilateral Approach* (1974). John C. Campbell, Guy de Carmoy, Shinichi Kondo.

6 *Energy: A Strategy for International Action* (1975). John C. Campbell, Guy de Carmoy, Shinichi Kondo.

7 *OPEC: The Trilateral World, and the Developing Countries: New Arrangements for Cooperation, 1976–1980* (1975). Richard N. Gardner, Saburo Okita, B. J. Udink.

8 *The Crisis of Democracy* (New York, New York University Press, 1975). Michel Crozier, Samuel P. Huntington, Joji Watanuki.

9 *A New Regime for the Oceans* (1976). Michael Hardy, Ann L. Hollick, Johan Jorgen Hølst, Douglas M. Johnston, Shigeru Oda.

10 *Seeking a New Accommodation in World Commodity Markets* (1976). Carl E. Beigie, Wolfgang Hager, Sueo Sekiguchi.

11 *The Reform of International Institutions* (1976). C. Fred Bergsten, Georges Berthoin, Kinhide Mushakoji.

12 *The Problem of International Consultations* (1976). Egidio Ortona, J. Robert Schaetzel, Nobuhiko Ushiba.

13 *Collaboration with Communist Countries in Managing Global Problems: An Examination of the Options* (1977). Chihiro Hosoya, Henry Owen, Andrew Shonfield.

14 *Towards a Renovated International System* (1977). Richard N. Cooper, Karl Kaiser, Masataka Kosaka.

15 *An Overview of East–West Relations* (1978). Jeremy R. Azrael, Richard Löwenthal, Tohru Nakagawa.

16 *Reducing Malnutrition in Developing Countries: Increasing Rice Production in South and Southeast Asia* (1978). Umberto Colombo, D. Gale Johnson, Toshio Shishido.

17 *Energy: Managing the Transition* (1978). Hanns W. Maull, Keichi Oshima, John C. Sawhill.

18 *Collective Bargaining and Employee Participation in Western Europe, North America and Japan* (1979). George C. Lodge, Hideaki Okamoto, Benjamin C. Roberts.

19 *Industrial Policy and the International Economy* (1979). John Pinder, Takeshi Hosomi, William Diebold.

20 'Labour Market Problems and Policies in Modern Trilateral Societies: Reducing Unemployment and Smoothing Adaption' (1980: not published). Heinz Markmann, Richard R. Nelson, Tadashi Hanami.

21 *Trade in Manufactured Products with Developing Countries: Reinforcing North–South Partnership* (1981). Albert Fishlow, Jean Carrière, Sueo Sekiguchi.

22 *The Middle East and the Trilateral Countries* (1981). Garrett Fitzgerald, Arrigo Levi, Hideo Kitahara, Joseph Sisco.

23 *'Trilateralism' and the International Economy of the 1980s: Three Essays* (1982). Miriam Camps, Ryokichi Hirono, Karsten Laursen.

24 *East–West Trade at a Crossroads: Economic Relations with the Soviet Union and Eastern Europe* (1982). Robert V. Roosa, Armin Gutowski, Michiya Matsukawa.

25 *Sharing International Responsibilities Among the Trilateral Countries* (1983). Nobuhiko Ushiba, Graham Allison, Thiérry de Montbrial.

26 *Trilateral Security: Defense and Arms Control Policies in the 1980s* (1983). Gerard C. Smith, Paolo Vittorelli, Kiichi Saeki.

27 *Facilitating Development in a Changing Third World: Finance, Trade, Aid* (1983). Takeshi Watanabe, Jacques Lesourne, Robert S. McNamara.

28 *Democracy Must Work: A Trilateral Agenda for the Decade* (1984). David Owen, Zbigniew Brzezinski, Saburo Okita.

29 *Agricultural Policy and Trade: Adjusting Domestic Programs in an International Framework* (1985). D. Gale Johnson, Kenzo Hemmi, Pierre Lardinois.

30 *East Asian Security and the Trilateral Countries* (1985). Masashi Nishihara.

31 *Prospects for East–West Relations* (1986). William G. Hyland, Karl Kaiser, Hiroshi Kimura.

32 *Conditions for Partnership in International Economic Management* (1986). C. Fred Bergsten, Etienne Davignon, Isamu Miyazaki.

33 *Restoring Growth in a Debt-Laden Third World* (1987). Martin Feldstein, Hervé de Carmoy, Koei Narasawa, Paul R. Krugman.

34 *Science and Technology in Trilateral Relations: Competition and Cooperation* (1987). Takashi Mukaibo, Harold Brown, Luis Solana, Fumio Kodama, Lewis Branscomb.

TRIALOGUE 1973–85

Trialogue was published by the New York office of the Commission.

1 *Bulletin on Developments in the Commission* (October 1973). Contributors not named.

2 *Bulletin on Developments in the Commission* (November 1973). Contributors not named.

3 *Bulletin on Developments in the Commission* (December 1973–January 1974). Contributors not named.

4 *Bulletin on Developments in the Commission* (February–March 1974). Contributors not named.

5 *Bulletin on Developments in the Commission* (May–July 1974). Contributors: Kazuhige Hirasawa, Harold Brown.

6 *Commission Recommends Cooperation with Oil-Exporters, Proposes New Aid Agency, Consults with Ford and Kissinger* (Winter 1974–5). Contributors: Nobuhiko Ushiba, Paul Delouvrier, George W. Ball, Andrew Shonfield.

7 *Trilateral Leaders Discuss Global Redistribution of Power and Problems of Trilateral Community, Meet with Miki and Miyazawa* (Summer 1975). Contributors: Takeshi Watanabe, Saburo Okita, Ralf Dahrendorf, Zbigniew Brzezinski.

8 *Is Reform an Illusion? A Trilateral Perspective on International Problems; World Bank Establishes 'Third Window' Trilateral Commission Proposal Realised* (Fall 1975). Contributors: Christopher J. Makins, Charles B. Heck.

9 *Economic Cooperation and Resource Management Top Paris Agenda: Chirac, Carli, Cheysson, Address Meeting* (Winter 1975–6). Contributors: Guido Carli, Claude Cheysson, Kinhide Mushakoji.

10 *Looking Back . . . and Forward* (Spring 1976). Contributors: Richard N. Cooper, Richard N. Gardner, Philip H. Trezise, John C. Campbell, Samuel P. Huntington, John H. Perkins, P. Nyboe Anderson, Marina Whitman, Peter Dobell, Takeshi Watanabe.

11 *Improper Corporate Payoffs Termed a 'Cancer' which Weakens Firms, Subverts Markets, and Threatens Democratic Values* (Summer 1976). Contributors: Lloyd N. Cutler, Prime Minister Pierre Trudeau, Zbigniew Brzezinski.

12 *The Governability Debate Continued* (Fall 1976). Contributors: Peter Jenkins, Walter Dean Burnham, Yonosuke Nagai, Umberto Colombo.

13 *Trade Issues and Macroeconomic Coordination Highlight Trilateral Tokyo Meeting* (Winter 1976–7). Contributors: Marina Whitman, Thiérry De Montbrial, Saburo Okita, Iichiro Hatoyama, Kiichi Miyazawa, President Carter, Zbigniew Brzezinski, Richard Cooper, David Rockefeller.

14 *Managing Global Problems: Avenues for Trilateral–Communist Collaboration* (Summer 1977). Contributors: Fred Sanderson, John Pinder, Gerald Parsky, Fuji Kamiya, Yevgeniy Rusakov.

15 *Trilateral Meeting in Bonn – Discusses East–West Relations and Strategies to Increase Food Production in LDCs; Assesses Nuclear Energy and Non-Proliferation Policies* (Fall 1977). Contributors: Gerard C. Smith, Kinya Niizeki, André Giraud, Zbigniew Brzezinski, Bunroku Yoshino, Chancellor Brandt, Henry A. Kissinger, Otto Graf Lambsdorff.

16 *The London Summit Revisited* (Winter 1977–8). Contributors: Henry Owen, Meinhard Miegel, Bunroku Yoshino, Fabio Basagni.

17 *Trilateral Proposal Debated – Doubling Rice Production in Asia* (Spring 1978). Contributors: James P. Grant, Saburo Okita, Francis Wells, Kenzo Henmi, Montague Yudelman.

18 *Energy, Industrial Relations and Trilateral Economic Problems Major Issues at Trilateral Meeting in Washington DC* (Summer 1978). Contributors: Harold Brown, Klaus von Dohnanyi, W. Michael Blumenthal, Nobuhiko Ushiba, Etienne Davignon, Kiichi Miyazawa.

19 *A Dimension of North–South, East–West, and Trilateral Relations – the Politics of Human Rights* (Fall 1978). Contributors: Henry A. Kissinger, Andrei Sakharov, Claude Cheysson, Ali A. Mazrui, Ribot Hatano, Horst Ehmke, Tom Farer, Romesh Thapar, Mihajlo Mihajlov, Jean-Marie Benoist, Gordon Fairweather.

240

20 *10th Trilateral Meeting – Discusses Payments Imbalances; Industrial Policies; Assesses China's Role in the International Community; Reviews Recent Developments in Japan, N. America, W. Europe* (Summer 1979). Contributors: Prime Minister Masayoshi Ohira, Otto Graf Lambsdorff, Kiichi Miyazawa, Yasuo Takeyama, Walter M. Heller, Endymion Wilkinson, Yusuke Kashiwagi, Michel Oksenberg, Kiichi Saeki.

21 *Security in the 1980s; The Great SALT II Debate – America's Strategy in the Age of Parity – A Changing Balance in Europe – What Role for Japan? – The Scope of SALT III* (Fall 1979). Contributors: Harold Brown, Alexander Haig, François de Rose, Karl Kaiser, Takuya Kubo, Toru Yano.

22 *Trilateral Relations – At the Threshold of the New Decade* (Winter 1980). Contributors: Robert R. Bowie, Otto Graf Lambsdorff, Nobuhiko Ushiba, Ulf Lantzke, Gerard C. Smith, George W. Rathjens, Ian Smart, Gaston Thorn, Yasushi Hara, Graham Allison, David Rockefeller.

23 *1980 Trilateral Commission Plenary, London – Discuss State of Trilateral Relations; The Security Balance; The Middle East* (Spring 1980). Contributors: Kiichi Miyazawa, Lord Carrington, Christopher Bertram, Sir Shridath S. Ramphal.

24 *The Trilateral Countries and the Middle East – What Chances for Peace?* (October, 1980). Contributors: Joseph J. Sisco, Shlomo Avineri, Edward Said, Saburo Okita, Udo Steinbach, William Scranton, Abdel Hamid Abdel-Ghani, HRH Prince Saud.

25 *Trilateral–Soviet Relations in Transition* (Winter 1980–1). Contributors: Seweryn Bialer, Willy Brandt, Nagao Hyodo, Zbigniew Brzezinski, Hiroshi Kimura, François de Rose.

26 *Washington Plenary Meeting of the Trilateral Commission – The Middle East and the Trilateral Countries; The International Economy in the 1980s; Current Developments in the Trilateral Countries; Changes in the Soviet Union and Eastern Europe* (Spring 1981). Contributors: Alexander Haig, Alan Greenspan, James Hoge, William Cohen, Hervé de Carmoy, Theo Sommer, Ariyoshi Okumura, Masashi Nishihara, Seweryn Bialer, Michael Kaser, Fuji Kamiya, Rodrigo Botero.

27 *Japan: A Partnership in Progress* (Summer/Fall 1981). Contributors: Nobuhiko Ushiba, Gerald L. Curtis, Takakazu Kuriyama, Otto Graf Lambsdorff, Robert Ingersoll, Martin G. Gilman, Wilhelm Haferkamp.

28 *North and South: After Cancun – Where To?* (Summer/Fall 1981). Contributors: Takeshi Watanabe, Pierre Elliott Trudeau, Haskell G. Ward, Javier Perez de Cuellar, H. Konan Bedie, Jean-Jacques Servan-Schreiber.

29 *Tokyo Plenary Meeting of Trilateral Commission – East–West Trade at a Crossroads; Sharing International Responsibilities Among the Trilateral Countries; Strengthening GATT* (Spring 1982). Contributors: Toshio Komoto, Zbigniew Brzezinski, Adam Malik, Hideo Kitahara, Edmund Wellenstein, Robert Strauss.

30/1 *Security and Disarmament* (Summer/Fall 1982). Contributors: Mitchell Sharp, Gerard C. Smith, Raymond Aron, Makoto Momoi, Zbigniew Brzezinski, Alois Mertes, Indira Ghandi, Joseph S. Nye, David Owen, Takahiro Yokomichi, Carlo Trezza.

32 *Middle East Opportunities* (Winter 1983). Contributors: Moshe Arens,

Ahmed Sidki Dajani, HRH Prince Hassan, Hideo Kitahara, Arrigo Levi, Yitzhak Rabin, Bassam Shaka, Aziz Sidki, Joseph Sisco, Ghassan Tueni, The Middle-East Team.

33 *Rome Plenary Meeting of Trilateral Commission* (Spring 1983). Contributors not named.

34 *Heart of Europe* (Spring/Fall 1983). Contributors: Georges Berthoin, Leszek Kolakowski, Ernst Kux, Zbigniew Brzezinski, Richard von Weizsacker, Czeslaw Milosz, Bruno Kreisky, Milovan Djilas, Yoshiya Kato, Robert A. D. Ford.

35 *Sovereignty and Intervention* (March 1984). Contributors: Richard N. Gardner, André Glucksmann, Altaf Gauhar, Mario Vargas Llosa, Jerome Kohn, Melvyn Hill.

36 *Washington DC Plenary Meeting of Trilateral Commission* (April 1984). Contributors: Daniel Yenkelovich, Henri Simonet, Mitchell Sharp, Naohiro Amaya, George P. Schultz, Jacques de Larosière, Jesus Silva-Herzog.

37 *Tokyo Plenary Meeting of Trilateral Commission* (April 1985). Contributors: Takeshi Watanabe, David Rockefeller, Georges Berthoin, Martin Feldstein, Karl Kaiser, Hiroshi Kimura, W. Tom Johnson, Edmund Wellenstein, Masataka Kosaka, Han Sung-joo, Sarasin Viraphol, Gerado Sicat, William Henderson, Koichi Kato, Sun Shangquing, Masashi Nishihara, D. Gale Johnson, Kenzo Hemmi, Pierre Lardinois.

NOTES

1 INTRODUCTION

1 The Trilateral Commission defines itself as 'a non-governmental, policy-oriented discussion group of about 300 distinguished citizens from Western Europe, North America and Japan formed to encourage mutual understanding and closer cooperation among these three regions on common problems . . . In this setting, the founders of the Commission believed it important that cooperation among Western Europe, North America (including Canada) and Japan be sustained and strengthened – not only on issues among these regions but in a global framework as well', *The Trilateral Commission: Questions and Answers* (New York, Trilateral Commission, 1980), p. 1.

2 The term 'global political economy' refers to both an integrated entity and analysis of political and economic structures and processes at a world or global level. The term is used in preference to the term 'international political economy' which carries the implication that economic interactions between states (rather than nations *per se*) are the major focus of political economy beyond the domestic level. The conceptualisation of this is, of course, a matter of debate between rival perspectives. For summaries see P. A. Gourevitch, 'The Second Image Reversed: the International Sources of Domestic Politics', *International Organisation*, vol. 32 (1978), pp. 929–52; R. J. Barry Jones, 'International Political Economy: Perspectives and Prospects', *Review of International Studies*, vol. 8 (1982), pp. 39–52; R. Tooze, 'In Search of International Political Economy', *Political Studies*, vol. 32 (1984), pp. 637–46. For collections of essays which use the term 'international political economy' see W. Ladd Hollist and F. Lamond Tullis (eds.), *An International Political Economy Year Book*, vol. 1 (Boulder, Colorado, Westview Press, 1985), S. Strange (ed.), *Paths to International Political Economy* (London, Frances Pinter, 1985). The nomenclature 'international political economy' is used throughout the literature. The earliest systematic use of the term 'global political economy' known to the author is H. Hveem, 'The Global Dominance System: Notes on a Theory of Global Political Economy', *Journal of Peace Research*, vol. 4 (1973), pp. 319–40.

3 The term 'establishment' is not precisely coterminous with 'upper' or 'ruling' class, although it consists of a triumvirate of international bankers, lawyers and corporate executives especially in New York City, as well as

243

government officials in Washington DC, and Bostonian and other Ivy League academics. It operates out of the public forum, it is a 'self-recruiting group of men (virtually no women) who have a shared philosophy toward, and have exercised practical influence on, the course of American defence and foreign policy', G. Hodgson, 'The Establishment', in R. W. Tucker and W. Watts (eds.), *Beyond Containment: US Foreign Policy in Transition* (Washington DC, Potomac Associates, 1973), p. 138. Hodgson adds, 'The American Foreign Policy Establishment is now divided even on the question of its own existence' (p. 130).

4 On these concepts, see A. Gramsci, *Selections from the Prison Notebooks of Antonio Gramsci*, translated and edited by Q. Hoare and G. Nowell Smith (New York, International Publishers, 1971), hereafter referred to as *Prison Notebooks*; see on hegemony: pp. 53–60, 80f, 104–6, 125ff; the state: pp. 52–4, 116–17, 239–75; organic intellectuals: pp. 6–20; civil society: pp. 12–13, 235–64; and historic bloc: pp. 360, 366, 377. For their application to the method of international relations see: R. W. Cox, 'Gramsci, Hegemony and International Relations: An Essay in Method', *Millennium*, vol. 12 (1983), pp. 162–75. These concepts are applied to the analysis of the Trilateral Commission in S. Gill, 'Hegemony, Consensus and Trilateralism', *Review of International Studies*, vol. 12 (1986), pp. 205–21.

5 F. Halliday, 'State and Society in International Relations: A Second Agenda', *Millennium*, vol. 16 (1987), pp. 215–30.

6 An exception is K. van der Pijl, *The Making of an Atlantic Ruling Class* (London, Verso, 1984).

7 E. Krippendorf, 'The Dominance of American Approaches in International Relations', *Millennium*, vol. 16 (1987), pp. 207–14.

8 This is a recurrent theme, for example, in S. Smith (ed.), *International Relations: British and American Perspectives* (Oxford, Basil Blackwell, 1985). See, in particular, the essays by the editor, 'Foreign Policy Analysis', pp. 45–55, M. Clarke, 'Transnationalism', pp. 146–70, and S. Gill, 'From Atlanticism to Trilateralism', pp. 185–212.

9 R. W. Cox, 'Social Forces, States and World Orders', revised version, in R. O. Keohane (ed.), *Neorealism and its Critics* (New York, Columbia University Press, 1986).

10 For example, F. Duchêne, K. Mushakoji and H. Owen, *The Crisis of International Cooperation* (New York, Trilateral Commission, 1974). Duchêne was formerly private secretary to the architect of the European Community, Jean Monnet, and the Director of the London-based International Institute for Strategic Studies; Mushakoji was Rector of the United Nations University in Tokyo and President of the International Political Science Association; Owen was Director of Foreign Policy Studies at the Brookings Institution in Washington DC, and later Ambassador-at-Large (and United States organiser for the seven-power economic summits) in the Carter administration.

11 B. Roberts, 'The Enigmatic Trilateral Commission: Boon or Bane?', *Millennium*, vol. 9 (1982), pp. 185–202.

12 The appointees included Walter Mondale (Vice-President), Cyrus Vance (Secretary of State), Harold Brown (Secretary of Defense), Michael

Blumenthal (Secretary of Treasury), and Zbigniew Brzezinski (National Security Advisor). Brzezinski had been the Director of the Trilateral Commission before taking office.

13 H. Sklar (ed.), *Trilateralism: Elite Planning For World Management* (Boston, South End Press, 1980).

14 J. R. Rosenau and O. R. Holsti identify three interdependent 'belief systems' within American foreign policy elites: 'Neo-isolationism' (e.g., the recent writings of George Kennan), 'Cold War Internationalism' (e.g., many members of the first Reagan administration), and the 'Post Cold War Internationalism' (e.g., much of the Carter administration). See 'US Leadership in a Shrinking World: The Breakdown of Consensuses and the Emergence of Conflicting Belief Systems', *World Politics*, vol. 35 (1983), pp. 368–92.

15 J. Larrain, *The Concept of Ideology* (London, Hutchinson, 1979).

16 On essential contestability see W. Connolly, *The Terms of Political Discourse* (Oxford, Basil Blackwell, 1983).

17 G. Therborn, *The Ideology of Power and the Power of Ideology* (London, New Left Books, 1980), p. 79.

18 Ibid., p. 80.

19 On American views on Europe see S. Gill, 'American Perceptions and Policies', in S. Gill (ed.), *Atlantic Relations: Beyond the Reagan Era* (Brighton, Wheatsheaf Books, 1989). An interesting study of Japanese–European elite perceptions is R. Immerman, 'European Attitudes Towards Japan: Trilateralism's Weakest Link', *Executive Seminar in National and International Affairs, Department of State, 1979–80* (Washington DC, US Department of State, April 1980).

20 Cox, 'Social Forces, States and World Orders', revised version, p. 207.

21 R. W. Cox, 'Ideologies and the New International Economic Order: Reflections on Some Recent Literature', *International Organisation*, vol. 33 (1979), pp. 257–302.

22 F. List, *The National System of Political Economy* (New York, Garland, 1974); see also, J. Gallagher and R. Robinson, 'The Imperialism of Free Trade', *Economic History Review*, second series, vol. 6 (1953), pp. 1–15.

2 REALIST AND LIBERAL PERSPECTIVES

1 Thucydides, *The History of the Peloponnesian War* (New York, Galaxy Books, 1960); N. Machiavelli, *The Prince* (Harmondsworth, Penguin, 1975).

2 E. H. Carr, *The Twenty Years' Crisis* (New York, Harper Torchbooks, 1964); H. J. Morgenthau, *Politics Among Nations: The Struggle for Power and Peace* (New York, Alfred Knopf, 1985); R. Gilpin, 'The Richness of the Tradition of Political Realism', *International Organisation*, vol. 38 (1984), pp. 287–304. See, as a counterpoint to Gilpin: H. and M. Sprout, 'Tribal Sovereignty vs. Interdependence', in M. Smith, R. Little and M. Shackleton (eds.), *Perspectives on World Politics* (London, Croom Helm/Open University Press, 1981), pp. 245–57.

3 Keohane (ed.), *Neorealism and its Critics*, p. 159.

4 T. Lowi, *The End of Liberalism* (New York, W. W. Norton, 1979).

5 List, *The National System of Political Economy*, cited in G. Kitching, *Development and Underdevelopment in Historical Perspective* (London, Methuen, 1982), p. 144.

6 H. Kohn, 'Nationalism', in D. Weiner (ed.), *Dictionary of the History of Ideas* (New York, Charles Scribner's Sons, 1973), p. 329.

7 T. L. Hughes, 'The Crack Up', *Foreign Policy* (1980), no. 40, pp. 33–60. See also G. Quester, 'Consensus Lost', *Foreign Policy* (1980), no. 40, pp. 18–32; R. W. Tucker, *The Purposes of American Power* (New York, Lehrman Institute/Praeger, 1981).

8 Interview with Professor Richard Falk, Princeton University, Princeton, NJ, 16 November 1981.

9 See D. K. Simes, 'Disciplining Soviet Power', *Foreign Policy* (1981), no. 43, pp. 33–53; R. Legvold, 'Containment Without Confrontation', *Foreign Policy* (1980), no. 40, pp. 74–98. Earlier Simes noted, 'Concern about the Soviet threat is growing in the United States. Cooperation with the Russians is once again perceived as unwise, if not unpatriotic . . . There is an urge to do something, to show the Kremlin that the United States is not about to be pushed around', D. K. Simes, 'The Anti-Soviet Brigade', *Foreign Policy* (1979–80), no. 37, p. 28.

10 R. Gilpin, *War and Change in World Politics* (Princeton, NJ, Princeton University Press, 1981), p. 211.

11 K. N. Waltz, *Theory of International Politics* (Reading, Mass., Addison-Wesley, 1979).

12 Gilpin, 'The Richness of the Tradition of Political Realism', pp. 296–7.

13 C. F. Bergsten, E. Davignon, I. Miyazaki, and W. Lawson, *Conditions for Partnership in International Economic Management* (New York, Trilateral Commission, 1986).

14 Gilpin, *War and Change in World Politics*, p. 129.

15 Gilpin, 'The Richness of the Tradition of Political Realism', pp. 295–6.

16 Ibid., p. 296.

17 On the wider elaboration of this argument see, D. P. Calleo, *Beyond American Hegemony: The Future of the Western Alliance* (Brighton, Wheatsheaf Books, 1987).

18 J. Greenless, 'Japan Brushes up its English', *Times Higher Educational Supplement*, 10 October 1986.

19 F. Adjami, 'The Global Logic of the Neoconservatives', *World Politics*, vol. 30 (1978), p. 464; S. Hoffman, *Primacy or World Order: American Foreign Policy Since the Cold War* (New York, McGraw-Hill, 1978), pp. 246–9, 263.

20 A. Smith, *An Enquiry into the Nature and Causes of the Wealth of Nations* (Harmondsworth, Penguin, 1984).

21 D. Ricardo, *Principles of Political Economy and Taxation* (Harmondsworth, Penguin, 1971).

22 R. Falk, 'A New Paradigm for International Legal Studies: Prospects and Proposals', *Yale Law Journal*, vol. 84 (1975), pp. 969–1021.

23 R. O. Keohane and J. S. Nye, *Power and Interdependence* (Boston, Little Brown, 1977); see also, R. Cooper, *The Economics of Interdependence: Economic Policy in the Atlantic Community* (New York, McGraw-Hill/Council on Foreign Relations, 1968).

24 Keohane and Nye, *Power and Interdependence*, pp. 24–9.
25 J. G. Ruggie, 'International Regimes, Transactions and Change – Embedded Liberalism in the Post-War Economic Order', *International Organisation*, vol. 36 (1982), pp. 379–415.
26 M. Camps, *The Management of Interdependence: A Preliminary View* (New York, Council on Foreign Relations, 1974).
27 M. Olson, *The Logic of Collective Action* (Cambridge, Mass., Harvard University Press, 1965); C. Kindleberger, *Power and Money* (New York, Basic Books, 1970), and 'Dominance and Leadership in the International Economy: Exploitation, Public Goods and Free Rides', *International Studies Quarterly*, vol. 25 (1981), pp. 242–54.
28 Olson, *The Logic of Collective Action*.
29 R. T. Kudrle, 'The Several Faces of the Multinational Corporation', in Hollist and Tullis (eds.), *An International Political Economy Year Book*, vol. 1, pp. 187–8.
30 S. Gill and D. Law, *The Global Political Economy: Perspectives, Problems and Policies* (Brighton, Wheatsheaf Books; Baltimore, Johns Hopkins University Press, 1988), p. 44.
31 B. S. Frey, *International Political Economics* (Oxford, Basil Blackwell, 1984), p. 130.
32 B. S. Frey, 'The Public Choice View of International Political Economy', *International Organisation*, vol. 38 (1984), p. 217.
33 Ruggie, 'International Regimes, Transactions and Change'.
34 Bergsten, *et al.*, *Conditions for Partnership in International Economic Management*, p. 10.
35 K. Kaiser, W. Lord, T. de Montbrial, D. C. Watt, *Western Security: What Has Changed? What Should Be Done?* (New York and London, Council on Foreign Relations/Royal Institute of International Affairs, 1981), pp. 45, 21. See also N. Ushiba, G. T. Allison and T. de Montbrial, *Sharing International Responsibilities* (New York, Trilateral Commission, 1983), pp. 14–19.
36 Ushiba, *et al.*, *Sharing International Responsibilities*, p. 21.
37 Interview with Zbigniew Brzezinski, Washington DC, 28 February 1982.

3 MARXIST PERSPECTIVES: THE QUESTION OF HEGEMONY REDEFINED

1 E. Mandel, *The Second Slump: A Marxist Analysis of Recession in the Seventies* (London, Verso, 1979).
2 For a review of these theories, see A. Brewer, *Marxist Theories of Imperialism* (London, Routledge and Kegan Paul, 1980), pp. 79–130. See V. I. Lenin, *Imperialism* (New York, International Publishers, 1939), especially pp. 114–15; N. Bukharin, *Imperialism and World Economy* (London, Merlin Press, 1976).
3 K. Kautsky, 'Ultra-Imperialism', *New Left Review* (1970), no. 59, pp. 41–6.
4 B. Rowthorn, 'Imperialism in the Seventies – Unity or Rivalry?', *New Left Review* (1971), no. 69, pp. 31–54. See also E. Mandel, 'Where is America Going?', *New Left Review* (1969), no. 54, pp. 3–15; M. Nicolaus, 'USA – The Universal Contradiction', *New Left Review* (1970), no. 59, pp. 3–18; E.

Mandel, 'The Laws of Uneven Development', *New Left Review* (1970), no. 59, pp. 19–40; B. Rowthorn, 'Imperialism in the Seventies: Unity or Rivalry?', *New Left Review* (1971), no. 69, pp. 31–54; J. Petras and R. Rhodes, 'The Reconsolidation of US Hegemony', *New Left Review* (1976), no. 97, pp. 37–53; F. Block, 'Communication', *New Left Review* (1976), no. 99, pp. 112–14; A. Szymanski, 'Is US Imperialism Resurgent?', *New Left Review* (1977), no. 101–2, pp. 144–52; and J. Petras and R. Rhodes, 'Reply to Critics', *New Left Review* (1977), no. 101–2, pp. 153–60.

5 N. D. Turkatenko, 'Origins and aims of the Trilateral Commission', *Ssa – Economika, Politika, Ideologija* (1977), no. 9, translated in *IDOC Bulletin* (1977), no. 11–12, pp. 5–6.

6 E. Mandel, *Europe versus America* (London: New Left Books, 1970), p. 13, emphasis in original. See also E. Mandel, 'The Laws of Uneven Development', *New Left Review* (1970), no. 59, pp. 19–38.

7 Gilpin, *War and Change in World Politics*, pp. 179–80.

8 Petras and Rhodes, 'The Reconsolidation of US Hegemony', p. 39.

9 J. Frieden, 'The Trilateral Commission: Economics and Politics in the 1970s', *Monthly Review* (1977), pp. 1–18. See also M. Lansberg, 'Multinational Corporations and the Crisis of Capitalism', *Insurgent Sociologist*, vol. 7 (1976), pp. 19–33; S. Hymer, 'The Internationalisation of Capital', *Journal of Economic Issues*, vol. 6 (1972), pp. 91–112.

10 I. Wallerstein, *The Capitalist World Economy* (Cambridge, Cambridge University Press, 1979). See also A. G. Frank, *Dependent Accumulation and Underdevelopment* (London, Macmillan, 1978); S. Amin, *Unequal Development* (New York, Monthly Review Press, 1976); A. Emmanuel, *Unequal Exchange: A Study of the Imperialism of Trade* (London, New Left Books, 1972).

11 R. Brenner, 'The Origins of Capitalist Development: A Critique of Neo-Smithian Marxism', *New Left Review* (1977), no. 104, pp. 25–92.

12 S. Amin, G. Arrighi, A. G. Frank and I. Wallerstein, *Dynamics of Global Crisis* (London, Macmillan, 1982), p. 235, my emphasis.

13 A. Bergesen, 'Modeling Long Waves of Crisis in the World System', in A. Bergesen (ed.), *Crises in the World-System* (Beverly Hills: Sage, 1983), p. 78.

14 Wallerstein, *The Capitalist World Economy*, p. 293.

15 Ibid., pp. 117–18.

16 See, for example, section 6 of H. Sklar, *Trilateralism*, pp. 339–434, especially K. Bird, 'Co-opting the Third World Elites: Trilateralism and Saudi Arabia', pp. 341–51; P. Nesbitt, 'Trilateralism and The Rhodesian Problem: An Effort at Managing the Zimbabwean Liberation Struggle', pp. 379–402.

17 Wallerstein, *The Capitalist World Economy*, p. 279.

18 Ibid., pp. 281–2.

19 This section draws on Gill, 'Hegemony, Consensus and Trilateralism'.

20 R. Simon, 'Gramsci's Concept of Hegemony', *Marxism Today*, March 1977, p. 84n. Simon points out that Marx did, however, use the term in a similar sense to Gramsci in parts II and IV of *The Eighteenth Brumaire of Louis Bonaparte*.

21 Gramsci, *Prison Notebooks*, p. 263. For Gramsci's critique of the idea of the 'nightwatchman' or minimalist state, see *Prison Notebooks*, pp. 261–3.
22 Ibid., p. 12.
23 Ibid., p. 238.
24 Ibid., p. 244.
25 Ibid., p. 262.
26 Ibid., p. 184.
27 Ibid., pp. 180–3.
28 Ibid., p. 181.
29 Ibid.
30 Ibid., pp. 181–2.
31 A. Showstack-Sassoon, *Gramsci's Politics* (London, Croom Helm, 1980), pp. 119–22. My interpretation of Gramsci has been influenced by Showstack-Sassoon, Joll, Larrain and Cox. There are a variety of other possible interpretations of Gramsci. See C. Mouffe (ed.), *Gramsci and Marxist Theory* (London, Routledge and Kegan Paul, 1979), and E. Laclau, *Politics and Ideology in Marxist Theory* (London, New Left Books, 1977).
32 Gramsci, *Prison Notebooks*, p. 366.
33 Ibid., p. 161.
34 Ibid., p. 168.
35 Cox, 'Social Forces, States and World Orders'.
36 Cox, 'Gramsci, Hegemony and International Relations', p. 169.
37 Ibid., p. 171.
38 Ibid.
39 Ibid., pp. 171–2.
40 J. Joll, *Gramsci* (Glasgow, Fontana, 1977), pp. 99–100.
41 Showstack-Sassoon, *Gramsci's Politics*, p. 116.
42 Gramsci, *Prison Notebooks*, p. 97.
43 Cited in Z. Brzezinski, 'Memorandum – The Trilateral Policy Program', 18 September 1973, *Mimeo*, p. 13, my emphasis.
44 J. Larrain, *Marxism and Ideology* (London, Macmillan, 1983), pp. 78–9, 80, 85.
45 Showstack-Sassoon, *Gramsci's Politics*, p. 134.
46 G. Berthoin, G. C. Smith and T. Watanabe, 'Foreword' to *Trilateral Commission Task Force Reports: 1–7* (New York, New York University Press, 1977), p. viii. See also Z. Brzezinski, *Between Two Ages: America's Role in the Technetronic Era* (New York, Viking Books, 1970), pp. 293–310, and an earlier chapter, 'The Quest For a Universal Vision', pp. 65–74.
47 Joll, *Gramsci*, pp. 100, 112.
48 L. H. Shoup and W. Minter, *Imperial Brains Trust: The Council on Foreign Relations and United States Foreign Policy* (New York, Monthly Review Press, 1977).

4 THE DECLINE OF AMERICAN HEGEMONY: MYTH AND REALITY

1 See, for example, G. Arrighi, 'A Crisis of Hegemony', in Amin *et al.*, *Dynamics of Global Crisis*, pp. 55–108; S. Strange, 'Interpretations of a Decade', in L. Tsoukalis (ed.), *International Monetary Relations in the 1970s*

(London, RIIA/Sage, 1985) pp. 1–43; and B. Russett, 'The Mysterious Case of Vanishing Hegemony; or, Is Mark Twain Really Dead?', *International Organisation*, vol. 89 (1985), pp. 206–31; S. Gill, 'American Hegemony: Its Limits and Prospects in the Reagan Era', *Millennium*, vol. 15 (1986), no. 3, pp. 311–36.

2 D. Bell, 'The End of American Exceptionalism', in N. Glazer and I. Kristol (eds.), *The American Commonwealth 1976* (New York, Basic Books, 1976), pp. 193–224.

3 R. Rosecrance (ed.), *America as an Ordinary Country: U.S. Foreign Policy and the Future* (Ithaca, Cornell University Press, 1976).

4 P. Kennedy, *The Rise and Fall of the Great Powers: Economic Change and Military Conflict From 1500 to 2000* (London, Unwin Hyman, 1988). These arguments also correspond to the views on the breakup of the international economic order under conditions of declining hegemony. See D. Sylvan, 'The Newest Mercantilism', *International Organisation* (1981), vol. 35, pp. 375–9. He discusses F. Block, *The Origins of International Economic Disorder* (Berkeley: University of California Press, 1977); R. Gilpin, *US Power and the Multinational Corporation* (New York, Basic Books, 1975); and S. Krasner, *Defending the National Interest* (Princeton, NJ, Princeton University Press, 1978). See also I. Wallerstein, *The Modern World System II* (New York, Academic Press, 1980), pp. 38–39; Gilpin, *War and Change in World Politics*, p. 156.

5 Calleo, *Beyond American Hegemony*, p. 220.

6 C. Chase-Dunn, 'International Economic Policy in a Declining Core State', in W. P. Avery and D. P. Rapkin (eds.), *America in a Changing World Political Economy* (London, Longman, 1983), pp. 77–96.

7 W. J. Baumol, 'Productivity Growth, Convergence and Welfare', *American Economic Review*, vol. 76 (1986), pp. 1072–85.

8 S. Melman, *Pentagon Capitalism: The Political Economy of War* (New York, McGraw-Hill, 1970); R. W. De Grasse, Jr, *Military Expansion, Economic Decline* (New York, M. E. Sharpe for the Council on Economic Priorities, 1983).

9 See the symposium in *International Studies Quarterly*, vol. 30 (1986), no. 4. The editors to the symposium note: 'The fragmentation of elites into a number of opposite poles, each holding to its own unique system of beliefs, signals the onset of an ideological crisis. Characteristic of such a crisis is the disintegration of the consensual basis of collective American action in world affairs, a resulting sense of lost direction' (p. 373).

10 See M. Crozier, *et al.*, *The Crisis of Democracy* (New York, New York University Press, 1975); D. Bell, *The Cultural Contradictions of Capitalism* (New York, Basic Books, 1976).

11 R. Gilpin, *The Political Economy of International Relations* (Princeton, NJ, Princeton University Press, 1987), p. 394.

12 Much of this literature found its way into the American journal *International Organisation*. For a bibliography and a critique see D. Snidal, 'The Limits of Hegemonic Stability Theory', *International Organisation*, vol. 39 (1985), pp. 579–614.

13 Keohane, *After Hegemony*; see also R. O. Keohane and J. S. Nye, 'Two Cheers for Multilateralism', *Foreign Policy* (1985), no. 60, pp. 148–67, and C. F. Bergsten, 'The Problem?', *Foreign Policy* (1985), no. 59, pp. 132–44.

14 See, for example, C. F. Bergsten, *et al.*, *Conditions for Partnership in International Economic Management* (New York, Trilateral Commission, 1986).

15 See D. Snidal, 'The Game THEORY of International Politics', *World Politics*, vol. 39 (1986), pp. 25–57. See also the whole edition of *World Politics*, vol. 38 (October, 1986), which is devoted to game theory and the question of international co-operation.

16 Calleo, *Beyond American Hegemony*, p. 107.

17 This idea of structural dominance is, of course, akin to Keohane and Nye's view of asymmetrical interdependence in *Power and Interdependence*. However, in Keohane's *After Hegemony*, it is as if Keohane had abandoned the use of this earlier conception. In his recent book, Keohane manifests a concern more for the constraints of interdependence for the United States than seeing how unequal interdependence may be a potential power resource for the dominant nation.

18 J. L. Hervey, 'The Internationalisation of Uncle Sam', *Economic Perspectives: Federal Reserve Bank of Chicago*, vol. 10 (1986), no. 3, p. 4.

19 G. de Jonquières and A. Kaletsky, 'The Enemy Within', *Financial Times*, 11 May 1987.

20 John Agnew, *The United States in the World-Economy* (Cambridge, Cambridge University Press, 1987), p. 139.

21 G. de Jonquières and A. Kaletsky, 'We are Hoist with our own Petard', *Financial Times*, 20 May 1987. See also, G. de Jonquières and A. Kaletsky, 'Beware the Simple Solution', *The Financial Times*, 18 May 1987.

22 Gill and Law, *The Global Political Economy*, p. 342.

23 R. Coombs, 'Rising in the East, Setting in the West', *Times Higher Education Supplement*, 6 February 1987.

24 See, for example, S. Strange, 'The Persistent Myth of Lost Hegemony', *International Organisation*, vol. 41 (1987), pp. 551–74; S. Strange, *Casino Capitalism* (Oxford, Basil Blackwell, 1986).

25 H. Nau, 'Where Reaganomics Works', *Foreign Policy* (1984–5), no. 57, pp. 22–3. Nau may have been aware of this when he was in government during 1981–4.

26 K. Ohmae, *Triad Power: The Coming Shape of Global Competition* (New York, Free Press, 1985).

27 See, for example, J. W. Fulbright, *The Pentagon Propaganda Machine* (New York, Viking Press, 1971); J. W. Fulbright (ed.), *American Militarism, 1970* (New York, Viking Press, 1969).

28 According to figures from the International Institute for Strategic Studies, and the independent US Council on Economic Priorities, US defence outlays in 1986–8 would, if appropriated by the Congress, have totalled over $1 trillion. Soviet expenditures were in effect virtually impossible to compare but support total armed forces of 5.15 million people as opposed to 2.13 million in the United States. Western estimates of Soviet expenditures have varied widely, ranging between 10 and 20 per cent of its NNP

(net national product). On Soviet policy see M. McGuire, *Military Objectives in Soviet Foreign Policy* (Washington DC, Brookings Institution, 1987).

29 F. Halliday, *The Making of the Second Cold War* (London, New Left Books, 1986), pp. 232–3.

30 Ibid., p. 235.

31 See A. L. Friedberg, 'The Assessment of Military Power', *International Security* (1987), vol. 12, pp. 190–202. Friedberg reviews: T. Gervasi, *The Myth of Soviet Military Supremacy* (New York, Harper and Row, 1986); W. T. Less and R. F. Staar, *Soviet Military Policy Since World War II* (Stanford, California, Hoover Institution Press, 1986). The essay points out the great difficulty of measuring relative military power, but warns against static forms of measurement (or 'simple force exchange models', upon which most government presentations have been constructed); the importance of estimates based on trends ('movies' rather than 'snapshots'); and stresses the importance of building perceptions of capabilities and intentions into assessments of varied 'functional and geographical theaters', pointing out that measurement of the situation in East Asia has been relatively neglected, at the expense of the European theatre.

32 In addition to massive Pentagon military expenditures, the Department of Defense also has huge outlays for research and development (R and D). In addition, American private companies account for nearly 50 per cent of the total R and D spending of all OECD countries. Since military R and D was 28 per cent of the 1985 United States total, America accounts for over 60 per cent of the OECD total for combined 'military' and 'civilian' R and D. Much of this private R and D expenditure would be 'public' in a state socialist country. Thus, taken to include private outlays, American military expenditures may be higher than even Halliday suggests. See P. Marsh, 'A Disturbing Outlook', *Financial Times*, 3 December 1985.

33 Halliday, *The Making of the Second Cold War*, pp. 57–8.

34 The real costs to the United States and its allies (and indeed to the Soviet Union) must be measured in terms of the opportunity costs of military expenditures in terms of long-term growth potential forgone. The bulk of the evidence from independent writers like Melman and de Grasse suggests that high military expenditures undermine the potential growth in productivity, as well as using up resources which could improve other aspects of American life. On the other hand, military expenditures have had certain Keynesian, demand-boosting effects in the short term.

35 S. Chan, 'The Impact of Defence Spending on Economic Performance', *Orbis*, vol. 29 (1985), p. 431.

36 Kaiser *et al.*, *Western Security*, p. 18.

37 J. Adams, 'US Offers $32 bn deal on fighter', *Sunday Times*, 6 March 1988.

38 H. Sprout and M. Sprout, 'National Priorities: Demands, Resources, Dilemmas', *World Politics*, vol. 24 (1972), pp. 311–12, cited in Gilpin, *War and Change in World Politics*, p. 174.

39 J. L. Bodaracco Jr and D. B. Yoffie, '"Industrial Policy": It Can't Happen Here', *Harvard Business Review*, vol. 6 (1983), p. 100.

40 Lester Thurow notes that by the early 1980s it was significant that in the biggest American cities, 8 per cent of those entering the work force were

functionally illiterate, and when American 17-year-olds left high school they knew less than half as much mathematics as their Japanese counterparts. American high school and college leaving test scores had fallen by 10 per cent in the previous fifteen years. By the mid-1980s Japan produced twice as many engineers per capita as the United States. See L. Thurow, 'America, Europe and Japan', *The Economist*, 9 November 1985, pp. 21–6.

41 C. Joyce, 'Science Under Reagan: the first four years', *New Scientist*, 24 January 1985, pp. 24–5.

42 Russett, 'The Mysterious Case of Vanishing Hegemony', p. 231.

43 M. Nishihara, *East Asian Security* (New York, Trilateral Commission, 1985), pp. 42–3.

44 Ibid., pp. 42–3.

45 Snidal, 'The Limits of Hegemonic Stability Theory'.

46 Russett, 'The Mysterious Case of Vanishing Hegemony', pp. 213–18.

47 Strange, 'The Persistent Myth of Lost Hegemony'.

48 S. Gill, 'American Hegemony and the International Economic Order', lecture given to Graduate School of International Relations, Geneva, 7 March 1988, *Mimeo*.

5 TOWARDS AN AMERICAN-CENTRED TRANSNATIONAL HEGEMONY?

1 Van der Pijl, *The Making of an Atlantic Ruling Class*, pp. 35–75.

2 United Nations Centre on Transnational Corporations, *Transnational Corporations in World Development: Trends and Prospects* (New York, United Nations, 1988).

3 *The Economist*, 24 January 1987.

4 A. Hoogvelt, 'The New International Division of Labour', in R. Bush, G. Johnston and D. Coates (eds.), *The World Order: Socialist Perspectives* (Oxford, Polity Press/Basil Blackwell, 1987), p. 75. Theorists at Reading University are cited in note 9, below. See also J. M. Stopford and J. H. Dunning, *Multinationals, Company Performance and Global Trends* (London, Macmillan, 1983).

5 W. Dullforce, 'Gatt revises trade growth forecast to 3 per cent', *Financial Times*, 26 November 1985.

6 William Cline notes, 'From 1950 through 1975, merchandise trade of industrial countries grew at an average rate of 8 per cent annually, contributing importantly to historically high growth rates, averaging over 4 per cent. Moreover, the relation between trade and growth has an accelerationist feature, attributable in part to the high responsiveness of imports to income growth (income elasticity) as well as inventory behaviour for traded goods' in W. R. Cline (ed.), *Trade Policy in the 1980s* (Washington DC, Institute for International Economics, 1983), p. 5.

7 The value of outward direct investment (excluding portfolio investment), measured in accumulated capital stock abroad within the advanced capitalist economies, in billions of dollars (end of year) rose from 105.3 in 1967 to 287.2 in 1976, with the United States providing the lion's share, at 56.6 per cent of the 1967 total and 47.5 per cent in 1976, with the United Kingdom

next in line with 16.6 per cent in 1967 and 11.2 per cent in 1976. Japan's total rose from 1.4 to 6.7 and West Germany's share of foreign direct investment rose from 2.8 to 6.9 per cent in the same period (Ushiba *et al.*, *Sharing International Responsibilities*, pp. 80–5).

The geographical distribution of British overseas investments in 1973 (in millions of US dollars) included the following shares: Western Europe 38.5 per cent ($1,446.8m), North America 31.5 per cent ($1,184.8m), Japan 0.5 per cent ($18.1m). In 1982 these figures were Western Europe 8.5 per cent ($374.4m), North America 61.5 per cent ($2,722.3m), Japan 0.5 per cent ($24m). The recent British figures reflect a massive shift towards North American investment, which had risen to 40.4 per cent of its total in 1978. French and German investments also reflect similar shifts towards North America. French investments, in millions of US dollars in 1978 were distributed as follows: European Community 33.9 per cent ($859.2m), the United States 15.3 per cent ($387.6m), and in 1983 the figures were European Community 21.8 ($402.2m) and the United States 27.8 per cent ($514.3m). West Germany invested 69.8 per cent of its foreign investment in Europe in 1973, and only 6.4 per cent in the United States. The European percentage fell to 45.1 in 1978, and the United States share of German investments rose to 32.7. In 1983, the figures were: Europe 36.3 per cent ($1,115.4m) and the United States 35.1 ($1,078m). During this period German investments in Asia, as a percentage of its total, fell from 5.4 to 4.3 per cent (Nishihara, *East Asian Security*, pp. 94–9).

8 This is partly reflected in the following table from *The Financial Times*, 8 August 1987:

Publicly recorded take-overs in the United States

Purchasers	Number of Deals 1980	1981	1982	1983	1984	1985	1986
United Kingdom	50	80	54	41	48	78	89
Canada	57	62	36	28	36	25	64
West Germany	14	14	6	2	4	12	19
Japan	9	9	4	6	6	9	16
Sweden	8	7	4	3	8	7	11
Netherlands	6	8	5	7	5	17	9
France	20	14	12	7	7	4	6

9 J. Stopford, J. Dunning and K. Haberlich (eds.), *The World Directory of Multinational Enterprises* (London, Macmillan, 1980), p. xv.

10 In 1972 the distribution of United States foreign direct investment included the following geographic shares: Canada 27.3 per cent, Europe 32.7 per cent, Japan 2.5 per cent, Latin America 17.8 per cent. In 1982, these figures (current value in millions of American dollars in brackets) were as follows: Canada 20.1 per cent ($44,509m); Europe 45.1 per cent ($99,877m); Japan 3.1 per cent ($6,872m); Latin America 14.9 per cent ($33,039m) (Nishihara, *East Asian Security*, pp. 94–9).

11 Japanese overseas direct investment also shows a consistent trend in the

late 1970s and 1980s towards the United States, Canada, and Latin America, as well as the European Community: in 1977 North America took 26.2 per cent of the total ($735m) and this rose to 33.2 per cent ($2,701m) in 1983. Japan's European investments rose from 7.8 per cent in 1977 ($220m) to 12.2 per cent ($990m) in 1982. Japan invested 23.1 per cent of its total in Latin America in 1983 (up from 16.3 per cent in 1977), and 22.7 per cent in Asia (mainly in Hong Kong, Singapore and Indonesia) as compared with 30.8 per cent in 1977. It is worth noting, however, that the absolute size of Japanese foreign direct investment has, until recently, remained fairly small compared with that of other major investing countries (United States investments in Latin America were worth $33,039m in 1982, compared with Japan's $1,878m) (Nishihara, *East Asian Security*, pp. 94–9).

12 Most Japanese transnationals and banks still had, by the mid-1980s, a relatively small percentage of their employees working overseas, which reflected the still underdeveloped process of transnationalisation of Japanese capital. Japanese manufacturing was still heavily concentrated in Japan, with Toyota having only 20 per cent of its workers abroad, Matsushita Electric 3 per cent, Hitachi 18 per cent and NEC 9 per cent. This contrasted with IBM (40 per cent of its employees overseas), General Motors (40 per cent), Exxon (54 per cent), Ford Motors (53 per cent), and Shell Transport and Trading (69 per cent). The world's biggest bank in 1985, Dai-Ichi Kangyo, had only 4 per cent of its employees overseas, the second biggest, Fuji Bank, only 2 per cent, whereas the third biggest, Sumitomo, had 21 per cent. The biggest United States bank, Citicorp, had 48 per cent of its workers abroad, Chase Manhattan 39 per cent, and BankAmerica 19 per cent. Barclays had 27 per cent, Hong Kong and Shanghai (mainly British owned) 76 per cent. The most international of the Japanese banks in these terms was the Bank of Tokyo, with 64 per cent of its employees overseas: it was, therefore, a significant exception. ('Global Finance and Investment', *Wall Street Journal*, Special report, 29 September 1986, pp. 17D–22D.) The general level of overseas engagement in industrial production is reflected in the following table.

Average foreign content of the world's 350 largest industrial corporations ($US m and %)

Item	Year	Total ($)	Foreign	Foreign share (%)
Sales	1971	1,769	527	30
	1980	7,084	2,822	40
Net assets	1971	956	300	31
	1980	2,417	803	33
Net earnings	1971	83	41	49
	1980	266	140	53
Employment	1971	63,318	23,958	39
	1980	68,669	31,914	46

Source: M. Taylor and N. Thrift (eds.), *Multinationals and the Restructuring of the World Economy* (London, Croom Helm, 1986), p. 2. Based on statistics from United Nations, Centre on Transnational Corporations.

13 'Global Finance and Investment', *Wall Street Journal*, 29 September 1986, p. 17D.

14 Kudrle, 'The Several Faces of the Multinational Corporation', p. 175. My emphasis.

15 J. L. Hervey, 'The Internationalisation of Uncle Sam', *Economic Perspectives*, Federal Reserve Bank of Chicago, vol. 10 (1986), p. 4.

16 'Global Finance and Investment', *Wall Street Journal*, 29 September 1986, pp. 17D–22D.

17 Ruggie, 'International Regimes, Transactions and Change'; van der Pijl, *The Making of an Atlantic Ruling Class*, pp. 90–109.

18 For data see: K. van der Pijl, 'The Political Economy of Atlantic Relations', paper to *British International Studies Association*, annual conference, Reading, 15–17 December 1986. Published as 'Restructuring the Atlantic Ruling Class', in Gill (ed.), *Atlantic Relations*, pp. 62–87.

19 Van der Pijl, 'Restructuring the Atlantic Ruling Class'.

20 T. Lowi, *The End of Liberalism: The Second Republic of the United States* (New York, W. W. Norton, second edition, 1979).

21 J. Pinder, T. Hosomi, W. Diebold, *Industrial Policy and the International Economy* (New York, Trilateral Commission, 1979), p. 67.

22 Pinder *et al.*, *Industrial Policy and the International Economy*, p. 68.

23 OECD, *Toward Full Employment and Price Stability* (Paris, OECD, 1977).

24 P. Cockburn, 'Oil Price Fall Forces Moscow to Cut Imports', *Financial Times*, 4 April 1986. Oil makes up about 60 per cent of Soviet hard currency earnings.

25 A. Kaletsky, 'Unkind Cut for Wage Slaves Pursuing a Dream', *Financial Times*, 20 January 1987.

26 T. Dodsworth, 'The Wage Deal that Bucked a Trend', *Financial Times*, 5 October 1983; and 'Unions Bow to Management's New Found Strength', *Financial Times*, 14 May 1985.

27 Kaletsky, 'Unkind Cut for Wage Slaves Pursuing a Dream'.

28 Ibid.

29 R. Whymant, 'Unions Lose Their Fighting Spirit', *Guardian*, 1 July 1986.

30 Kaletsky, 'Unkind Cut for Wage Slaves Pursuing a Dream'.

31 C. F. Bergsten, 'The Problem?', *Foreign Policy* (1985), no. 59, p. 138.

32 H. R. Nau, 'Where Reaganomics Works', *Foreign Policy* (1984–5), no. 57, pp. 22–3.

33 H. R. Nau, 'Or The Solution?', *Foreign Policy* (1985), no. 59, p. 147.

34 Ibid., pp. 148–9.

35 Arrighi, 'A Crisis of Hegemony'.

36 M. Davis, 'Reaganomics' Magical Mystery Tour', *New Left Review* (1985), no. 149, pp. 45–65, at p. 47.

37 See D. Law, 'The Baker Initiatives and Macroeconomic Co-operation', in Gill (ed.), *Atlantic Relations*, pp. 138–56.

38 Halliday, *The Making of the Second Cold War*, p. 235.

39 See S. Smith, 'Strategic Relations in the Reagan Era', in Gill (ed.), *Atlantic Relations*, pp. 157–78.

40 See R. N. Gardner, S. Okita and B. J. Udink, *OPEC, The Trilateral World*,

and the Developing Countries: New Arrangements for Cooperation (New York, Trilateral Commission, 1975); and by the same authors, *A Turning Point in North–South Economic Relations* (New York, Trilateral Commission, 1974); C. E. Beigie, W. Hager and S. Sekiguchi, *Seeking a New Accommodation in World Commodity Markets* (New York, Trilateral Commission 1976).

41 For an initial attempt at the development of the concept of the power of capital, see Gill and Law, *The Global Political Economy*, pp. 83–101.

42 For other views on structural power, see H. Ward, 'Structural Power – A Contradiction in Terms?', *Political Studies* vol. 35 (1987), pp. 593–610; D. Marsh, 'Interest Group Activity and Structural Power', in D. Marsh (ed.), *Capital and Politics in Western Europe* (London, Frank Cass, 1983); C. E. Lindblom, *Politics and Markets* (New York, Basic Books, 1977), pp. 170–88. For a recent and more comprehensive attempt to theorise the structural power of capital at the global level, see S. Gill and D. Law 'Global Hegemony and the Structural Power of Capital', *International Studies Quarterly* (December 1989).

43 It is widely known that the largest transnationals have total sales exceeding the GNP of many small and medium-sized countries. For details of assets and sales of the top 100 industrial and financial corporations see: 'Global Finance and Investment', *Wall Street Journal*, 29 September 1986.

44 On the liberalisation of the financial structure, and on exchange and commodity markets, see Strange, *Casino Capitalism*.

45 P. A. Volcker, 'Economic Strategy', remarks made to Trilateral Commission luncheon, 14 November 1985, Washington DC (based on transcript).

46 Gill and Law, *The Global Political Economy*, pp. 81–102.

47 See D. Lascelles, 'A Time to Map New Strategies', *Financial Times*, World Banking Special Supplement, 22 May 1986, p. 1.

48 S. Strange, 'Paying the Price of Expansion', review of S. Marris, *Deficits and the Dollar: the World Economy at Risk* (Washington DC, Institute for International Economics, 1985), *Times Higher Educational Supplement*, 25 April 1986. Marris shows how Reagan's monetarist rhetoric was linked to Keynesian measures such as the 1981 Economic Recovery Tax Act, which boosted investment and raised the M1 indicator of the United States money supply between August 1982 and August 1983 by 13 per cent. This raised domestic demand by 20 per cent, and increased investment's share in GNP by 4 per cent. Strange observes, 'What it also did – though it was not planned nor anticipated – was to draw in an "ample supply" of savings from the rest of the world, which by 1985 was financing 45 per cent of net investment in the United States. The result may have been to keep U.S. interest rates (the cost of financing the U.S. government's budget deficit) as much as 5 percentage points lower than they would otherwise have been' (p. 17).

49 Strange, *Casino Capitalism*, p. 5.

50 M. M. Amen, 'Recurring Influences on Economic Policy-Making: Kennedy and Reagan Compared', in P. M. Johnston and W. R. Thompson

(eds.), *Rhythms in Politics and Econonics* (New York, Praeger, 1985), pp. 181–200.

51 D. Rockefeller, 'Address to Chase Manhattan Financial Forum', Montreal, 9 March 1972, *Mimeo*, pp. 10–11.

52 R. N. Cooper, 'International Economic Cooperation: Is it Desirable? Is it Likely?', *Bulletin of the American Academy of Arts and Sciences*, vol. 39 (1985), pp. 11–35.

53 A further example of an important personnel change was in July 1986, when Barber Conable, ex-Chairman of the United States House Ways and Means Committee took over from Alden Clausen (ex-President of Bank-America), as Chairman of the World Bank. The previous Chairman was Robert S. MacNamara. All three have been Trilateral Commissioners.

54 Volcker, 'Economic Strategy', my emphasis.

6 PRIVATE INTERNATIONAL RELATIONS COUNCILS

1 Gramsci, 'Number and Quality in Representative Systems of Government', *Prison Notebooks*, pp. 191–2.

2 S. Gill, 'From Atlanticism to Trilateralism', in S. Smith (ed.), *International Relations*.

3 Van der Pijl, *The Making of an Atlantic Ruling Class*, pp. 38–9, 41, 43–4.

4 Ibid., pp. 78–80.

5 K. Polanyi, *The Great Transformation* (Boston, Beacon Press, 1944); Carr, *The Twenty Years' Crisis*.

6 On ACUSE, and Monnet's links with important members of the American establishment, see A. Grosser, *The Western Alliance* (New York, Vintage, 1982), pp. 102–6. Monnet was also close to Kohnstamm, Bernhard's private secretary, and to a host of European leaders including Adenauer of West Germany, Schuman of France, de Gasperi of Italy, and Spaak of Belgium.

7 T. Skocpol, 'Political Responses to Capitalist Crisis: Neo-Marxist Theories of the State and the Case of the New Deal', *Politics and Society* (1980), vol. 10, pp. 155–201; T. Ferguson, 'From Normalcy to New Deal', *International Organisation* (1984), vol. 38, pp. 41–94.

8 P. A. Gourevitch, 'Breaking With Orthodoxy: the Politics of Economic Policy Responses in the Depression of the 1930s', *International Organisation* (1984), vol. 38, pp. 196–217; Ruggie, 'International Regimes, Transactions and Change'.

9 Shoup and Minter, *Imperial Brains Trust*.

10 Van der Pijl, *The Making of an Atlantic Ruling Class*, pp. 108–10, 114, 116–18.

11 Skocpol, 'Political Responses to Capitalist Crisis'.

12 Ferguson, 'From Normalcy to New Deal', p. 68.

13 Van der Pijl, *The Making of an Atlantic Ruling Class*, pp. 178–82.

14 Grosser, *The Western Alliance*, p. 111.

15 Ibid., pp. 98–128.

16 G. Lichtheim, *The New Europe* (New York, Praeger, 1963), pp. 217–18.

17 A. Hatch, *Prince Bernhard of the Netherlands* (New York, Doubleday, 1962), pp. 237–8. This was Bernhard's official biography.

18 Corporations and banks whose leaders have attended Bilderberg include ARCO, Exxon, Royal-Dutch Shell, BP, Compagnie Française des Pétroles, IBM, General Motors, Ford, Unilever, British-American Tobacco, Beechams, Courtaulds, Rio-Tinto Zinc Group, Massey-Ferguson, British Leyland, Hawker Siddeley, Dassault, Chase Manhattan, First National City Bank (Citicorp), Chemical Bank, Brown Brothers Harriman, Tube Investments, Mercantile Investment Trust, Barclays, Kleinwort Benson, Banque Lambert, S. G. Warburg, Rothschilds, de Nederlandse Bank, Bergens Privatbank, Union Bank of Switzerland, Société Bancaire de Paris, as well as the Deutsche Bundesbank, the Bank of England, Banca d'Italia, International Monetary Fund, and the World Bank. Media which have been represented include NBC and CBS, *The New York Times*, *Scientific American*, *Time*, *Christian Science Monitor*, *The Times* (London), *The Observer*, *Le Monde*, *L'Express*, *Le Nouvel Observateur*, *Die Zeit*, *La Stampa*, and *Journal de Genève*. Key American law firms represented include Sullivan and Cromwell, and Milbank, Tweed, Hadley and McCloy. In addition there have been individuals associated with foundations (e.g. Ford, Rockefeller, Carnegie), and think-tanks (e.g. the Council on Foreign Relations, Brookings, Chatham House, Harvard Center for International Affairs, the International Institute for Strategic Studies, the French, German, Norwegian and Italian Institutes of International Relations). Nearly all of these have been represented on the Trilateral Commission.

19 E. Pasymowski and C. Gilbert, 'Bilderberg: the Cold War Internationale', *Congressional Record*, vol. 117 (1971), part 24, 92nd Congress, p. 32053.

20 Hatch, *Prince Bernhard of the Netherlands*, p. 240.

21 *Official Record, Bilderberg Conference* held at Garmisch-Partenkirchen, 23–5 September 1955, p. 5.

22 Hatch, *Prince Bernhard of the Netherlands*, p. 243.

23 Interview with Right Hon. Reginald Maudling, London, 27 November 1978. The agendas, attendance lists, and parts of many of the discussion papers of the Bilderberg meetings are contained in *Freemen Digest* (Nov.–Dec. 1978), available from 1331 South State Street, PO Box G, Provo, Utah 84601. This contains interviews with long-standing members of the steering committee: William P. Bundy, Ernst van der Breugel, Joseph E. Johnson, George C. Ball and Charles W. Muller. This appears to be the most comprehensive set of documents concerning Bilderberg ever to have been published.

24 Bilderberg has, of course, been a *bête noir* of the right in the United States, notably of the John Birch Society and the Liberty Lobby. See S. M. Lipset (himself a Bilderberger), *The Politics of Unreason* (New York, Harper and Row, 1970), pp. 258–61, for a discussion of this. John Birchers see themselves as in the tradition of the Anti-Masonic party of the 1820s, although what they see as the 'real menace today' is the league of Bilderbergers (and Trilateralists) with the communists, rather than Masonry. McCarthyism can also be interpreted in terms of this nativist tradition. See statement by Rep. Joe E. Elvins of Tennessee, 'Press Reports Secret Meeting of Inter-

national Leaders', *Congressional Record*, vol. 120 (1974), part 21, 93rd Congress, pp. 27643–5.

25 N. von Hoffman, 'Bilderbergers as Prey', *Washington Post*, 25 July 1975, reprinted in *Congressional Record*, vol. 121 (1975), 94th Congress, 1st session, part 2, extension of remarks, p. E 4251.

26 Statement by Rep. John D. Rarick, 'Secret Bilderberg Meeting and the Logan Act', *Congressional Record*, vol. 117 (1971), part 13, 92nd Congress, pp. 16698–9; V. A. Doyle, 'The Logan Act', *Congressional Record*, vol. 117 (1971), part 13, 92nd Congress, pp. 16699–70; 'Bilderberg Case: Reply from US Attorney General's Office', *Congressional Record*, vol. 117 (1971), part 19, 92nd Congress, pp. 25649–50.

27 Pasymowski and Gilbert, 'Bilderberg: the Cold War Internationale', p. 32053.

28 M. Kohnstamm, 'Summary of Discussion Which took Place at the Bilderberg Conference in Cambridge England – 2 April 1967', Confidential correspondence from Max Kohnstamm to H. R. H. Bernhard. Cited in Pasymowski and Gilbert, 'Bilderberg: the Cold War Internationale', p. 32055.

29 Official Record, Bilderberg Barbizon Conference, 18–20 March 1955.

30 Pasymowski and Gilbert, 'Bilderberg: the Cold War Internationale', p. 32055.

31 Hatch, *Prince Bernhard of the Netherlands*, p. 240.

32 J. D. B. Miller, *The World of States* (London, Croom Helm, 1981), pp. 94–116.

33 D. Calleo, *The Imperious Economy* (Cambridge, Mass, Harvard University Press, 1982), pp. 62–8.

34 Cited in A. J. Reichley, *Conservatives in an Age of Change* (Washington DC, Brookings Institution, 1981), p. 225.

35 Interview with C. Fred Bergsten, Washington DC, 19 March 1982.

36 'Testimony of Professor Richard N. Cooper, Yale University', in *New Realities and New Directions in United States Foreign Economic Policy*, Report by the Subcommittee on Foreign Economic Policy of the House Committee on Foreign Affairs, 28 February 1972.

37 C. F. Bergsten, R. O. Keohane, J. S. Nye, 'International Economics and International Politics: A Framework for Analysis' in C. F. Bergsten and L. B. Krause (eds.), *World Politics and International Economics* (Washington D.C., Brookings Institutions, 1975), p. 18.

38 Z. Brzezinski, 'The Trilateral Relationship', Johns Hopkins School of Advanced International Studies (SAIS), *SAIS Review*, vol. 18 (1974), p. 6.

39 Ibid., p. 5.

40 Interview with Lord Roll of Ipsden, London, 16 November 1978.

41 Official Record, Bilderberg Megève Conference, 19–21 April 1974.

42 Members of the *Interplay* editorial board included Lord Harlech and Sir Kenneth Younger, both of whom were respectively the Chairman and Director of Chatham House; Jean-Claude Casanova, Professor of Politics at the Ecole des Sciences Politiques; Kurt Birrenbach, President of Thyssen; future German Chancellor Helmut Schmidt; Max Kohnstamm; George Ball; Robert Bowie; Aurelio Peccei, the founder of the Club of Rome;

Marion Donhoff, editor of *Die Zeit*; Christian Herter; Arthur Schlesinger Jr; Robert Manning; and Marshall Schulman.

43 *Interplay* authors included Hedley Bull, David Watt, Werner Feld, Adam Ulam, Maurice Duverger, Edward Banfield, Harlan Cleveland, Sir Denis Brogan, Alfred Grosser, François Duchêne, Ronald Steel, Zbigniew Brzezinski, J. D. B. Miller, Richard Pipes, Pierre Hassner, Alastair Buchan, Chalmers Roberts, Samuel H. Beer, Charles P. Kindleberger and Robert Triffin.

44 *Interplay*, vol. 1 (July 1967), no. 1, p. 5, my emphasis.

45 See vols. 1–4 (1967–71); F. Duchêne, 'Europe's Eleventh Hour', *Interplay*, vol. 1 (1968), no. 9, pp. 35–41.

46 H. Scott Stokes, 'Yukio Mishima: The Last Samurai', *Interplay*, vol. 4 (1971), no. 2, pp. 28–35.

47 T. C. Rhee, 'Same Bed, Different Dreams', *Interplay*, vol. 3 (1970), no. 11, pp. 4–10.

48 The reports included: 'Reshaping the International Economic Order' (1972), 'Reassessing North–South Economic Relations' (1972), 'World Trade and Domestic Adjustment' (1973), 'Towards the Integration of World Agriculture' (1973), 'Cooperative Approaches to World Energy Problems' (1974), and 'Trade in Primary Commodities: Conflict or Cooperation?' (1974). (All are Washington DC, Brookings Institution publications.) Other significant Trilateral Commission members involved in Brookings tripartite conferences included: Gardner Ackley and Paul McCracken (both former members of the United States Council of Economic Advisors, CEA), Bruce Maclaury and Robert Solomon (both of Brookings), Alan Greenspan (ex-CEA), Thiérry de Montbrial (Ecole Polytechnique, and Head of the French Institute of International Relations), Wolfgang Hager (European University Institute), B. J. Udink (former Minister of Development, Netherlands), Carl E. Beigie (C. D. Howe Research Institute, Montreal), Hiroshi Hori (Kansai Electric Co.) and Motoo Kaji (University of Tokyo). Both Udink and Beigie have written for the Trilateral Commission. The 1974 report on world energy problems was written in conjunction with the Trilateral Commission's own energy task force, and included Guy de Carmoy, Shinichi Kondo, and John C. Campbell, the three Trilateral Commission rapporteurs.

49 P. H. Trezise, 'Foreword' to *Economic Prospects and Policies in Industrial Countries* (Washington DC, Brookings Institution, 1977), p. iii.

50 T. Dye, *Who's Running America?* (Englewood Cliffs, NJ, Prentice-Hall, 1979), second edition, pp. 153–4. For further information on the Rockefeller industrial interests, and wider political and social connections see pp. 153–61. An earlier assessment of the size and scale of Rockefeller interests in banking, energy, high-technology industry, education, foundations, and fine art, is in P. Collier and D. Horowitz, *The Rockefellers: An American Dynasty* (New York, Holt, Rinehart and Winston, 1976).

51 Interview with C. Fred Bergsten, Washington DC, 19 March 1982; interview with François Duchêne, Brighton, 31 January 1978.

52 J. Reston, 'Japan Demands Equality', *New York Times*, 2 March 1973.
53 Interview with Takashi Watanabe, London, 25 March 1980.

7 AIMS, ACTIVITIES, ORGANISATION AND MEMBERSHIP OF THE TRILATERAL COMMISSION

1 'The Trilateral Commission' internal document, *Mimeo*, 1973, p. 4.
2 Ibid., p. 4.
3 Interview with Tadashi Yamamoto, Munich, 24 April 1983.
4 'The Trilateral Commission', p. 8.
5 Z. Brzezinski, 'Memorandum: The Trilateral Policy Program – A Report on Present and Prospective Trilateral Task Force Work', *Mimeo*, 18 September 1973, p. 8. First emphasis is in the original, the second is mine.
6 Brzezinski, 'Memorandum: The Trilateral Policy Program', p. 8.
7 'Statement of Purposes', *Trialogue* (1973), no. 2, pp. 1–2.
8 These were reports Nos. 11, 12 and 14, titles and authors of which are listed in full in Appendix 4. See also Report No. 2. See R. D. Putnam and N. Bayne, *Hanging Together: The Seven-Power Summits* (London, Heinemann for RIIA, 1984), pp. 44–6.
9 Putnam and Bayne, *Hanging Together*, p. 47.
10 Lord Carrington, 'Secretary of State's Speech to the Trilateral Commission', London, 24 March 1980.
11 'The Trilateral Commission', pp. 8–9.
12 Brzezinski, 'Memorandum: The Trilateral Policy Program', p. 2.
13 Ibid., pp. 3–6.
14 'The Constituencies of the Tricom', Ford Foundation Document 790–0465, *Mimeo*, March/April 1979, p. 1.
15 Trilateral Commission, *Annual Report 1983–84*, p. 1.
16 'Process of Organisation', Trilateral Commission internal document, *Mimeo*, 1973, p. 4.
17 Ibid., p. 5.
18 S. Hoffman, *Primacy or World Order: American Foreign Policy Since the Cold War* (New York, McGraw-Hill, 1978), p. 27.
19 M. Bundy, G. Kennan, R. S. McNamara and G. Smith, 'Nuclear weapons and the Atlantic Alliance', *Foreign Affairs*, vol. 60 (Spring 1982), pp. 753–68.
20 For details on such corporations in the 1970s, see R. J. Barnet, *The Lean Years: Politics in the Age of Scarcity* (New York, Simon and Schuster, 1980), pp. 239–94.
21 The Japan–United States Economic Relations Group was established by President Carter and Prime Minister Ohira after their joint communiqué of 2 May 1979, and consisted of eight members, six of whom were in the Trilateral Commission.
22 T. Hajime, 'Rockefeller's Men in Tokyo', *AMPO*, Pacific Area Resources Centre, Tokyo, Japan, 1978, p. 41.
23 Interview with Paul Delouvrier, London, 25 March 1980; interview with Gardner Ackley, Ann Arbor, Michigan, 27 July 1979. This point was also developed in interviews with François Duchêne, Brighton, 31 January 1978, and Zbigniew Brzezinski, Washington D.C., 28 February 1982.

24 This phrase is Hervé de Carmoy's. Interview, London, 24 March 1980.
25 'Global Finance and Investment', *Wall Street Journal*, 29 September 1986, pp. 17D–21D. All top 10 companies had members, and members worked for 16 of the top 20, and 27 of the top 40 companies. Also 9 of the top 10, 18 of the top 20, and 25 of the top 30 banks were represented. Of the world's largest insurers, members were associated with 9 of the top 10 and 14 of the top 20. Commission members were associated with 6 of the top 10 and 16 of the top 25 securities and financial services firms.
26 H. Patrick and H. Rusovsky, *Asia's New Giant* (Washington DC, Brookings Institution, 1976), p. 498.
27 For example, in America, major economic associations and foundations with board members or directors who are also Commissioners include the Committee on Economic Development, the Conference Board, the Business Council, the Trade Board, American Council on Capital Formation, the AFL–CIO, American Institute for Free Labor Development. Likewise, Japanese members are influential in the following: the very powerful Federation of Economic Organisations (Keidanren), the Federation of Employers Organisations, Council of Science and Technology, Japan Committee for Economic Development, Asia Community Trust, Japan Economic Foundation, Japan Foreign Trade Council, the Japan Auto Workers Union, and, as has been noted, Japan–US Economic Relations ('Wise Men's') Group.
   West European members are associated with leadership of: the Spanish Employers Association, Netherlands Bankers Association, Irish Management Institute, Association of French Banks, the Federation of Belgian Industries, German Federation of Chambers of Commerce, Federation of German Banks, Federation of German Industries, German Trade Union Federation, the Federation of Norwegian Trade Unions, the Italian Confederation of Workers Syndicates, the British Institute of Directors.
28 At the former of these two levels, the Commission has members influential in: the European Movement, European Commission, OECD, Atlantic Institute, Bilderberg, Institute of International Finance, Brandt Commission, British Atlantic Committee, Ditchley Foundation, Anglo-German Association, Atlantic Treaty Association, North Atlantic Council, the Club of Rome, the Saltzburg seminars, and the Nobel Peace Prize Committee.
29 American economists include Gardner Ackley, at the time of writing Professor at the University of Michigan; Walter Heller, Professor at the University of Minnesota and a former chairman of CEA during the Kennedy and Johnson administrations; Alan Greenspan, also a former CEA chairman and, from 1987, Chairman of the Board of Governors at the Federal Reserve; Henrik Houthakker, Professor of Economics at Harvard, and an ex-member of the CEA; and Professor Gale Johnson, Chairman of the University of Chicago Department of Economics. Among political scientists, Richard Holbrooke, former editor of *Foreign Policy* magazine and former United States Assistant Secretary of State for East Asia and Pacific Affairs in the Carter Administration, and Winston Lord, former President of the Council on Foreign Relations and Reagan's Ambassador to China are members. This is in addition to the likes of Kissinger, Brzezinski, Huntington, and Allison.

30 Interview with Gardner Ackley, Ann Arbor, Michigan, 27 July 1979.
31 Dye, *Who's Running America?*, pp. 161–3; van der Pijl, *The Making of an Atlantic Ruling Class*, pp. 270–1.
32 Dye, *Who's Running America?*, pp. 213, 225, 226.
33 See, for example, C. Wright Mills, *The Power Elite* (Oxford, Oxford University Press, 1956); G. William Domhoff, *The Higher Circles* (New York, Vintage Books, 1971); J. Scott, *Classes, Corporations and Capitalism* (London, Hutchinson, 1979).
34 T. R. Dye, 'Who Owns America? Strategic Ownership Positions in Industrial Corporations', *Social Science Quarterly*, vol. 6 (1983), pp. 863–70, especially p. 868. See also Scott, *Classes*, p. 177, and M. Useem, 'The Inner Group of the American Capitalist Class', *Social Problems* (February 1978), no. 25, pp. 225–40.
35 Dye, 'Who Owns America?', table 2, p. 867.
36 Trilateral Commission, *Annual Report 1983–84*, p. 23.
37 Trilateral Commission, *Annual Report 1983–84*. See also, Trilateral Commission (North America), 'Support, Year ended June 30, 1985, Schedule 1', *Mimeo*. Most of the initial funding (1973–80) came from private individuals (such as David Packard, Patrick E. Haggerty, and of course David Rockefeller), and from firms such as ARCO, BankAmerica, Bechtel, Boeing, Cargill, CBS, Coca-Cola, Deere, Exxon, Ford, General Electric, General Foods, General Motors, Gulf Oil, Honeywell, IBM, Sears Roebuck, Standard Oil, Texas Instruments, Time Inc., Wells Fargo Bank, Weyerhaeuser, and Xerox. Other support came from foundations (notably the Ford, Rockefeller and Mellon Foundations, Rockefeller Brothers Fund, German Marshall Fund of the United States and Sumitomo Fund for Policy Research Studies). See 'Current and Former Major Financial Supporters in the United States (Since the Founding of the Trilateral Commission in 1973)' (New York, Trilateral Commission, 15 October 1980). Since 1980, additional corporate contributors have been Hunt Oil, IT&T, *Los Angeles Times*, 3M, Northrop, NCR, Peat Marwick, Pepsico, Goldman Sachs, RJ Reynolds, Rockwell, TRW, United Brands, and the *Washington Post*. During 1985 the following corporations also made contributions: ABC, American Family Life Assurance, BF Goodrich, WR Grace, Gulf and Western, Macy's, McGraw-Hill, Irving Trust, Mobil Oil, *New York Times*, and Shell. Additional foundation support came from the Annenberg Fund. (Noteworthy here is the fact that the Annenbergs are close friends of the Reagans. The two families usually stay together in Palm Springs, California, for Christmas.)
38 For example, if 100 members travel from Europe and North America first class to Tokyo at a fare of US$ 2,500, and stay for four nights at a Tokyo hotel, which would cost at least $300 per night, this alone would amount to $370,000. It would be reasonable to suppose that members personally spend about $500,000 to attend plenary meetings. Actual expenditures may be much higher since attendance at some meetings has risen to over 200, with up to 20 additional invited observers. In addition, travel costs for national and regional meetings must be counted as well as the costs of absence from work and other obligations.

39 Trilateral Commission, *Annual Report, 1983–84*, p. 16.
40 Interview with Sir Philip de Zulueta, London, 16 January 1978; interview with Christopher Makins, former Deputy Director of the Commission, Washington DC, 7 August 1979.
41 Interview with Barber B. Conable (then Ranking Republican, House Ways and Means Committee), Washington DC, 11 June 1979.
42 Trilateral Commission, *Annual Report, 1980–81*.
43 C. S. Karpel, 'Cartergate: the Death of Democracy', *Penthouse* (November 1977), pp. 69–73, 90, 104, 106, 130.
44 Interview with Charles Heck, New York City, 11 March 1982.
45 D. Pedersen, 'Trilateral Alarm', *Des Moines Sunday Register – Iowa News*, 27 April 1980. N. Lemann, 'A Call to Farms', *Texas Monthly* (December 1978), pp. 69–70.
46 M. T. Klare, 'The Traders versus the Prussians', *Seven Days*, 28 March 1977, pp. 32–3.
47 Interview with Paul Delouvrier, London, 25 March 1980; interview with George Franklin, New York, 21 June 1979. Franklin said Carter read all Commission task force reports before his campaign for president got into full swing. Carter was also personally very active in distributing reports to members of the Democratic Party.

8 THEORETICAL AND PRACTICAL ASPECTS OF THE TRILATERAL COMMISSION

1 *Trialogue* (Fall 1977), no. 15, pp. 5, 10.
2 Ibid., pp. 8–9.
3 *Trialogue* (Summer 1978), no. 18, p. 4.
4 Calleo, *The Imperious Economy*, pp. 141–44.
5 *Trialogue* (Summer 1977), no. 14, p. 12.
6 Interview with Mrs Lucy Wilson Benson, Arlington, Va, 2 December 1981. Benson was responsible for arms export programmes in the State Department during the Carter administration.
7 *Trialogue* (Fall 1977), no. 15, pp. 16–17.
8 Z. Brzezinski, 'American Policy and Global Change', *Trialogue* (Fall 1977), no. 15, p. 12.
9 Ibid.
10 Ibid., p. 13.
11 Ibid., p. 3.
12 *Trialogue* (Summer 1978), no. 18, pp. 17–18.
13 Ibid., p. 20.
14 Trilateral Commission, *Annual Report 1980–81*, p. 1.
15 Interview with Tadashi Yamamoto, London, 23 March 1980.
16 *Trialogue* (Spring 1980), no. 23, pp. 14–15.
17 Interviews with George Franklin, New York City, 17 November 1981 and 10 March 1982.
18 *Trialogue* (Spring 1980), no. 23, p. 7, my emphasis.
19 *Trialogue* (Winter 1980/81), no. 25, p. 4.
20 Kaiser *et al.*, *Western Security*.

21 Ibid., pp. 19–22.
22 *Trialogue* (Spring 1982), no. 29, p. 10.
23 Roosa *et al.*, *East–West Trade at the Crossroads*, pp. 115–16.
24 *Trialogue* (Spring 1984), no. 35, pp. 3–4.
25 Ibid.
26 Ibid., pp. 21–5.
27 *Trialogue* (April 1984), no. 36, pp. 43–4.
28 Calleo, *The Imperious Economy*, p. 146.
29 Bruce MacLaury, President of Brookings, André Lamfalussy, Head of the Economic and Monetary Department of the Bank for International Settlements (and a member of the Group of thirty experts reviewing the international financial system), and Masao Fujioka, Director of the Export–Import Bank of Japan, were the rapporteurs. See *Trialogue* (Fall 1979), no. 21, p. 6.
30 Z. Brzezinski, 'Building a Wider World Order? Averting a Global Breakdown?', *Trialogue* (Spring 1982), no. 29, pp. 28–9.
31 Bergsten *et al.*, *Conditions for Partnership in International Economic Management*, p. 6, note 2.
32 S. Ostry, 'The World Economy: Marking Time', in *America and the World 1983* (New York, Council on Foreign Relations, 1984), pp. 538–41.
33 Ostry, 'The World Economy: Marking Time', pp. 552–4; Raymond Barre, 'Some Remarks on the Trilateral Relations', Rome, 17 April 1983; see also Walter Heller, 'US Economic Recovery and Deficits', *Trilateral Memorandum*, no. 7 (Rome), 18 April 1983, in which he argues that there had been a 'quiet revolution in Reaganomics' from 'super-supply-side dogma' to 'demand-side pragmatism', and gave a bullish outlook on growth, unemployment and low inflation. See also his 'Mr Reagan is Keynesian Now', *Wall Street Journal*, 23 March 1983, which analyses the upward trend in government expenditure under Reagan.
34 R. Strauss, E. Wellenstein and B. Yoshino, 'After the GATT Ministerial', *Trilateral Memorandum*, no. 1 (Rome), 14 April 1983.
35 *Trialogue* (April 1984), no. 36, p. 5.
36 D. Owen, S. Okita and Z. Brzezinski, 'Exploiting Summitry', *New York Times*, 8 April 1984; H. Rowen, 'Trilateral Group debates Japan's Commitments', *Washington Post*, 2 April 1984. See also, D. Owen *et al.*, *Democracy Must Work: A Trilateral Agenda for the Decade* (New York, New York University Press, 1984).
37 Trilateral Commission, *Annual Report (1984–85)*, pp. 11–12.
38 'US and Japan Strike Deal on Yen Package', *Financial Times*, 30 April 1984; *Financial Times*, editorial, 'Freer Access to Japan', 30 May 1984.
39 *Trialogue* (April 1985), no. 37, pp. 4–5.
40 T. Mukaibo, H. Brown, L. Solana, F. Kodama, L. Branscomb, *Science and Technology in Trilateral Relations: Competition and Cooperation*, Discussion Draft (New York, Trilateral Commission, 1987), pp. 1–5.
41 Ibid., pp. 75–80.
42 Ibid., p. 53.
43 Ibid., pp. 81–3.
44 Ibid., p. 88.
45 P. Kamura, *International Relations in Japan – A Policy Research and Analysis*

Perspective (Tokyo, Japan Center for International Exchange/Rockefeller Foundation, 1981).

46 S. Gill, 'Some Questions and an Overview of Trends', in Gill (ed.), *Atlantic Relations*, pp. 1–13.

47 Owen *et al.*, *Democracy Must Work*, p. 4.

9 HEGEMONY, KNOWLEDGE AND THE LIMITS OF INTERNATIONALISM

1 On such limits and structural constraints, see Gill and Law, *The Global Political Economy*, pp. 320–30; R. W. Cox, 'Economic Reform and the Social Structure of Accumulation in Socialist Countries', Paper presented at the 14th Congress of the International Political Science Association, 28 August–1 September 1988, Washington DC.

2 C. J. Hamelink, *Cultural Autonomy in Global Communications* (London, Longman, 1983). See pp. 1–25, data from pp. 12–13, based on UNCTAD sources.

3 In the long term the emergence of a more competitive, extensive and international market for educational products is to be anticipated. International competition in this sphere is likely to 'internationalise' and perhaps homogenise the content of curricula, or at least to modify 'national' curricula and products in ways which make them more accessible to foreign consumers. An example of this is the EEC's ERASMUS project intended to be the educational counterpart to the completion of the internal market by 1992 (ERASMUS will take much longer). The ERASMUS credit-transfer system is designed to allow free movement of higher education students (and faculty exchanges) throughout the EEC, and individual institutions will act in consortia to compete for consumers. The design of the credit-transfer system is largely based on American models and practices, and would, in time, be open to transatlantic consumers.

4 'Global Finance and Investment', *Wall Street Journal*, 29 September 1986, p. 17D.

5 Further evidence supporting this argument is in Strange, 'The Persistent Myth of Lost Hegemony'.

6 D. Gordon, 'The Global Economy: New Edifice or Crumbling Foundations?', *New Left Review* (1988), no. 168, p. 25.

7 This is the product of the Advisory Group on Economic Structural Adjustment for International Harmony. Its final report was submitted to Japan's Prime Minister Nakasone (who had set up the group in 1985) on 7 April 1986.

8 Feldstein *et al.*, *Restoring Growth In a Debt-Laden Third World*, p. 133.

9 M. G. Gilman, 'Japan's Financial Coming of Age', *Trialogue*, no. 27, pp. 27–32.

10 I. Shapiro, 'The Risen Sun', *Foreign Policy* (1980–1), no. 41, pp. 62–81. The phrase comes from the title of a Japanese bestseller by Keigo Okonogi called *The Age of the Moratorium Man*.

11 E. F. Vogel, 'Pax Nipponica?', *Foreign Affairs*, vol. 65 (1986), p. 757. See also p. 763.

12 W. G. Hyland, K. Kaiser and H. Kimura, *Prospects for East–West Relations* (New York, Trilateral Commission, 1986).

13 N. R. Malcolm, remarks made after presentation of 'Soviet Views on Atlantic Relations in the Reagan Era', *British International Studies Association*, Annual Conference, Reading, 15–17 December 1986. This insight would appear to have been confirmed by subsequent developments. A group of key Trilateral Commissioners held discussions with Gorbachev and other Soviet leaders in Moscow on 16–18 January 1989. This, and other meetings and activities, led to the publication of a report by Valéry Giscard d'Estaing, Yashuhiro Nakasone and Henry Kissinger, *East–West Relations* (New York, Trialteral Commission, 1989). Building upon work also completed on Asia and the Pacific during 1987–8, the report argued for a firm but constructive engagement with the 'new look' in Soviet foreign policy, a thorough overhaul and synthesis of Trilateral security concepts for the 1990s and proposed a general framework for Western strategy. See also, Richard Holbrooke, Roderick MacFarquhar and Kazuo Nukazawa, *East Asia in Transition: Challenges for the Trilateral countries* (New York, Trilateral Commission, 1988).

14 J. Plender, 'Capital Flows and Gunboats', *Financial Times*, 2 March 1987.

15 M. Tran, 'British Fight US Trade Bill', *Guardian*, 2 April 1988.

16 L. Kolakowski, *Main Currents of Marxism*, vol. 2 (Oxford, Oxford University Press, 1978), p. 525, cited in J. Elster, 'Belief, Bias and Ideology', in M. Hollis and S. Lukes (eds.), *Rationality and Relativism* (Oxford, Basil Blackwell, 1982).

17 Therborn, *The Ideology of Power and the Power of Ideology*, p. 84.

18 Interview with Professor Robert Bowie, Washington DC, 3 December 1981.

19 Wright Mills, *The Power Elite*.

20 Immerman, 'European Attitudes Towards Japan: Trilateralism's Weakest Link'.

21 See Waltz, *Theory of International Politics*; L. Althusser, *For Marx*, translated by B. Brewster (London, Allen Lane for Penguin Press, 1969); L. Althusser and E. Balibar, *Reading Capital*, translated by B. Brewster (London, New Left Books, 1970). A historical materialist conception of structure involves common and repeated patterns of action. Structures are not simply categories invented by theorists, rather they are aggregates of responses to given, historically specific, conditions. They involve habits, expectations and anticipations, that is how people conceive and act upon 'the limits of the possible'. By contrast, for Althusser, action and history are cast out of an objective 'science' of structures.

SELECT BIBLIOGRAPHY

BOOKS

Agnew, J., *The United States in the World-Economy* (Cambridge, Cambridge University Press, 1987).

Althusser, L., *For Marx*, translated by B. Brewster (London, Allen Lane for Penguin Press, 1969).

Althusser, L. and E. Balibar, *Reading Capital*, translated by B. Brewster (London, New Left Books, 1970).

Ambrose, S., *Rise to Globalism: American Foreign Policy, 1938–76* (Harmondsworth, Pelican Books, 1976).

Amin, S., *Unequal Development* (New York, Monthly Review Press, 1976).

Amin, S., G. Arrighi, A. G. Frank and I. Wallerstein, *Dynamics of Global Crisis* (London, Macmillan, 1982).

Avery, W. P. and D. P. Rapkin (eds.), *America in a Changing World Political Economy* (London, Longman, 1983).

Barnet, R. J., *The Lean Years: Politics in the Age of Scarcity* (New York, Simon and Schuster, 1980).

Real Security; Restoring American Power in a Dangerous Decade (New York, Simon and Schuster, 1981).

The Alliance (New York, Simon and Schuster, 1983).

Bell, D., *The Cultural Contradictions of Capitalism* (New York, Basic Books, 1976).

Bell, D. and I. Kristol, *The Crisis in Economic Theory* (New York, Basic Books, 1983).

Bergesen, A. (ed.), *Crises in the World-System* (Beverley Hills, Sage, 1983).

Bergsten, C. F., *The Dilemmas of the Dollar: the Politics of U.S. International Monetary Policy* (New York, New York University Press, 1975).

Bergsten, C. F. and L. B. Krause (eds.), *World Politics and International Economics* (Washington DC, Brookings Institution, 1975).

Bergsten, C. F., T. Horst and T. Moran, *American Multinationals and American Interests* (Washington DC, Brookings Institution, 1978).

Blake, D. H. and R. S. Walters, *The Politics of Global Economic Relations* (Englewood Cliffs, NJ, Prentice-Hall, 1976).

Block, F., *The Origins of International Economic Disorder* (Berkeley, University of California Press, 1977).

Breton, A., *The Economic Theory of Representative Government* (Chicago, Aldine, 1974).

Brewer, A., *Marxist Theories of Imperialism* (London, Routledge and Kegan Paul, 1980).

Brzezinski, Z., *Between Two Ages: America's Role in the Technetronic Era* (New York, Viking Books, 1970).

Buchanan, J. M. and G. Tullock, *The Calculus of Consent* (Ann Arbor, University of Michigan Press, 1962).

Buci-Glucksman, C., *Gramsci and the State*, translated by D. Fernbach (London, Lawrence and Wishart, 1980).

Bukharin, N., *Imperialism and World Economy* (London, Merlin Press, 1976).

Bull, H., *The Anarchical Society* (New York, Columbia University Press, 1977).

Bush, R., G. Johnston and D. Coates (eds.), *The World Order: Socialist Perspectives* (Oxford, Policy Press/Basil Blackwell, 1987).

Calleo, D. P., *The Imperious Economy* (Cambridge, Mass., Harvard University Press, 1982).

Beyond American Hegemony: The Future of the Western Alliance (Brighton, Wheatsheaf Books, 1987).

Calleo, D. and B. Rowland, *America and the World Political Economy* (Bloomington, Indiana University Press, 1973).

Camps, M., *The Management of Interdependence: A Preliminary View* (New York, Council on Foreign Relations, 1974).

Carr, E. H., *The Twenty Years' Crisis* (New York, Harper Torchbooks, 1964).

Carter, J., *Why Not the Best?* (Nashville, Tenn., Broadman Press, 1975).

Cline, W. R. (ed.), *Trade Policy in the 1980s* (Washington DC, Institute for International Economics, 1983).

Cohen, B., *The Question of Imperialism: The Political Economy of Dominance and Dependence* (New York, Basic Books, 1973).

Organising the World's Money: The Political Economy of International Monetary Relations (New York, Basic Books, 1977).

Collier, P. and D. Horowitz, *The Rockefellers: An American Dynasty* (New York, Holt, Rinehart and Winston, 1976).

Connolly, W., *The Terms of Political Discourse* (Oxford, Basil Blackwell, 1983).

Cooper, R. N., *The Economics of Interdependence: Economic Policy in the Atlantic Community* (New York, McGraw-Hill/Council on Foreign Relations, 1968).

Cooper, R. N. (ed.), *A Reordered World: Emerging International Economic Problems* (Washington DC, Potomac Associates/Basic Books, 1973).

Cox, R. W., *Production, Power and World Order: Social Forces in the Making of History* (New York, Columbia University Press, 1987).

De Grasse, Jr, R. W., *Military Expansion, Economic Decline* (New York, M. E. Sharpe for the Council on Economic Priorities, 1983).

Destler, I. M. and H. Sato (eds.), *Coping with U.S.–Japanese Economic Conflicts* (Lexington, Mass., D. C. Heath, 1982).

Domhoff, G. W., *The Higher Circles* (New York, Vintage Books, 1971).

Downs, A., *An Economic Theory of Democracy* (New York, Harper and Row, 1957).

Dye, T. R., *Who's Running America?* (Englewood Cliffs, NJ, Prentice-Hall, 1979).

Emmanuel, A., *Unequal Exchange: A Study of the Imperialism of Trade* (London, New Left Books, 1972).

Ferguson, T. and J. Rogers (eds.), *The Hidden Election: Politics and Economics in the 1980 Presidential Campaign* (New York, Pantheon Books, 1981).

Frank, A. G., *Dependent Accumulation and Underdevelopment* (London, Macmillan, 1978).

Frey, B. S., *International Political Economics* (Oxford, Basil Blackwell, 1984).

Friedman, M., *Capitalism and Freedom* (Chicago, University of Chicago Press, 1975).

Froebel, F., J. Heinrichs and O. Kreye, *The New International Division of Labour* (Cambridge, Cambridge University Press, 1980).

Fulbright, J. W. (ed.), *American Militarism, 1970* (New York, Viking Press, 1969).

The Pentagon Propaganda Machine (New York, Viking Press, 1971).

Gardner, R., *Sterling–Dollar Diplomacy* (New York, McGraw-Hill, 1969).

Giddens, A., *A Contemporary Critique of Historical Materialism*, vol. 2. *The Nation State and Violence* (Oxford, Polity Press/Basil Blackwell, 1985).

Gill, S. (ed.), *Atlantic Relations: Beyond the Reagan Era* (Brighton, Wheatsheaf Books, 1989).

Gill, S. and D. Law, *The Global Political Economy: Perspectives, Problems and Policies* (Brighton and Baltimore, Md., Wheatsheaf Books/Johns Hopkins University Press, 1988).

Gilpin, R., *US Power and the Multinational Corporation* (New York, Basic Books, 1975).

War and Change in World Politics (Princeton, NJ, Princeton University Press, 1981).

The Political Economy of International Relations (Princeton, Princeton University Press, 1987).

Goldfrank, W. (ed.), *The World System of Capitalism* (Beverly Hills, Sage Publications, 1979).

Goldthorpe, J. H. (ed.), *Order and Conflict in Contemporary Capitalism: Studies on the Political Economy of West European Nations* (Oxford, Clarendon Press, 1984).

Gramsci, A., *The Modern Prince and Other Writings*, selected and translated by L. Marks (International Publishers, New York, 1957).

Selections from the Prison Notebooks of Antonio Gramsci, translated by Q. Hoare and G. Nowell Smith (New York, International Publishers, 1971).

Selections from Political Writings, 1910–1920, with additional texts by Bordiga and Tasca, selected and edited by Q. Hoare, translated by J. Matthews (New York, International Publishers, 1977).

Selections from Political Writings, 1921–1926, with additional texts by other Italian Communist leaders, translated and edited by Q. Hoare (New York, International Publishers, 1978).

Hamelink, C. J., *Cultural Autonomy in Global Communications* (London, Longman, 1983).

Gordon, L., *Growth Policies and the International Order* (New York, McGraw-Hill, for Council on Foreign Relations 1980s Project, 1979).

Habermas, J., *Legitimation Crisis* (London, Heinemann, 1975).

Halliday, F., *The Making of the Second Cold War* (London, New Left Books, 1986).

Hatch, A., *Prince Bernhard of the Netherlands* (New York, Doubleday, 1962).

Hayek, F. A., *Knowledge, Evolution and Society* (London, Adam Smith Institute, 1983).

Hirsch, F. and J. Goldthorpe (eds.), *The Political Economy of Inflation* (Cambridge, Mass., Harvard University Press, 1978).

Hoffman, S., *Primacy or World Order: American Foreign Policy Since the Cold War* (New York, McGraw-Hill, 1978).

Hollist, W. Ladd and F. Lamond Tullis (eds.), *An International Political Economy Year Book*, vol. 1 (Boulder, Colo., Westview Press, 1985).

Holsti, O. R., R. M. Silverson and A. L. George (eds.), *Change in the International System* (Boulder, Colo., Westview Press, 1980).

Holsti, O. R. and J. N. Rosenau, *American Leadership in World Affairs: Vietnam and the Breakdown of Consensus* (Boston, Allen and Unwin, 1984).

Huntington, S. P., *American Politics: the Promise of Disharmony* (Cambridge, Mass., Belknap Press of Harvard University Press, 1981).

Johnston, P. M. and W. R. Thompson (eds.), *Rhythms in Politics and Economics* (New York, Praeger, 1985).

Joll, J., *Gramsci* (Glasgow, Fontana, 1977).

Kamura, P., *International Relations in Japan – A Policy Research and Analysis Perspective* (Tokyo, Japan Center for International Exchange/ Rockefeller Foundation, 1981).

Katzenstein, P. (ed.), *Between Power and Plenty* (Madison, University of Wisconsin Press, 1978).

Kennedy, P., *The Rise and Decline of the Great Powers: Economic Change and Military Conflict from 1500 to 2000* (London, Unwin Hyman, 1988).

Keohane, R. O., *After Hegemony: Cooperation and Discord in the World Political Economy* (Princeton, Princeton University Press, 1984).

(ed.), *Neorealism and its Critics* (New York, Columbia University Press, 1986).

Keohane, R. O. and J. S. Nye (eds.), *Transnational Relations and World Politics* (Cambridge, Mass., Harvard University Press, 1972).

Power and Interdependence (Boston, Mass., Little Brown, 1977).

Keynes, J. M., *The General Theory of Employment, Interest and Money* (New York, Harcourt Brace, 1964).

Kindleberger, C. P., *Power and Money* (New York, Basic Books, 1970).

The World In Depression, 1929–39 (Berkeley, University of California Press, 1973).

Kitching, G., *Development and Underdevelopment in Historical Perspective* (London, Methuen, 1982).

Klamer, A., *The New Classical Macroeconomics* (Brighton, Wheatsheaf Books, 1984).

Krasner, S. D., *Defending the National Interest* (Princeton, NJ, Princeton University Press, 1978).

Structural Conflict: The Third World against Global Liberalism (Berkeley, University of California Press, 1985).

(ed.), *International Regimes* (special issue of *International Organisation*, vol. 36, Spring 1982).

Kuhn, T., *The Structure of Scientific Revolutions* (Chicago, University of Chicago Press, 1962).

Laclau, E., *Politics and Ideology in Marxist Theory* (London, New Left Books, 1977).

Landes, D. S., *The Unbound Prometheus: Technological Change and Industrial Development in Western Europe from 1750 to the Present Day* (Cambridge, Cambridge University Press, 1969).

Larrain, J., *The Concept of Ideology* (London, Hutchinson, 1979).

Marxism and Ideology (London, Macmillan, 1983).

Lenin, V. I., *Imperialism: The Highest Stage of Capitalism* (New York, International Publishers, 1939).

Lichtheim, G., *The New Europe* (New York, Praeger, 1963).

Lindberg, L. N. and C. S. Maier (eds.), *The Politics of Inflation and Economic Stagnation: Theoretical Approaches and International Case Studies* (Washington DC, Brookings Institution, 1985).

Lindblom, C. E., *Politics and Markets: The World's Political-Economic Systems* (New York, Basic Books, 1977).

List, F., *The National System of Political Economy* (New York, Garland, 1974).

Lowi, T., *The End of Liberalism* (New York, W. W. Norton, 1979).

Machiavelli, N., *The Prince* (Harmondsworth, Penguin, 1975).

Magaziner, I. and R. Reich, *Minding America's Business* (New York, Harcourt Brace Jovanovitch, 1982).

Mandel, E., *Europe versus America* (London, New Left Books, 1970).

The Second Slump: A Marxist Analysis of Recession in the Seventies, translated by Jon Rothschild (London, Verso, 1979).

Marsh, D. (ed.), *Capital and Politics in Western Europe* (London, Frank Cass, 1983).

Marx, K., *Karl Marx: Selected Writings* edited by D. McLellan (Oxford, Oxford University Press, 1977).

McGuire, M., *Military Objectives in Soviet Foreign Policy* (Washington, DC, Brookings Institution, 1987).

Melman, S., *Pentagon Capitalism: The Political Economy of War* (New York, McGraw-Hill, 1970).

Miller, J. D. B., *The World of States* (London, Croom Helm, 1981).

Modelski, G. (ed.), *Transnational Corporations and World Order* (San Francisco, W. W. Freeman, 1979).

Morgenthau, H. J., *Politics Among Nations: The Struggle for Power and Peace* (New York, Alfred Knopf, 1985).

Mouffe, C. (ed.), *Gramsci and Marxist Theory* (London, Routledge and Kegan Paul, 1979).

Lipset, S. M., *The Politics of Unreason* (New York, Harper and Row, 1970).

Mills, C. Wright, *The Power Elite* (Oxford, Oxford University Press, 1956).

Nisbet, R., *The Twilight of Authority* (Oxford, Oxford University Press, 1975).

Odell, J. S., *U.S. International Monetary Policy* (Princeton, NJ, Princeton University Press, 1982).

OECD, *Towards Full Employment and Price Stability* (McCracken Report) (Paris, OECD, 1977).

Ohmae, K., *Triad Power: The Coming Shape of Global Competition* (New York, Free Press, 1985).

Olson, M., *The Logic of Collective Action* (Cambridge, Mass., Harvard University Press, 1965).

Owen, H. (ed.), *The Next Phase in Foreign Policy* (Washington DC, Brookings Institution, 1973).

Oye, K. A. *et al.* (eds.), *Eagle Entangled: U.S. Foreign Policy in a Complex World* (New York, Longman, 1979).

Eagle Defiant: U.S. Foreign Policy in the 1980s (Boston, Mass., Little Brown, 1983).

Patrick, H. and H. Rusovsky, *Asia's New Giant* (Washington DC, Brookings Institution, 1976).

Poggi, G., *The Development of the Modern State* (London, Hutchinson, 1978).

Polanyi, K., *The Great Transformation: The Political and Economic Origins of Our Time* (Boston, Mass., Beacon Press, 1957).

Poulantzas, N., *Political Power and Social Classes* (London, New Left Books, 1973).

Putnam, R. D. and N. Bayne, *Hanging Together: The Seven-Power Summits* (London, Heinemann for Royal Institute of International Affairs, 1984).

Reich, R., *The Next American Frontier* (Harmondsworth, Penguin, 1983).

Reichley, A. J., *Conservatives in an Age of Change* (Washington DC, Brookings Institution, 1981).

Ricardo, D., *Principles of Political Economy and Taxation* (Harmondsworth, Penguin, 1971).

Rosecrance, R. (ed.), *America as an Ordinary Country: U.S. Foreign Policy and the Future* (Ithaca, Cornell University Press, 1976).

Rousseas, S., *Capitalism and Catastrophe* (Cambridge, Cambridge University Press, 1979).

Rowland, B. (ed.), *Balance of Power or Hegemony: The Inter-War Monetary System* (New York, New York University Press, 1976).

Schell, J., *The Time of Illusion: an Historical and Reflective Account of the Nixon Era* (New York, Vintage Books, 1976).

Schumpeter, J. A., *Capitalism, Socialism and Democracy* (New York, Harper and Row, 1950).

Scott, J., *Classes, Corporations and Capitalism* (London, Hutchinson, 1979).

Shonfield, A. (ed.), *International Economic Relations of the Western World, 1959–71*, two vols. (London, Oxford University Press, 1976).

Shoup, L. H. and W. Minter, *Imperial Brains Trust: The Council on Foreign Relations and United States Foreign Policy* (New York, Monthly Review Press, 1977).

Showstack-Sassoon, A., *Gramsci's Politics* (London, Croom Helm, 1980).

Sklar, H. (ed.), *Trilateralism: Elite Planning for World Management* (Boston, Mass., South End Press, 1980).

Smith, A., *An Enquiry into the Nature and Causes of the Wealth of Nations* (Harmondsworth, Penguin Books, 1984).

Smith, M., R. Little and M. Shackleton (eds.), *Perspectives on World Politics* (London, Croom Helm/Open University Press, 1981).

Smith, S. (ed.), *International Relations: British and American Perspectives* (Oxford, Basil Blackwell, 1985).

Spiro, H. J., *A New Foreign Policy Consensus?* (London, Sage Publications, 1979).

Steinfels, P., *The Neo-Conservatives* (New York, Simon and Schuster, 1980).

Stopford, J. M. and J. H. Dunning, *Multinationals, Company Performance and Global Trends* (London, Macmillan, 1983).

Stopford, J. M., J. H. Dunning and K. Haberlich (eds.), *The World Directory of Multinational Enterprises* (London, Macmillan, 1980).

Strange, S., *Casino Capitalism* (Oxford, Basil Blackwell, 1986).

(ed.), *Paths to International Political Economy* (London, Frances Pinter, 1985).

Strange, S. and R. Tooze (eds.), *The International Politics of Surplus Capacity: Competition for Market Shares in the World Recession* (London, Allen and Unwin, 1981).

Taylor, M. and N. Thrift (eds.), *Multinationals and the Restructuring of the World Economy* (London, Croom Helm, 1986).

Therborn, G., *The Ideology of Power and the Power of Ideology* (London, New Left Books, 1980).

Thucydides, *The History of the Peloponnesian War* (New York, Galaxy Books, 1960).

Tsoukalis, L. (ed.), *The Political Economy of International Money* (London, RIIA/Sage, 1985).

Tucker, R. W., *The Purposes of American Power* (New York, Lehrman Institute/ Praeger, 1981).

Tucker, R. W. and W. Watts (eds.), *Beyond Containment: US Foreign Policy in Transition* (Washington DC, Potomac Associates, 1973).

United Nations Centre on Transnational Corporations, *Transnational Corporations in World Development: Trends and Prospects* (New York, United Nations, 1988).

Van der Pijl, K., *The Making of an Atlantic Ruling Class* (London, Verso, 1984).

Vernon, R., *Sovereignty at Bay* (New York, Basic Books, 1971).

Wallerstein, I., *The Capitalist World Economy* (Cambridge, Cambridge University Press, 1979).

The Modern World System II (New York, Academic Press, 1980).

Waltz, K. N., *Theory of International Politics* (Reading, Mass., Addison-Wesley, 1979).

Wolfe, A., *The Limits of Legitimacy: Political Contradictions of Contemporary Capitalism* (New York, Free Press, 1977).

ARTICLES

Amen, M. M., 'Recurring Influences on Economic Policy-Making: Kennedy and Reagan Compared', in P. M. Johnston and W. R. Thompson (eds.), *Rhythms in Politics and Economics*, pp. 181–200

Barraclough, G., 'The Great World Crisis', *New York Review of Books*, 23 January 1975, pp. 20–9.

Baumol, W. J., 'Productivity Growth, Convergence and Welfare', *American Economic Review*, vol. 76 (1986), pp. 1072–85.

Bell, D., 'The End of American Exceptionalism', in N. Glazer and I. Kristol (eds.), *The American Commonwealth 1976* (New York, Basic Books, 1976), pp. 193–224.

'The Future World Disorder', *Foreign Policy* (1977), no. 27, pp. 109–35.

Bergsten, C. F., 'The New Economics and US Foreign Policy', *Foreign Affairs* (1972), vol. 50, pp. 199–222.

'The Problem?', *Foreign Policy* (1985), no. 59, pp. 132–44.

Brenner, R., 'The Origins of Capitalist Development: A Critique of Neo-Smithian Marxism', *New Left Review* (1977), no. 104, pp. 25–92.

Brzezinski, Z., 'Japan's Global Engagement', *Foreign Affairs*, vol. 50 (1972), pp. 270–82.

'US Foreign Policy: The Search for Focus', *Foreign Affairs*, vol. 51 (1973), pp. 708–27.

Bundy, M., G. Kennan, R. S. McNamara and G. A. Smith, 'Nuclear weapons and the Atlantic Alliance', *Foreign Affairs*, vol. 60 (Spring 1982), pp. 753–68.

Chase-Dunn, C., 'International Economic Policy in a Declining Core State', in Avery and Rapkin (eds.), *America in a Changing World Political Economy*, pp. 77–96.

Cooper, R. N., 'Trade Policy is Foreign Policy', *Foreign Policy* (1972–3), no. 9, pp. 18–37.

Cox, R. W., 'Ideologies and the New International Economic Order: Reflections on Some Recent Literature', *International Organisation*, vol. 33 (1979), pp. 257–302.

'Gramsci, Hegemony and International Relations: An Essay in Method', *Millennium*, vol. 12 (1983), pp. 162–75.

'Social Forces, States and World Orders', revised version, in R. O. Keohane (ed.), *Neorealism and its Critics* (New York, Columbia University Press, 1986), pp. 204–54.

'Economic Reform and the Social Structure of Accumulation in Socialist Countries'. Paper presented at the 14th World Congress of the International Political Science Association, 28 August – 1 September 1988, Washington DC.

Davis, M., 'The Political Economy of Late Imperial America', *New Left Review* (1984), no. 143, pp. 6–38.

'Reaganomics' Magical Mystery Tour', *New Left Review* (1985), no. 149, pp. 45–65.

Dimitrakos, D. P., 'Gramsci and the Contemporary Debate on Marxism', *Philosophy of Social Science*, vol. 16 (1986), pp. 459–88.

Dye, T. R., 'Who Owns America? Strategic Ownership Positions in Industrial Corporations', *Social Science Quarterly*, vol. 6 (1983), pp. 863–70.

Elster, J., 'Belief, Bias and Ideology', in M. Hollis and S. Lukes (eds.), *Rationality and Relativism* (Oxford, Basil Blackwell, 1982).

Falk, R., 'A New Paradigm for International Legal Studies: Prospects and Proposals', *Yale Law Journal*, vol. 84 (1975), pp. 969–1021.

Ferguson, T., 'From Normalcy to New Deal', *International Organisation*, vol. 38 (1984), pp. 41–94.

Frey, B. S., 'The Public Choice View of International Political Economy', *International Organisation*, vol. 38 (1984), pp. 199–223.

Friedberg, A. L., 'The Assessment of Military Power', *International Security*, vol. 12 (1987), pp. 190–202.

Frieden, J., 'The Trilateral Commission: Economics and Politics in the 1970s', *Monthly Review* (1977), pp. 1–18.

Gallagher, J. and R. Robinson, 'The Imperialism of Free Trade', *Economic History Review*, second series, vol. 6 (1953), pp. 1–15.

Gill, S., 'Hegemony, Consensus and Trilateralism', *Review of International Studies*, vol. 12 (1986), pp. 205–21.

'American Hegemony: Its Limits and Prospects in the Reagan Era', *Millennium*, vol. 15 (1986), no. 3, pp. 311–36.

'From Atlanticism to Trilateralism', in S. Smith (ed.), *International Relations: British and American Perspectives*, pp. 185–212.

Gill, S. and D. Law, 'Global Hegemony and the Structural Power of Capital', *International Studies Quarterly* (December 1989).

Gilpin, R., 'The Richness of the Tradition of Political Realism', *International Organisation*, vol. 38 (1984), pp. 287–304.

Gordon, D., 'The Global Economy: New Edifice or Crumbling Foundations?, *New Left Review* (1988), no. 168, pp. 24–64.

Gourevitch, P. A., 'The Second Image Reversed: the International Sources of Domestic Politics', *International Organisation*, vol. 32 (1978), pp. 929–52.

'Breaking With Orthodoxy: the Politics of Economic Policy Responses in the Depression of the 1930s', *International Organisation*, vol. 38 (1984), pp. 196–217.

Halliday, F., 'State and Society in International Relations: A Second Agenda', *Millennium*, vol. 16 (1987), pp. 215–30.

Hoogvelt, A., 'The New International Division of Labour', in R. Bush *et al.* (eds.), *The World Order: Socialist Perspectives*, pp. 65–86.

Hughes, T. L., 'The Crack Up', *Foreign Policy* (1980), no. 40, pp. 33–60.

Hveem, H., 'The Global Dominance System: Notes on a Theory of Global Political Economy', *Journal of Peace Research*, vol. 4 (1973), pp. 319–40.

Hymer, S., 'The Internationalisation of Capital', *Journal of Economic Issues*, vol. 6 (1972), pp. 91–111.

Immerman, R., 'European Attitudes Towards Japan: Trilateralism's Weakest Link', *Executive Seminar in National and International Affairs, Department of State, 1979–80* (Washington DC, US Department of State, April 1980).

Jones, R. J. B., 'International Political Economy: Perspectives and Prospects', *Review of International Studies*, vol. 8 (1982), pp. 39–52.

Kautsky, K., 'Ultra-Imperialism', *New Left Review* (1970), no. 59, pp. 41–6.

Keohane, R. O. and J. S. Nye, 'Two Cheers for Multilateralism', *Foreign Policy* (1985), no. 60, pp. 148–67.

Kindleberger, C. P., 'Dominance and Leadership in the International Economy: Exploitation, Public Goods and Free Rides', *International Studies Quarterly*, vol. 25 (1981), pp. 242–54.

Klare, M. T., 'The Traders versus the Prussians', *Seven Days*, 28 March 1977, pp. 32–3.

Krippendorf, E., 'The Dominance of American Approaches in International Relations', *Millennium*, vol. 16 (1987), pp. 207–14.

Kudrle, R. T., 'The Several Faces of the Multinational Corporation', in Hollist and Tullis (eds.), *An International Political Economy Yearbook*, vol. 1, pp. 175–97.

Lansberg, M., 'Multinational Corporations and the Crisis of Capitalism', *Insurgent Sociologist*, vol. 7 (1976), pp. 19–33.

Law, D., 'The Baker Initiatives and Macroeconomic Co-operation', in S. Gill (ed.), *Atlantic Relations: Beyond the Reagan Era*.

Legvold, R., 'Containment Without Confrontation', *Foreign Policy* (1980), no. 40, pp. 74–98.

Mandel, E., 'Where is America Going?', *New Left Review* (1969), no. 54, pp. 3–15.

'The Laws of Uneven Development', *New Left Review* (1970), no. 59, pp. 19–38.

Moran, M., 'Politics, Banks and Markets: an Anglo-American Comparison', *Political Studies*, vol. 32 (1984), pp. 173–89.

Nicolaus, M., 'USA – The Universal Contradiction', *New Left Review* (1970), no. 59, pp. 3–18.

Nye, J. S., 'US Power and Reagan Policy', *Orbis*, vol. 26 (1982), pp. 391–412.

Petras, J. and R. Rhodes, 'The Reconsolidation of US Hegemony', *New Left Review* (1976), no. 97, pp. 37–53.

'Reply to Critics', *New Left Review* (1977), no. 101–2, pp. 153–60.

Roberts, B., 'The Enigmatic Trilateral Commission: Boon or Bane?', *Millennium*, vol. 9 (1982), pp. 185–202.

Rosenau, J., and O. R. Holsti, 'US Leadership in a Shrinking World: The Breakdown of Consensuses and the Emergence of Conflicting Belief Systems', *World Politics*, vol. 35 (1983), pp. 368–92.

Rowthorn, B., 'Imperialism in the Seventies: Unity or Rivalry?', *New Left Review* (1971), no. 69, pp. 31–54.

Ruggie, J. G., 'International Regimes, Transactions and Change – Embedded Liberalism in the Post War Economic Order', *International Organisation*, vol. 36 (1982), pp. 379–415.

Russett, B. M., 'The Mysterious Case of Vanishing Hegemony; or, Is Mark Twain really dead?', *International Organisation*, vol. 39 (1985), pp. 206–31.

Shapiro, I., 'The Risen Sun', *Foreign Policy* (1980–1), no. 41, pp. 62–81.

Simes, D. K., 'Disciplining Soviet Power', *Foreign Policy* (1981), no. 43, pp. 33–53.

Simon, R., 'Gramsci's Concept of Hegemony', *Marxism Today*, March 1977.

Skocpol, T., 'Political Responses to Capitalist Crisis: Neo-Marxist Theories of the State and the Case of the New Deal', *Politics and Society*, vol. 10 (1980), pp. 155–201.

Smith, S., 'Strategic Relations in the Reagan Era', in Gill (ed.), *Atlantic Relations: Beyond the Reagan Era*, pp. 157–78.

Snidal, D., 'The Limits of Hegemonic Stability Theory', *International Organisation*, vol. 39 (1985), pp. 579–614.

'The Game THEORY of International Politics', *World Politics*, vol. 39 (1986), pp. 25–57.

Sprout, H. and Sprout, M., 'Tribal Sovereignty vs. Interdependence', in M. Smith, R. Little and M. Shackleton (eds.), *Perspectives on World Politics* (London, Croom Helm/Open University Press, 1981), pp. 245–57.

Strange, S., 'Interpretations of a Decade', in L. Tsoukalis (ed.), *The Political Economy of International Money* (London, Croom Helm, 1985).

'Protectionism and World Politics', *International Organisation*, vol. 39 (1985), pp. 233–59.

'The persistent myth of lost hegemony', *International Organisation*, vol. 41 (1987), pp. 551–74.

Sylvan, D., 'The Newest Mercantilism', *International Organisation*, vol. 35 (1981), pp. 375–9.

Symposium in *World Politics*, vol. 38 (1985), October (On game theory and international co-operation).

Symposium in *International Studies Quarterly*, vol. 30 (1986), no. 4. (On consensus and belief systems among American foreign policy elites.)

Szymanski, A., 'Is US Imperialism Resurgent?', *New Left Review* (1977), no. 101–2, pp. 144–52.

Tooze, R., 'In Search of International Political Economy', *Political Studies*, vol. 32 (1984), pp. 637–46.

Turkatenko, N. D., 'Origins and aims of the Trilateral Commission', *Ssa – Economika, Politika, Ideologija* (1977), no. 9, translated in *IDOC Bulletin* (1977), no. 11–12, pp. 5–6.

Ullman, R. H., 'Trilateralism: Partnership for What?', *Foreign Affairs*, vol. 55 (1976), pp. 3–18.

Useem, M., 'The Inner Group of the American Capitalist Class', *Social Problems* (February 1978), no. 25, pp. 225–40.

van der Pijl, K., 'Restructuring the Atlantic Ruling Class', in Gill (ed.), *Atlantic Relations: Beyond the Reagan Era*, pp. 62–87.

Ward, H., 'Structural Power – A Contradiction in Terms?', *Political Studies*, vol. 35 (1987), pp. 593–610.

INDEX

Lightning Source UK Ltd.
Milton Keynes UK
UKOW04f2308190615

253793UK00001B/68/P